Best of Bridge
Home Preserving

120 Recipes for Jams, Jellies, Marmalades, Pickles & More

Robert
ROSE

D1445928

Disclaimer
The recipes in this book have been carefully tested by our kitchen and our tasters. To the best of
our knowledge, they are safe and nutritious for ordinary use and users. For those people with food
or other allergies, or who have special food requirements or health issues, please read the suggested
contents of each recipe carefully and determine whether or not they may create a problem for you.
All recipes are used at the risk of the consumer.

We cannot be responsible for any hazards, loss or damage that may occur as a result of any
recipe use.

For those with special needs, allergies, requirements or health problems, in the event of any
doubt, please contact your medical adviser prior to the use of any recipe.

Design and Production: Joseph Gisini/PageWave Graphics Inc.
Editor: Sue Sumeraj
Proofreader: Sheila Wawanash
Indexer: Gillian Watts
Photographer: Colin Erricson
Associate Photographer: Matt Johannsson
Food Stylist: Kathryn Robertson
Prop Stylist: Charlene Erricson
Some jams photographed were provided by Yvonne Tremblay

Cover image: Blackberry Plum Jelly (page 120)

The publisher gratefully acknowledges the financial support of our publishing program by the
Government of Canada through the Canada Book Fund.

Published by Robert Rose Inc.
120 Eglinton Avenue East, Suite 800, Toronto, Ontario, Canada M4P 1E2
Tel: (416) 322-6552 Fax: (416) 322-6936
www.robertrose.ca

Printed and bound in China

1 2 3 4 5 6 7 8 9 PPLS 22 21 20 19 18 17 16 15 14

CONTENTS

INTRODUCTION

HOME PRESERVING USED TO BE DONE OUT OF NECESSITY. IF YOU WANTED TO EAT MORE THAN ROOT VEGETABLES, CABBAGE, SQUASH AND APPLES IN THE WINTER MONTHS, YOU CANNED FRESH FRUITS AND VEGETABLES IN THE SUMMER.

NOW, OUR HOMES HAVE FREEZERS, AND MOST OF THE FOODS WE LIKE TO EAT ARE AVAILABLE IN SUPERMARKETS, FROM COUNTRIES AROUND THE WORLD. YET THE POPULARITY OF HOME PRESERVING IS SOARING — AND FOR GOOD REASON: THERE IS A HUGE DIFFERENCE IN FLAVOR BETWEEN STORE-BOUGHT PRESERVES AND HOMEMADE PRESERVES MADE FROM HOME-GROWN PRODUCE (FROM YOUR GARDEN OR LOCAL FARMERS).

ONE TASTE AND YOU'LL KNOW THAT HOME PRESERVING IS WORTH THE EFFORT. WITH HOME CANNING, YOU KNOW WHAT IS GOING INTO YOUR FOOD. YOU CAN CREATE UNIQUE SPREADS AND CONDIMENTS WITH COMBINATIONS OF FRUITS AND/OR VEGETABLES, ALONG WITH HERBS, SPICES AND OTHER ADD-INS. THE RESULT IS A PRODUCT *YOU* MADE — WHICH GIVES IT ADDED VALUE FOR EVERYONE YOU SHARE YOUR PRESERVING TREASURES WITH.

7 GREAT REASONS TO PRESERVE

1. FRESHNESS: YOU CAN PRESERVE FOODS IN SEASON, WITH LITTLE DISTANCE BETWEEN FARM AND TABLE.

2. GREAT TASTE: BECAUSE YOU'RE USING IN-SEASON PRODUCE, YOU KNOW IT WAS PICKED AT THE PEAK OF RIPENESS, FOR THE BEST FLAVOR AND AROMA.

3. GOOD NUTRITION: VITAMINS AND MINERALS ARE ALSO AT THEIR PEAK IN FRUITS AND VEGETABLES PICKED AT THEIR FINEST HOUR.

4. ECONOMICAL PRICE: WHEN SUPPLY IS PLENTIFUL, PRICES ARE LOWER.

5. OFF-SEASON ENJOYMENT: YOU CAN SAVOR YOUR FAVORITE FRUITS AND VEGETABLES ALL YEAR ROUND.

6. INDIVIDUALITY: YOU CAN TAILOR YOUR INGREDIENTS TO YOUR OWN TASTES, CREATING UNIQUE SPREADS AND CONDIMENTS.

7. GIFT-GIVING: HOMEMADE PRESERVES ADD A WELL-RECEIVED PERSONAL TOUCH THAT EVERYONE APPRECIATES.

THE BASICS: EVERYTHING YOU NEED TO KNOW

FOOD SAFETY

FOOD SAFETY IS THE CORNERSTONE OF CANNING. YOU WANT TO GET IT RIGHT SO YOU CAN FEEL CONFIDENT WHEN EATING THE FOOD LATER ON. BE ASSURED THAT IF YOU FOLLOW CURRENT, SAFE PRACTICES, ALL WILL BE WELL. ONCE YOU LEARN THE BASICS, THE INFORMATION APPLIES TO ANY OF THE SWEET OR SAVORY PRESERVES IN THIS BOOK, FROM JAMS AND JELLIES TO PICKLES AND RELISHES.

THE PRIMARY MICROORGANISMS THAT CAN SPOIL FOOD AND CAUSE ILLNESS ARE BACTERIA (SUCH AS *CLOSTRIDIUM BOTULINUM*), MOLDS AND YEASTS. SOME COME FROM THE SOIL AND CANNOT BE WASHED OFF; OTHERS ARE IN THE AIR AND LAND ON OUR FOOD. NATURALLY OCCURRING ENZYMES CAN ALSO CAUSE FOOD SPOILAGE.

HEAT AND ACIDITY PREVENT THESE MICROORGANISMS FROM HAVING AN ADVERSE EFFECT ON CANNED FOODS. HEATING THE FOOD ADEQUATELY AND REMOVING OXYGEN FROM THE JARS IS ESSENTIAL. THE RECIPES IN THIS BOOK ARE PRESERVED USING THE BOILING WATER CANNING METHOD, WHICH IS SUITABLE FOR HIGH-ACID FOODS. LOW-ACID FOODS WITHOUT ADDED ACID MUST BE CANNED IN A PRESSURE CANNER (FOR MORE INFORMATION, VISIT HTTP://NCHFP.UGA.EDU). IT IS NO LONGER CONSIDERED

SAFE TO USE PARAFFIN WAX ON TOP OF JAMS AND
JELLIES.

TO ENSURE THAT YOUR PRESERVES ARE SAFE, FOLLOW
THE RECIPE CAREFULLY, ADD THE EXACT AMOUNT OF
INGREDIENTS CALLED FOR, AND PROCESS JARS IN A
BOILING WATER CANNER FOR THE SPECIFIED AMOUNT OF
TIME. CURRENT RECIPES, SUCH AS THE ONES IN THIS
BOOK, HAVE THE MOST UP-TO-DATE PROCESSING TIMES,
WHICH SHOULD BE STRICTLY ADHERED TO.

HEAT

ALL OF THE PRESERVING RECIPES IN THIS BOOK ARE
PROCESSED USING THE BOILING WATER CANNER METHOD,
WHICH IS EASY TO FOLLOW AND IS VERY EFFECTIVE FOR
THE SAFE CANNING OF HIGH-ACID FOODS, PRODUCING A
RELIABLE SEAL.

PROCESSING JARS IN A BOILING WATER CANNER
(ALSO CALLED A BOILING WATER BATH) AFTER FILLING
THEM AND APPLYING THE LIDS IS IMPORTANT FOR THE
SAFE LONG-TERM ROOM TEMPERATURE STORAGE OF
YOUR PRESERVES. HEATING FOOD AT A HIGH ENOUGH
TEMPERATURE, FOR A LONG ENOUGH TIME, ENSURES THAT
NATURAL ENZYMES PRESENT IN FOOD ARE DEACTIVATED
AND MICROORGANISMS ARE DESTROYED. THE PROCESS
REMOVES OXYGEN FROM THE JARS AND, IN COMBINATION
WITH THE SPECIALLY DESIGNED LIDS, GIVES THEM AN
AIRTIGHT SEAL THAT PREVENTS MICROORGANISMS FROM
GETTING IN. A GOOD VACUUM SEAL WILL BE MAINTAINED
FOR THE DURATION OF THE JARS' STORAGE. WHILE JARS

MAY SEAL (AS VERIFIED BY THE LIDS CURVING INWARD) WITHOUT PROCESSING, THE STRENGTH OF THE SEAL IS GREATER AFTER PROCESSING. AN UNSEALED OR OPENED JAR MUST BE REFRIGERATED.

ACIDITY

MANY FOODS USED FOR CANNING, SUCH AS MOST FRUITS, HAVE A HIGH LEVEL OF ACIDITY (A PH BELOW 4.6), BUT MANY VEGETABLES, INCLUDING TOMATOES, ARE LOW-ACID (A PH OF 4.6 OR ABOVE) AND REQUIRE ADDED ACID TO DECREASE THE OVERALL PH OF THE PRESERVE TO A LEVEL SAFE FOR BOILING WATER CANNING. THE ACIDITY CAN BE INCREASED BY THE ADDITION OF A HIGH-ACID INGREDIENT SUCH AS LEMON JUICE, CITRIC ACID OR VINEGAR. PICKLES, RELISHES, SALSAS AND SAUCES (MADE PRIMARILY FROM VEGETABLES) ARE EXAMPLE OF PRESERVES THAT REQUIRE ADDED ACID TO BRING THEIR PH INTO THE ACCEPTABLE RANGE.

ACIDITY ALSO PLAYS AN IMPORTANT ROLE IN THE PRESERVATION AND TASTE OF PICKLES, RELISHES, CHUTNEYS, SALSAS AND SAUCES. TO ENSURE THE SAFETY OF YOUR PRESERVES, IT IS IMPORTANT NOT TO ADJUST THE AMOUNT OF ACID CALLED FOR IN A RECIPE.

OTHER SAFETY TIPS

- USE CURRENT, TESTED RECIPES THAT INCLUDE INSTRUCTIONS FOR PROCESSING IN A BOILING WATER CANNER. OLDER RECIPES ARE NOT NECESSARILY FOOD-SAFE AND CAN INCLUDE INGREDIENTS THAT ARE NO LONGER CONSIDERED SAFE FOR CONSUMPTION.

- NEVER USE ANIMAL PRODUCTS OR OILS IN PRESERVES THAT ARE PROCESSED IN A BOILING WATER CANNER. THE FOOD WILL NOT BE SAFE FOR ROOM TEMPERATURE STORAGE.

- USE ONLY HIGH-QUALITY PRODUCE. ANY PRODUCE THAT IS STARTING TO MOLD, ROT OR OTHERWISE DETERIORATE CAN RUIN YOUR PRESERVED PRODUCT.

- BE SURE ALL UTENSILS ARE CLEAN AND DRY BEFORE USING THEM TO PREPARE INGREDIENTS FOR PRESERVES. THIS INCLUDES YOUR HANDS!

- ONLY USE JARS AND LIDS SPECIFICALLY DESIGNED FOR CANNING. DO NOT REUSE JARS FROM COMMERCIALLY PREPARED PRODUCTS UNLESS THEY ARE MASON JARS THAT FIT TWO-PIECE METAL LIDS.

- IF IN DOUBT, THROW IT OUT. IF YOU'RE UNSURE WHETHER A PRESERVED PRODUCT HAS BEEN SEALED AND STORED PROPERLY, OR YOU DON'T KNOW HOW LONG IT'S BEEN STORED, IT'S BEST NOT TO EAT IT.

WHAT YOU'LL NEED

HARDWARE OR GENERAL MERCHANDISE STORES USUALLY CARRY THE FULL LINE OF CANNING PARAPHERNALIA: JARS, EXTRA LIDS, MAGNETIC WANDS, CANNING FUNNELS AND JAR LIFTERS, EXTRA LABELS, ETC. MANY OF THESE PRODUCTS, WHILE NOT ESSENTIAL, DO MAKE CANNING EASIER AND ARE WORTH THE SMALL INVESTMENT. SOME STORES SELL FULL CANNING KITS.

THE HOUSEWARES SECTIONS OF DEPARTMENT AND DISCOUNT STORES, SPECIALTY KITCHEN STORES AND SUPERMARKETS CARRY COOKWARE, UTENSILS AND GADGETS. IF YOU CAN, SPEND THE EXTRA MONEY FOR QUALITY GOODS.

EQUIPMENT

LARGE POT FOR BOILING WATER CANNING: ANY LARGE POT WITH A LID, WITH A MINIMUM CAPACITY OF 21 QUARTS (20 L), IS GOOD FOR STERILIZING JARS AND PROCESSING PRESERVES. YOU CAN ALSO USE A POT SPECIFICALLY DESIGNED FOR CANNING, SUCH AS PORCELAIN-COVERED STEEL. THE POT MUST BE DEEP ENOUGH TO ALLOW WATER TO COVER THE JARS BY AT LEAST 1 INCH (2.5 CM), WITH 2 INCHES (5 CM) BETWEEN THE TOP OF THE WATER AND THE TOP OF THE POT. IF YOU USE AN ELECTRIC STOVETOP, THE BOTTOM OF THE POT SHOULD EXTEND NO MORE THAN 2 INCHES (5 CM) BEYOND THE BURNER TO ENSURE EVEN HEAT DISTRIBUTION. IF YOU USE A GLASS OR CERAMIC COOKTOP, CHECK YOUR MANUAL TO MAKE SURE YOUR COOKTOP IS SUITABLE FOR HOME CANNING.

RACK FOR CANNER: A RACK ALLOWS WATER TO CIRCULATE UNDER AND AROUND THE JARS WITHIN THE CANNER. IT CAN BE A COMMERCIALLY MADE RACK (ONE OFTEN COMES WITH THE CANNER) OR A ROUND WIRE CAKE RACK THAT FITS INSIDE YOUR POT. COMMERCIAL RACKS USUALLY HAVE HANDLES AND ARE DESIGNED SO THEY CAN BE PERCHED ON THE SIDES OF THE CANNER WHILE YOU ADD JARS, THEN LOWERED INTO THE WATER FOR PROCESSING. ALTERNATIVELY, YOU CAN MAKE A RACK: USING STRONG

TWINE, TIE SIX SCREW BANDS (FROM TWO-PIECE CANNING LIDS) TOGETHER INTO A RING, THEN TIE ONE IN THE CENTER.

TO PREVENT RUSTING, BE SURE TO REMOVE THE RACK FROM THE CANNER AFTER REMOVING THE JARS AND LET IT DRY THOROUGHLY.

CANNING JARS WITH TWO-PIECE LIDS: CANNING JARS (MASON JARS) ARE MADE OF SPECIAL HEAT-RESISTANT GLASS FOR BOILING WATER CANNING. THE LIDS CONSIST OF METAL RINGS (ALSO KNOWN AS SCREW BANDS) AND ONE-TIME-USE METAL LIDS WITH A SEALING COMPOUND THAT NEEDS TO BE SOFTENED BEFORE USE.

MOST OF THE SWEET SPREADS IN THIS BOOK USE 8-OUNCE (250 ML) JARS (ALSO CALLED HALF-PINT JARS). SMALLER JARS ARE NICE BECAUSE YOU USE THEM UP MORE QUICKLY (THEREBY CONSUMING A FRESHER PRODUCT). IN ADDITION, YOU CAN TRY SEVERAL PRESERVES AT THE SAME TIME FOR MORE VARIETY, AND YOU HAVE MORE JARS TO SHARE. FOR POPULAR JAMS FOR LARGE FAMILIES, USE PINT (500 ML) JARS, AS THESE PRESERVES WILL BE CONSUMED MORE QUICKLY. FOR SAVORY PRESERVES, SUCH AS WINE, GARLIC, HERB AND PEPPER JELLIES, USE 4-OUNCE (125 ML) JARS — THEY'RE GREAT FOR GIFT-GIVING AND FOR PRESERVES EATEN IN SMALLER AMOUNTS. PICKLES, SALSAS AND SAUCES ARE USUALLY CANNED IN PINT (500 ML) JARS OR LARGER; RELISHES AND CHUTNEYS IN 8-OUNCE (250 ML) JARS. FOR PICKLES, YOU MAY PREFER JARS WITH A WIDER OPENING, FOR EASIER PACKING.

PLASTIC STORAGE LIDS: ONCE A JAR IS OPENED, IT IS BEST TO REPLACE THE METAL LID WITH A PLASTIC ONE DESIGNED FOR STORAGE, AS ACIDIC INGREDIENTS CAN CORRODE METAL LIDS DURING STORAGE AND CAUSE PREMATURE FOOD SPOILAGE.

LARGE POT FOR COOKING PRESERVES: CHOOSE A LARGE, DEEP, HEAVY-BOTTOMED POT; THIN-BOTTOMED POTS MAY CAUSE SCORCHING, AND POTS THAT ARE TOO SMALL WILL RESULT IN MESSY BOILOVERS. MOST SETS OF COOKING POTS INCLUDE A LARGE, WIDE POT OR A DUTCH OVEN WITH A LID. OTHER LARGE POTS, SUCH AS STOCKPOTS, MAY ALSO BE SUITABLE. THE POT SHOULD HAVE AN EXTRA LAYER OF METAL ON THE BOTTOM, SANDWICHED BETWEEN THE STAINLESS STEEL; IT IS USUALLY ALUMINUM OR COPPER, WHICH ARE GOOD HEAT CONDUCTORS. DO NOT USE ALL-ALUMINUM OR ALL-IRON POTS.

POTS WITH A LARGER DIAMETER ARE PREFERRED FOR FRUIT BUTTERS, MARMALADES, CONSERVES, SAUCES AND CHUTNEYS. THEY ALLOW FOR GREATER EVAPORATION OF WATER WHEN YOU ARE COOKING DOWN THE MIXTURE TO THICKEN IT. TRY A POT WITH A CAPACITY OF ABOUT $5\frac{1}{2}$ QUARTS, OR 22 CUPS (5.5 L). A POT THAT IS TALLER (DEEPER) AND A LITTLE NARROWER IS BETTER FOR MAKING JAMS AND ESPECIALLY JELLIES: THE JELLY LIQUID OFTEN BUBBLES UP HIGH AND COULD OVERFLOW A SHORTER POT. TRY ONE THAT IS $9\frac{1}{2}$ INCHES (24 CM) IN DIAMETER AND $6\frac{1}{2}$ INCHES (16 CM) DEEP, AND HOLDS ABOUT 28 CUPS (7 L). YOU NEED A POT WITH A DEPTH AT LEAST FOUR TIMES THAT OF THE CONTENTS BEFORE BOILING.

FOR RELISHES AND PICKLES, WHICH ARE NOT COOKED AS LONG AS SWEET SPREADS, USE A POT LARGE ENOUGH TO EASILY STIR TOGETHER INGREDIENTS AND ALLOW ROOM TO BOIL WITHOUT BOILING OVER.

SMALL SAUCEPAN: ANY SMALL SAUCEPAN CAN BE USED TO HEAT THE DISC PORTION OF METAL JAR LIDS, TO SOFTEN THE SEALING COMPOUND. YOU MAY ALSO USE A SMALL SAUCEPAN TO SOFTEN CITRUS PEEL.

BOWLS: LARGE AND SMALL BOWLS ARE USED FOR PREMEASURED FRUIT AND VEGETABLES, SUGAR, DRIED FRUIT, NUTS, SPICES, ETC. YOU'LL NEED STURDY BOWLS MADE OF A NON-REACTIVE MATERIAL SUCH AS STAINLESS STEEL, GLASS OR CERAMIC. IF YOU PLAN TO MAKE PICKLES OR RELISHES, A VERY LARGE BOWL OR CONTAINER IS ESSENTIAL FOR SOAKING PRODUCE IN SALT AND/OR BRINE. A DEEP, STRAIGHT-SIDED BOWL OR POT THAT IS ABOUT 9 TO 11 INCHES (23 TO 28 CM) ACROSS AND ABOUT 6 TO 7 INCHES (15 TO 18 CM) DEEP WILL FIT THE LARGEST RECIPES IN THIS BOOK.

OTHER EQUIPMENT: YOU'LL GET GOOD USE OUT OF A FOOD PROCESSOR, A FOOD MILL OR VICTORIO STRAINER, A MANDOLINE SLICER, A COLANDER, SIEVES, A KITCHEN SCALE AND A PLASTIC-COATED APRON.

UTENSILS

MEASURES: FOR ACCURATE MEASURING, YOU NEED GLASS LIQUID MEASURES AND METAL OR PLASTIC NESTING MEASURING CUPS AND SPOONS FOR DRY INGREDIENTS. DO NOT MEASURE SUGAR IN A LIQUID MEASURE, AND DO

NOT MEASURE LIQUIDS (WATER, JUICE, WINE, ETC.) IN THE CUPS USED FOR DRY INGREDIENTS. FOR JAMS AND JELLIES, A 4-CUP (1 L) LIQUID MEASURE CAN BE USED FOR LARGE QUANTITIES OF FRUIT (ONCE IT IS EMPTY, USE IT TO DISCARD SKIMMED FOAM). FOR PICKLES, RELISHES, CHUTNEYS AND SALSAS, IT'S BEST TO USE A DRY SINGLE-CUP MEASURE (OR SMALLER MEASURES AS NECESSARY) MULTIPLE TIMES. THE LARGE 8-CUP (2 L) MEASURING CUPS ARE GREAT TO USE AS BOWLS, BUT ARE NOT AS ACCURATE FOR MEASURING.

SPOONS: WOODEN SPOONS ARE GREAT FOR STIRRING, AND ONES WITH EXTRA-LONG HANDLES ARE IDEAL FOR AVOIDING HOT SPLASHES FROM BUBBLING PRESERVES. MARK WOODEN SPOON HANDLES SO YOU DO NOT INTERCHANGE THOSE YOU USE FOR SWEET AND SAVORY PRESERVES. ANOTHER OPTION IS HIGH-HEAT-RESISTANT SPOONS (SUCH AS EXOGLASS), WHICH LOOK LIKE WOODEN SPOONS BUT ARE MADE FROM A COMPOSITE MATERIAL THAT WITHSTANDS HIGH TEMPERATURES. THEY DON'T ABSORB FLAVORS FROM THE FOOD, ARE DISHWASHER SAFE AND DON'T HARBOR BACTERIA. THEY ARE MORE EXPENSIVE THAN WOODEN SPOONS AND OTHER PLASTICS, BUT ARE LONG-LASTING AND VERY DURABLE. PLASTIC OR MELAMINE SPOONS ARE NOT AS GOOD FOR THE CONSTANT STIRRING OF HOT MIXTURES.

USE A LARGE METAL SPOON (STAINLESS STEEL OR CHROME-PLATED) TO SKIM OFF FOAM FROM JAMS AND JELLIES, AND A SLOTTED METAL SPOON TO TRANSFER

PICKLED PRODUCTS INTO JARS (SO YOU CAN GET THE PROPER PROPORTION OF PICKLES TO LIQUID IN EACH JAR).

KNIVES: YOU NEED A GOOD-QUALITY CHEF'S KNIFE FOR CHOPPING AND A PARING KNIFE FOR PEELING AND TRIMMING. A KNIFE SHARPENER KEEPS KNIVES SHARP SO YOU CAN WORK FASTER AND AVOID CUTS DUE TO THE KNIFE SLIPPING.

CUTTING BOARDS: USE A LARGE PLASTIC CUTTING BOARD, WITH A GROOVE TO CATCH JUICES, WHEN CHOPPING CITRUS FRUIT, PINEAPPLE, PEACHES, ETC. A WOODEN BOARD IS GREAT FOR CUTTING VEGETABLES, ONIONS AND GARLIC, ETC. ALWAYS USE A SEPARATE, DEDICATED CUTTING BOARD FOR FRUIT, AS STRONG FLAVORS, LIKE ONION, WILL TRANSFER.

LADLE: A STAINLESS STEEL OR CHROME-PLATED LADLE IS THE PREFERRED TOOL FOR TRANSFERRING MOST PRESERVES TO JARS (THE EXCEPTION IS PICKLES, FOR WHICH YOU SHOULD USE A SLOTTED METAL SPOON, AS DISCUSSED ABOVE, OR TONGS).

CANNING FUNNEL: MOST OF THE CANNING FUNNELS AVAILABLE TODAY ARE PLASTIC OR SILICONE, BUT YOU WILL FIND SOME MADE OF STAINLESS STEEL. THESE WIDE-MOUTH FUNNELS MAKE IT EASIER TO LADLE PRESERVES, ESPECIALLY THICK MIXTURES, INTO JARS AND HELP KEEP THE JAR RIM AND SIDES CLEAN OF STICKY MIXTURES.

MAGNETIC WAND: THIS HANDY TOOL — A MAGNET ATTACHED TO THE END OF A PLASTIC WAND — IS USED

TO LIFT PREPARED JAR LIDS FROM HOT WATER. JUST TOUCH THE MAGNET TO THE CENTER OF THE METAL LID, PLACE THE LID ON TOP OF THE CLEAN JAR RIM AND DETACH WITH YOUR FINGER BY TOUCHING THE TOP OF THE LID. THESE WANDS ARE NOT EXPENSIVE, AND ARE SOLD ONLINE IF YOU CANNOT FIND THEM IN A HARDWARE OR GENERAL MERCHANDISE STORE.

HEADSPACE GAUGE/BUBBLE REMOVER: THIS HANDY PLASTIC TOOL, WHICH HAS NOTCHES AT $\frac{1}{4}$-INCH (0.5 CM) INTERVALS, IS USED TO MEASURE HEADSPACE (THE DISTANCE FROM THE TOP SURFACE OF THE MIXTURE TO THE JAR RIM) AND TO REMOVE AIR BUBBLES FROM INSIDE THE JAR.

RUBBER OR SILICONE SPATULA: USE A SPATULA TO SCRAPE SUGAR FROM THE INSIDE EDGES OF THE POT WHEN MAKING SWEET SPREADS (UNDISSOLVED SUGAR CAN CAUSE CRYSTALS LATER ON). A LONG, FLEXIBLE, NARROW SPATULA CAN BE USED TO REMOVE AIR BUBBLES IF YOU DON'T HAVE A BUBBLE REMOVER. LOOK FOR HIGH-HEAT-RESISTANT (SILICONE) SPATULAS IN KITCHEN STORES.

JAR LIFTER: THESE SPECIALIZED TONGS ARE COATED WITH SILICONE AND ARE DESIGNED TO FIT AROUND THE NECKS OF JARS. THEY MAKE LIFTING JARS EASIER AND SAFER.

SILICONE-COATED TONGS: LONG- OR SHORT-HANDLED METAL TONGS WITH HEATPROOF SILICONE COATING ON THE ENDS ARE IDEAL FOR PACKING HOT FOODS INTO JARS, ESPECIALLY WHEN YOU'RE TRYING TO NEATLY PACK FOODS SUCH AS ASPARAGUS, BEANS OR SLICES OF CUCUMBERS.

METAL TONGS WITHOUT SILICONE COATING ARE NOT SUITABLE, AS THE METAL CAN SCRATCH THE JARS.

SILICONE OVEN MITTS: THESE ARE HEAT- AND WATER-RESISTANT AND ARE VERY HELPFUL FOR HANDLING THE CANNING RACK AND HOT, WET JARS.

DISPOSABLE LATEX OR RUBBER GLOVES: WEAR THESE WHEN HANDLING HOT CHILE PEPPERS, TO PREVENT STINGING AND BURNS, AND WHEN HANDLING DARK-COLORED PRODUCE SUCH AS BEETS, CHERRIES AND RED CABBAGE, TO PREVENT STAINING ON YOUR HANDS. THEY'RE AVAILABLE AT PHARMACIES AND HARDWARE STORES.

POTATO MASHER OR PASTRY BLENDER: USE TO CRUSH FRUIT TO RELEASE JUICES.

KITCHEN TIMER: A DIGITAL TIMER ENSURES ACCURATE TIMING OF BOILING AND COOKING.

CANDY OR DIGITAL THERMOMETER: USE TO TEST THE TEMPERATURE FOR THE SETTING POINT (SEE PAGE 24).

LINT-FREE TOWELS: FINELY WOVEN TOWELS MADE OF NATURAL FIBERS (COTTON OR LINEN) ALLOW FOR THE BEST ABSORPTION WHEN DRAINING WASHED PRODUCE. AVOID TERRYCLOTH TOWELS, WHICH TEND TO LOSE FIBERS.

OTHER UTENSILS: CHEESECLOTH, A JELLY BAG, A CHERRY PITTER, A STRAWBERRY HULLER OR WIDE DRINKING STRAW (TO REMOVE STRAWBERRY HULLS), A VEGETABLE PEELER (Y-SHAPED IS BEST), A CITRUS ZESTER, GRATERS AND A CITRUS JUICER WILL ALL COME IN HANDY.

TERMINOLOGY

HOME PRESERVING COMES WITH ITS OWN SET OF TERMS, SOME OF WHICH MAY BE UNFAMILIAR TO YOU, OR MAY HAVE MUCH MORE PRECISE MEANINGS WHEN IT COMES TO CANNING THAN IS NECESSARY IN OTHER TYPES OF COOKING.

BOILING

- FULL BOIL, FULL ROLLING BOIL, HARD BOIL: A BOIL THAT CANNOT BE STIRRED DOWN, THAT BUBBLES CONSTANTLY AND VIGOROUSLY. MANY LARGE BUBBLES BREAK THE SURFACE AT A VERY RAPID PACE.

- BOIL: LARGE BUBBLES BREAK THE SURFACE AT A RAPID PACE. IF STIRRED, BUBBLES WILL CONTINUE TO BREAK THE SURFACE, BUT SLIGHTLY MORE SLOWLY.

- GENTLE BOIL: A STEADY BOIL THAT IS NOT TOO VIGOROUS BUT IS NOT AS SLOW AS SIMMERING. LARGER BUBBLES BREAK THE SURFACE AT A MODERATE PACE. IF STIRRED, BUBBLES WILL SUBSIDE SLIGHTLY, THEN RESUME AS SOON AS STIRRING STOPS.

- SIMMER: A CONSTANT, LIGHT BUBBLING OVER LOWER HEAT THAT SLOWLY COOKS THE FOOD.

- STEAMING HOT: THE LIQUID OR FOOD IS VERY HOT; STEAM RISES FROM THE SURFACE AND SMALL BUBBLES FORM BUT DO NOT RISE AND BREAK THE SURFACE.

CHOPPING

- COARSELY CHOPPED: PIECES ARE RANDOM IN SHAPE AND $3/4$ TO 1 INCH (2 TO 2.5 CM) IN SIZE.

- CHOPPED: PIECES ARE RANDOM IN SHAPE AND $\frac{1}{2}$ TO $\frac{3}{4}$ INCH (1 TO 2 CM) IN SIZE.

- FINELY CHOPPED: PIECES ARE RANDOM IN SHAPE AND $\frac{1}{8}$ TO $\frac{1}{4}$ INCH (3 MM TO 0.5 CM) IN SIZE.

- CUBED: PIECES ARE UNIFORM CUBE SHAPES AND ABOUT $\frac{1}{2}$ INCH (1 CM) IN SIZE.

- DICED: PIECES ARE UNIFORM CUBE SHAPES AND ABOUT $\frac{1}{4}$ INCH (0.5 CM) IN SIZE.

- MINCED: PIECES ARE RANDOM IN SHAPE AND VERY TINY (SMALLER THAN $\frac{1}{8}$ INCH/3 MM), BUT ARE STILL DISCERNIBLE PIECES (NOT MASHED OR PURÉED).

OTHER COMMON TERMS

- FINGERTIP-TIGHT: TO TIGHTEN THE JAR RING, WITH ONLY YOUR FINGERTIPS GRIPPING IT, JUST UNTIL THE RING IS SNUG, NOT AS TIGHT AS IT WILL GO. IF THE RING IS OVERTIGHTENED BEFORE PROCESSING, AIR WILL NOT BE ABLE TO ESCAPE THE JAR DURING PROCESSING, AND A GOOD SEAL WILL NOT FORM. TIGHTENING RINGS AFTER PROCESSING IS LIKELY TO DISTURB AND WEAKEN THE SEAL.

- HEADSPACE: THE SPACE LEFT BETWEEN THE SURFACE OF THE PRESERVE AND THE TOP RIM OF THE JAR. HEADSPACE MUST BE CAREFULLY MEASURED TO ALLOW ROOM FOR EXPANSION OF THE FOOD DURING HEAT PROCESSING AND TO ENSURE THE PROPER VACUUM SEAL UPON COOLING. CONTENTS FROM OVERFILLED JARS MAY SEEP OUT AND INTERFERE WITH THE SEAL.

UNDERFILLING WILL LEAVE MORE AIR IN THE JAR THAN CAN BE FORCED OUT DURING THE PROCESSING TIME, RESULTING IN A POOR SEAL.

- SETTING POINT, SET POINT, GELLING POINT, GEL POINT: THE POINT AT WHICH YOUR JAM, JELLY OR MARMALADE IS DONE, AT WHICH THE SUGAR, PECTIN AND ACID COME TOGETHER TO CREATE A GEL AND WILL SET. THERE ARE VARIOUS WAYS TO TEST FOR THE SETTING POINT (SEE PAGE 24).

UNDERSTANDING FRUIT'S NATURAL PECTIN

PECTIN IS A TYPE OF SOLUBLE FIBER AND IS HIGHEST IN AND UNDER THE SKIN OF FRUIT, AS WELL AS IN THE SEEDS AND FLESH. PECTIN, SUGAR AND HIGH ACIDITY (LOW PH) ARE NECESSARY FOR THE SETTING, OR GELLING, OF SWEET SPREADS SUCH AS JAMS, JELLIES, MARMALADES AND CONSERVES.

SOME FRUITS HAVE ABUNDANT NATURAL PECTIN, SO THEY DO NOT REQUIRE THE ADDITION OF COMMERCIAL PECTIN AND DO NOT NEED TO BE COOKED FOR VERY LONG BEFORE THEY WILL SET. FRUITS LOWER IN PECTIN MUST BE COOKED DOWN TO EVAPORATE WATER AND CONCENTRATE THE PECTIN. HIGH-PECTIN FRUIT CAN BE COMBINED WITH FRUIT THAT IS LOWER IN PECTIN TO ASSIST IN GELLING.

OVERRIPE FRUIT IS LOWER IN PECTIN AND ACID THAN RIPE FRUIT. UNDERRIPE FRUIT IS HIGHER IN ACID AND

PECTIN AND MAY BE USED IN SOME PRESERVES AS A PORTION (NO MORE THAN A QUARTER) OF THE OVERALL FRUIT. USING TOO MUCH UNDERRIPE FRUIT INCREASES ACIDITY, CAUSING PRESERVES TO SET TOO QUICKLY AND TOO FIRMLY, AND CAN CAUSE WEEPING (WATER OOZING FROM THE PRESERVE).

COMMERCIAL PECTINS ARE EXTRACTED FROM CITRUS FRUIT. SOME PRESERVES CANNOT BE MADE WITHOUT ADDED COMMERCIAL PECTIN, WHILE SOME RECIPES INCLUDE ADDED PECTIN FOR SPEEDIER COOKING AND TO MAKE THINGS EASIER FOR THOSE WHO HAVE TROUBLE DETERMINING THE SETTING POINT. THE RECIPES IN THIS BOOK HAVE IT ALL WORKED OUT FOR YOU.

LIQUID PECTIN BRANDS VARY IN THEIR INSTRUCTIONS ON WHETHER TO BOIL AFTER ADDING THE PECTIN. FOLLOW THE INSTRUCTIONS THAT COME WITH THE PECTIN FOR WHEN TO ADD.

HOW TO USE A JELLY BAG

PLACE THE JELLY BAG IN ITS HOLDER. RINSE THE BAG BY POURING ABOUT 2 CUPS (500 ML) BOILING WATER OVER IT; LET DRAIN. (THIS ALSO HELPS TO KEEP JUICE FROM SOAKING INTO THE BAG.) SET THE JELLY BAG OVER A LARGE BOWL OR POT; POUR IN COOKED FRUIT AND JUICE. COVER AND LET JUICE DRIP SLOWLY THROUGH THE JELLY BAG OVERNIGHT. DO NOT SQUEEZE THE JELLY BAG OR JELLY WILL BE CLOUDY. MOST OF THE JUICE WILL HAVE DRIPPED THROUGH AFTER ABOUT 4 HOURS; LONGER

DRIPPING WILL YIELD ABOUT $\frac{1}{2}$ CUP (125 ML) MORE LIQUID. DISCARD CONTENTS OF BAG, WASH THE BAG WITH WARM, SOAPY WATER AND LET IT DRY; STORE IN A PLASTIC BAG TO KEEP IT CLEAN.

IF YOU DON'T HAVE A JELLY BAG, YOU CAN USE SEVERAL LAYERS OF CHEESECLOTH LAYERED IN A FINE-MESH STRAINER, BUT THE JELLY MAY NOT BE AS CLEAR.

TESTING SOFT SPREADS FOR THE SETTING POINT

TESTING WHETHER A JAM, JELLY OR MARMALADE MADE WITHOUT ADDED PECTIN WILL SET ONCE IT COOLS CAN BE TRICKY. THERE ARE SEVERAL WAYS TO TEST, BUT IT IS RECOMMENDED TO USE THE TEMPERATURE METHOD IN COMBINATION WITH ONE OF THE OTHER METHODS. ALWAYS REMOVE THE POT FROM THE STOVE TO STOP THE COOKING WHILE YOU TEST.

- WRINKLE (OR PLATE) METHOD: PLACE ABOUT 2 TSP (10 ML) OF JAM, JELLY OR MARMALADE ON A CHILLED SMALL PLATE AND PLACE IT IN THE FREEZER FOR A MINUTE OR TWO, UNTIL COOLED TO ROOM TEMPERATURE. A SKIN WILL FORM ON TOP. IF YOU GENTLY PUSH IT WITH YOUR FINGER OR A FORK, IT WILL WRINKLE IF THE MIXTURE IS DONE. IT IS BEST TO KEEP TWO OR THREE PLATES CHILLED AND READY.

- SHEETING METHOD: USING A CLEAN, DRY, SMALL METAL SPOON, REMOVE SOME OF THE MIXTURE FROM THE POT. TILT THE SPOON SO THE MIXTURE RUNS OVER

THE SIDE ONTO A DISH. EARLY IN THE PROCESS, THE DROPS WILL BE RUNNY; AS THE MIXTURE CONTINUES TO COOK, THE DROPS WILL START TO COME TOGETHER. WHEN THE MIXTURE IS READY, THE DROPS WILL JOIN INTO ONE AND SHEET OFF THE SPOON IN WHAT LOOKS LIKE ONE LAYER.

- TEMPERATURE METHOD: USE A CANDY OR DIGITAL THERMOMETER. FIRST TEST THE BOILING POINT OF WATER, WHICH WILL VARY WITH ALTITUDE AND THE ATMOSPHERIC CONDITIONS THAT DAY. THEN TAKE THE TEMPERATURE OF THE JAM, JELLY OR MARMALADE. MAKE SURE TO PLACE THE THERMOMETER IN THE CENTER OF THE POT, NOT TOUCHING THE BOTTOM OR THE SIDES. THE SETTING POINT IS USUALLY 8°F (4°C) ABOVE THE BOILING POINT OF WATER AS DETERMINED BY YOUR THERMOMETER — THERE MAY BE A 1° MARGIN OF ERROR IN ITS ACCURACY. AT SEA LEVEL, THE SETTING TEMPERATURE WOULD BE 220°F (104°C). AS WATER EVAPORATES FROM YOUR MIXTURE, IT WILL INCREASE IN TEMPERATURE. IT MAY NOT SEEM TO CHANGE TOO QUICKLY AT FIRST BUT WILL INCREASE MORE QUICKLY AS THE JAM GETS CLOSER TO THE SETTING POINT.

A NOTE ON METRIC MEASUREMENTS

METRIC MEASUREMENTS ARE INCLUDED FOR ALL THE RECIPES. THEY ARE BASED ON *EQUIVALENT* MEASUREMENTS DEVELOPED FOR CANADIAN COOKS BY COOKING PROFESSIONALS AND HOME ECONOMISTS

WORKING FOR THE METRIC COMMISSION WHEN THE METRIC SYSTEM WAS FIRST INTRODUCED, RATHER THAN ON STRAIGHT CONVERSIONS FROM IMPERIAL TO METRIC. FOR CONVENIENCE, THE MEASURES WERE DESIGNED TO BE EVEN MULTIPLES OF FIVES AND TENS. THE RECIPES IN THIS BOOK WERE NOT TESTED IN METRIC, SO RESULTS MAY VARY. FOR BEST RESULTS, USE ALL IMPERIAL OR ALL METRIC MEASURES. USE TESTS FOR DONENESS, WHERE POSSIBLE, TO ENSURE THAT THE MIXTURE HAS REACHED THE SETTING POINT.

A NOTE ON YIELD

THE YIELD STATED FOR EACH RECIPE IS FOR THE APPROXIMATE NUMBER OF STANDARD CANNING JARS THE RECIPE WILL FILL. THERE WILL OFTEN BE MORE THAN THE AMOUNT STATED, DEPENDING ON HOW ACCURATELY YOU MEASURE, VARIABILITY IN THE MOISTURE CONTENT OF THE FRUIT OR VEGETABLES, THE AMOUNT OF PECTIN IN THE FRUIT, THE DIAMETER OF THE POT YOU USE AND VARIATIONS IN COOKING TIME. THE YIELD IS MEANT TO BE A GUIDELINE FOR THE NUMBER OF JARS AND LIDS TO PREPARE. PREPARE AT LEAST ONE ADDITIONAL JAR AND LID IN CASE YOU HAVE EXTRA PRESERVES OR IF A JAR BREAKS. YOU CAN ALSO PUT THE EXTRA PRESERVES IN A SMALL BOWL, CONTAINER OR NON-CANNING JAR FOR SAMPLING; ONCE COOLED, COVER AND REFRIGERATE FOR UP TO 3 WEEKS. OR USE A SPARE CANNING JAR WITH A PLASTIC LID (METAL LIDS ARE NOT NECESSARY IF IT IS NOT BEING PROCESSED).

DO NOT DOUBLE RECIPES. YOUR POT MAY OVERFLOW, EVEN IF IT DOES NOT LOOK ALL THAT FULL (ESPECIALLY JELLIES WHEN BOILING HARD). ALSO, COOKING IN TOO LARGE A QUANTITY MAY OVERCOOK FRUIT OR PREVENT THICKENING/GELLING OR AFFECT THE COOKING TIME.

HOW TO PROCESS IN A BOILING WATER CANNER

PRESERVING IS NOT DIFFICULT AND IS CERTAINLY MUCH MORE EFFICIENT IF YOU FOLLOW THESE SIMPLE GUIDELINES.

PREPARING THE CANNER

PROCESSING IS DONE IN A LARGE POT OF BOILING WATER WITH A RACK ON WHICH TO PLACE JARS. (DO NOT PLACE JARS DIRECTLY ON THE BOTTOM OF THE POT OR THEY MAY CRACK.) FILL THE CANNER WITH WATER, MAKING SURE THE WATER LEVEL WILL COVER JARS BY AT LEAST I INCH (2.5 CM) ONCE THEY ARE SUBMERGED. IT IS BETTER TO ADD MORE WATER IF YOU'RE NOT SURE, SINCE IT IS EASIER TO REMOVE SOME IF THE POT IS TOO FULL. IF THE WATER DOESN'T COVER THE JARS AND YOU HAVE TO ADD MORE, IT WILL SLOW DOWN THE PROCESSING.

COVER THE POT AND BRING THE WATER ALMOST TO A BOIL OVER MEDIUM-HIGH HEAT; THIS WILL TAKE 30 TO 60 MINUTES, DEPENDING ON YOUR STOVE AND POT. ONCE THE WATER IS ALMOST TO A BOIL, REDUCE THE HEAT TO KEEP IT AT A LOW SIMMER UNTIL YOU ARE READY TO ADD FILLED JARS. KEEP THE LID ON TO MINIMIZE EVAPORATION.

MAKE SURE THE CANNER IS READY BEFORE YOUR PRESERVES ARE SO THE FILLED JARS DON'T COOL DOWN.

PREPARING JARS

WASH JARS THOROUGHLY IN HOT, SOAPY WATER AND RINSE WELL, OR RUN THROUGH A SANITIZING CYCLE IN A DISHWASHER (START THIS BEFORE PREPARING THE CANNER IF YOU PLAN TO USE THE DISHWASHER). DO NOT TOWEL DRY. PREPARE AN EXTRA JAR OR TWO (EVEN ONE IN A SMALLER SIZE IS HELPFUL), JUST IN CASE YOU HAVE MORE PRODUCT THAN THE RECIPE SPECIFIES. JARS THAT ARE TO BE USED FOR FOODS THAT WILL BE PROCESSED FOR 10 MINUTES OR LONGER DO NOT NEED TO BE STERILIZED BEFORE FILLING. YOU MAY STERILIZE IF YOU WISH. INSPECT ALL JARS TO MAKE SURE THEY ARE FREE FROM CRACKS, CHIPS OR OTHER DAMAGE. DO NOT USE ANY THAT ARE EVEN SLIGHTLY DAMAGED, AS THEY CAN BREAK DURING FILLING OR PROCESSING.

THE JARS NEED TO BE HOT WHEN YOU FILL THEM. TO HEAT JARS, RUN THEM UNDER HOT TAP WATER SO THEY WARM UP SLIGHTLY. THEN PLACE THEM IN A POT OF HOT WATER, FILLING THE JARS WITH THE WATER. PLACE THE POT OVER LOW HEAT; DO NOT LET BOIL, BUT KEEP IT STEAMING. IF YOU HAVE A CANNER WITH A RACK THAT CAN BE RESTED BY THE HANDLES ON THE SIDES OF THE POT, YOU CAN PUT JARS FILLED WITH HOT WATER ON THE RACK AND KEEP THE WATER AT A LOW SIMMER TO KEEP THE JARS HOT. AGAIN, DO NOT LET THE WATER BOIL. IF THEY ARE IN THE DISHWASHER, TIME IT SO THE HOT JARS ARE

READY WHEN THE PRESERVES ARE. NEVER HEAT JARS IN THE OVEN. DRY HEAT CAN DAMAGE THE GLASS.

PREPARING LIDS

WASH AND RINSE THE NUMBER OF METAL DISCS AND RINGS NEEDED (ALWAYS PREPARE ONE OR TWO EXTRA, JUST IN CASE). FILL A SMALL SAUCEPAN WITH ABOUT 2 INCHES (5 CM) OF WATER. ADD THE METAL DISCS AND BRING TO A SIMMER OVER MEDIUM HEAT. DO NOT LET BOIL. ONCE THE WATER COMES TO A SIMMER, REMOVE THE POT FROM THE HEAT, COVER AND KEEP THE DISCS HOT. IF THE WATER COOLS, THE SEALING COMPOUND WILL HARDEN AND WILL NOT CREATE A PROPER SEAL ON THE JARS. DO NOT PREPARE THE LIDS ANY EARLIER THAN ABOUT 20 MINUTES BEFORE YOU PLAN TO FILL THE JARS.

FILLING JARS

ONCE YOU START COOKING OR HEATING THE FOOD, IT IS IMPORTANT TO PROCEED WITH THE ENTIRE RECIPE. DO NOT LET FOOD COOL OR SIT BEFORE FILLING AND PROCESSING JARS. IF THE COOKING TIME IS 30 MINUTES OR MORE, THE JARS AND LIDS CAN BE PREPARED WHILE THE FOOD IS COOKING. IF THE COOKING TIME IS LONGER THAN 1 HOUR, THE CANNER CAN BE PREPARED WHILE THE FOOD IS COOKING.

WHEN YOU'RE READY TO FILL THE JARS, WORK QUICKLY TO DO SO. USING A JAR LIFTER AND/OR YOUR HANDS WHILE WEARING SILICONE OVEN MITTS, REMOVE JARS, ONE AT A TIME IF SO DIRECTED IN THE RECIPE, FROM THE

HOT WATER, CANNER OR DISHWASHER AND DRAIN WELL.
DO NOT TOWEL DRY. IT'S A GOOD IDEA TO HAVE THE JAR
LIFTER IN ONE HAND AND A SILICONE OVEN MITT ON THE
OTHER TO BRACE THE JAR WHILE MOVING IT.

FOR JAMS AND OTHER SWEET SPREADS, SAUCES,
SALSAS, CHUTNEYS AND RELISHES, LADLE THE HOT
PRESERVES INTO HOT JARS, LEAVING THE HEADSPACE
SPECIFIED IN THE RECIPE (MEASURE IT WITH A RULER OR
NOTCHED BUBBLE REMOVER). A CANNING FUNNEL WILL
MAKE THIS EASIER. LIFT THE FUNNEL ABOVE THE RIM OF
THE JAR WHEN FILLING THE TOP PORTION OF THE JAR TO
BE SURE THE FOOD DOESN'T SPILL OVER THE EDGE AND
TO GET A GOOD VIEW OF THE LEVEL OF THE FOOD.

FOR PICKLES, PACK THE PRODUCE INTO THE HOT JARS
AS SPECIFIED (USING SILICONE-COATED TONGS FOR HOT
VEGETABLES). PLACE A CANNING FUNNEL IN THE MOUTH
OF THE JAR AND FILL THE JAR WITH THE HOT PICKLING
LIQUID, LEAVING THE AMOUNT OF HEADSPACE SPECIFIED IN
THE RECIPE.

IF THE JARS AND PRESERVES ARE HOT AND YOU FILL
QUICKLY, MOST OF THE AIR WILL GET PUSHED OUT AS YOU
FILL THE JARS. FOR PICKLES AND CHUNKY PRESERVES,
SUCH AS CHUTNEYS AND SALSAS, YOU MAY NEED TO
REMOVE AIR BUBBLES. TO DO SO, CAREFULLY INSERT A
BUBBLE REMOVER OR NARROW, NON-METALLIC SPATULA
BETWEEN THE FOOD AND THE SIDE OF THE JAR, ALL THE
WAY TO THE BOTTOM OF THE JAR, PRESSING GENTLY
INTO THE CENTER OF THE JAR TO REMOVE ANY AIR

BUBBLES TRAPPED IN THE FOOD. REPEAT THIS THREE OR FOUR TIMES AROUND THE JAR. THIS IS PARTICULARLY IMPORTANT FOR RAW-PACK PICKLES, WHICH TEND TO HAVE LOTS OF AIR TRAPPED BETWEEN THE PIECES.

AFTER REMOVING THE AIR BUBBLES, DOUBLE-CHECK THE HEADSPACE MEASUREMENT AND ADD MORE HOT PICKLING LIQUID OR PRESERVES, IF NEEDED, TO ADJUST IT. IF NECESSARY, USE A SMALL SPOON TO REMOVE ANY EXCESS. NEVER TOUCH THE INSIDE OF THE JAR WITH A METAL UTENSIL, AS THIS CAN DAMAGE THE JAR.

APPLYING LIDS AND FILLING THE CANNER

USING A PAPER TOWEL DIPPED IN CLEAN HOT WATER, WIPE THE RIM AND THREADS OF THE JAR, SWITCHING TO A CLEAN SECTION OF THE PAPER TOWEL AS IT GETS FOOD ON IT, TO BE SURE NO FOOD WILL INTERFERE WITH THE LID'S SEAL. USING A MAGNETIC LID LIFTER OR SILICONE-COATED TONGS, REMOVE A DISC FROM THE HOT WATER AND PLACE IT ON TOP OF THE JAR, THEN PLACE THE METAL RING OVER IT. SCREW THE RING ONTO THE JAR FIRMLY, BUT ONLY UNTIL FINGERTIP-TIGHT. IF THE RING IS TOO TIGHT, AIR CAN'T ESCAPE FROM THE JAR AND THE LID MAY FAIL TO SEAL. USING THE JAR LIFTER OR LIFTING CAREFULLY WITH YOUR HAND AROUND THE NECK OF THE FILLED JAR (NOT AROUND THE RING), PLACE THE JAR, WITHOUT TILTING AT ALL, ON THE RACK IN THE CANNER. REPEAT WITH THE REMAINING JARS, MAKING SURE THEY DO NOT TOUCH EACH OTHER OR THE SIDES OF THE CANNER.

PROCESSING

IF USING A RACK THAT RESTS ON THE SIDES OF THE CANNER WHILE YOU ADD JARS, USE THE HANDLES TO CAREFULLY LOWER THE RACK TO THE BOTTOM OF THE CANNER. THE WATER SHOULD COVER THE JARS BY AT LEAST 1 INCH (2.5 CM). TO MEASURE THE WATER LEVEL ABOVE THE JARS, DIP A WOODEN SPOON HANDLE VERTICALLY INTO THE WATER UNTIL IT JUST TOUCHES A LID, THEN MEASURE THE LENGTH OF THE WATER MARK ON THE HANDLE. IF THERE IS NOT ENOUGH WATER IN THE POT, ADD MORE BOILING WATER, POURING IT BETWEEN THE JARS, NOT ON TOP OF THEM.

IF THE WATER IS TOO DEEP AND THERE ISN'T AT LEAST 2 INCHES (5 CM) BETWEEN THE SURFACE OF THE WATER AND THE TOP OF THE POT, USE A GLASS MEASURING CUP OR A SAUCEPAN WITH A HANDLE TO SCOOP OUT SOME OF THE WATER, BEING CAREFUL NOT TO TOUCH THE JARS AND MAKING SURE THE JARS ARE STILL SUFFICIENTLY COVERED.

COVER THE POT AND BRING THE WATER TO A FULL ROLLING BOIL OVER HIGH HEAT. BEGIN TIMING ONCE THE WATER IS BOILING. LET THE WATER BOIL, TURNING THE HEAT DOWN SLIGHTLY IF IT STARTS TO BOIL OVER, BUT MAINTAINING A FULL BOIL. PROCESS FOR THE TIME SPECIFIED IN THE RECIPE, ADJUSTING FOR ALTITUDE IF NECESSARY (SEE PAGE 35).

FOR PICKLES, RELISHES, SAUCES AND OTHER PRESERVES THAT HAVE MORE LIQUID CONTENTS, IT IS IMPORTANT TO LET THE JARS STAND IN THE CANNER FOR

5 MINUTES WHEN THE PROCESSING TIME IS COMPLETE, WITH THE HEAT AND LID OFF. THIS ALLOWS THE PRESSURE IN THE JARS TO STABILIZE AND REDUCES THE CHANCE OF LIQUID LEAKING FROM JARS BEFORE THEY HAVE A CHANCE TO SEAL.

REMOVING JARS FROM THE CANNER

LIFT THE CANNER RACK TO THE EDGE OF THE CANNER, IF POSSIBLE. USING THE JAR LIFTER OR YOUR HAND IN A SILICONE OVEN MITT, GRASP THE NECK OF EACH JAR (NOT THE METAL RING) AND TRANSFER THE JARS, WITHOUT TILTING, TO A TOWEL-LINED HEAT-RESISTANT SURFACE, LEAVING SOME SPACE AROUND EACH JAR. DO NOT PLACE JARS ON A COLD SURFACE. A WOODEN CUTTING BOARD OR A STABLE WIRE COOLING RACK WORKS WELL.

LETTING JARS COOL

LET JARS COOL AT ROOM TEMPERATURE. DO NOT DRY OR TOUCH THE LIDS OR JARS, AND DO NOT RETIGHTEN RINGS. ANY MOVEMENT OF THE JARS AND LIDS CAN INTERFERE WITH A PROPER SEAL. WHILE THE JARS AND LIDS COOL, THE SEALING COMPOUND IN THE DISCS COOLS AND HARDENS, FORMING A TIGHT SEAL AROUND THE RIM OF THE JAR. YOU WILL HEAR A "POP" OR A "SNAP" SOUND AS A LID FORMS THE SEAL (THIS IS A GOOD SOUND!).

FOR PICKLES, CHUTNEYS AND OTHER SAVORY PRESERVES, IT'S BEST TO LET THE JARS COOL, WITHOUT MOVING THEM, FOR 24 HOURS. FOR SWEET SPREADS, ONCE THE JARS HAVE COOLED, CHECK FOR SET BY TILTING THE JAR SLIGHTLY. JELLIES WILL NOT MOVE WHEN SET;

SOME JAMS AND CONSERVES HAVE A SOFTER SET AND MAY MOVE SLIGHTLY; MARMALADES MAY TAKE UP TO A WEEK TO COMPLETELY SET.

WHEN THE PRESERVES HAVE COOLED OR SET, REMOVE THE METAL RINGS AND WIPE THE JARS WELL WITH A DAMP CLOTH, ESPECIALLY THE AREA THAT WAS UNDER THE RING (ANY FOOD LEFT WILL LIKELY GROW MOLD, WHICH MAY GET INTO YOUR JARS). CHECK TO MAKE SURE ALL THE LIDS HAVE SEALED. PROPERLY SEALED LIDS WILL BE SLIGHTLY CONCAVE. TO TEST THAT THEY ARE SEALED, PRESS THE MIDDLE OF THE LID WITH YOUR FINGER. YOU SHOULDN'T FEEL ANY MOVEMENT IN THE LID. A LID WITHOUT A PROPER SEAL WILL FLEX DOWN WHEN PRESSED AND THEN BACK UP AS YOU RELEASE YOUR FINGER.

ANY UNSEALED JARS SHOULD BE REFRIGERATED IMMEDIATELY AND USED WITHIN A FEW DAYS (OR UP TO 3 WEEKS FOR SWEET SPREADS). YOU CAN REPROCESS UNSEALED OR UNSET JARS OF JAMS, JELLIES, CONSERVES AND MARMALADES (BUT NOT SAVORY PRESERVES) WITHIN 24 HOURS. CHECK THE JAR FOR ANY IMPERFECTIONS AND CHANGE JARS IF NECESSARY. PREPARE JAR, USE A NEW DISC AND REHEAT (OR FURTHER COOK) THE MIXTURE, THEN RE-PROCESS. THIS CAN OFTEN DEGRADE THE QUALITY OF THE FOOD, SO IF ONLY ONE JAR IS UNSEALED, IT IS BEST TO EAT THE FOOD INSTEAD.

LABELING AND STORAGE

LABEL JARS WITH THE NAME OF THE CONTENTS AND THE DATE. IF YOU'RE PLANNING TO STORE YOUR JAMS IN

A BOX, YOU MIGHT WANT TO PLACE THE LABELS ON THE TOP OF THE LID RATHER THAN ON THE SIDE OF THE JAR. THAT WAY, YOU CAN READ THEM EASILY WHILE THE JARS ARE IN THE BOX. THE OTHER BENEFIT IS THAT THERE'S NO NEED TO PICK THE LABELS OFF THE JARS ONCE THEY'RE EMPTIED; AFTER EATING THE PRESERVE, JUST DISCARD THE METAL LID, AS IT CANNOT BE REUSED ANYWAY.

STORE SEALED, LABELED JARS IN A COOL, DRY, DARK PLACE. WARMTH, TEMPERATURE FLUCTUATIONS, DAMPNESS OR LIGHT WILL DETERIORATE THE FLAVOR AND COLOR OF YOUR PRESERVES. THE IDEAL STORAGE TEMPERATURE IS 40°F TO 50°F (4°C TO 10°C). PROPERLY STORED, YOUR PRESERVES WILL KEEP FOR UP TO 1 YEAR.

HIGH ALTITUDE PROCESSING

IF YOU LIVE AT AN ALTITUDE ABOVE 1,000 FEET (306 M), YOU'LL NEED TO ADJUST THE PROCESSING TIMES GIVEN IN THE RECIPES AS FOLLOWS:

- 1,000 TO 3,000 FEET (306 TO 915 M): INCREASE TIME BY 5 MINUTES

- 3,001 TO 6,000 FEET (916 TO 1,830 M): INCREASE TIME BY 10 MINUTES

- 6,001 TO 8,000 FEET (1,831 TO 2,440 M): INCREASE TIME BY 15 MINUTES

- 8,001 TO 10,000 FEET (2,441 TO 3,050 M): INCREASE TIME BY 20 MINUTES

SOURCE: COURTESY OF JARDEN CORPORATION.

USING YOUR PRESERVES

TIME TO ENJOY THE RESULTS! RINSE AND WIPE JARS AND LIDS AFTER STORING. AS LONG AS PROPER PROCESSING METHODS WERE FOLLOWED AND THE FOOD WAS STORED PROPERLY, THE RISK OF SPOILAGE IS LOW. HOWEVER, IT'S BEST TO INSPECT JARS FOR ANY SIGNS OF SPOILAGE BEFORE OPENING. THE LID SHOULD STILL BE SEALED — IF IT'S NOT, THROW OUT THE CONTENTS OF THE JAR. LOOK FOR SIGNS OF A BULGING LID, BUBBLES RISING IN THE FOOD OR AN UNNATURAL COLOR. DISCARD ANY FOOD THAT YOU SUSPECT MAY BE SPOILED.

TO OPEN THE LID, PLACE THE DULL SIDE OF A KNIFE HORIZONTALLY BETWEEN THE NARROWEST THREAD ON THE JAR AND THE METAL DISC AND ANGLE THE KNIFE, EXERTING GENTLE PRESSURE AGAINST THE LID TO POP IT OFF. YOU SHOULD HEAR A DISTINCT SOUND INDICATING THE RELEASE OF THE VACUUM. YOU CAN ALSO USE THE ROUNDED END OF A CHURCH KEY-STYLE BOTTLE OPENER TO LIFT THE LID.

CHECK THE INSIDE OF THE LID, THE INSIDE OF THE JAR AND THE TOP OF THE FOOD FOR ANY SIGNS OF MOLD, AND SMELL TO MAKE SURE THERE ARE NO OFF-AROMAS. IT IS NOT SAFE JUST TO REMOVE MOLD FROM THE TOP OF A PRESERVE, AS MOLD HAS ROOTS AND BRANCHES THAT REACH DEEP INTO THE MIXTURE. TO BE SAFE, DISCARD ANY FOOD THAT SHOWS SIGNS OF MOLD.

AFTER OPENING, REFRIGERATE PRESERVES AND USE WITHIN 1 MONTH.

QUICK TIPS FOR SUCCESS

- BE SURE YOU HAVE ALL OF THE NECESSARY EQUIPMENT AND INGREDIENTS AND THE AMOUNT OF TIME NEEDED TO COMPLETE THE RECIPE WITHOUT DELAYS.

- ALWAYS FOLLOW THE RECIPE EXACTLY, MEASURING INGREDIENTS ACCURATELY.

- DO NOT DOUBLE RECIPES.

- SPICES AND SEASONINGS CAN BE VARIED TO YOUR TASTE, BUT DO NOT ALTER THE TYPE OR AMOUNT OF VEGETABLES, FRUIT, ACID, SUGAR OR SALT IN A RECIPE UNLESS A TIP SAYS THIS IS OKAY.

- FRAGRANT, RIPE (AND SOME UNDERRIPE) FRESH FRUIT WILL GIVE TASTIEST RESULTS.

- DO NOT INTERCHANGE LIQUID PECTIN AND PECTIN CRYSTALS. CHECK THE "BEST BEFORE" DATE.

- ONCE YOU START COOKING OR HEATING THE FOOD, IT IS IMPORTANT TO PROCEED WITH THE ENTIRE RECIPE. DO NOT LET FOOD COOL OR SIT BEFORE FILLING AND PROCESSING JARS.

- REMOVE ANY AIR BUBBLES TRAPPED IN THE FOOD AFTER FILLING THE JARS.

- PROCESS JARS IN A BOILING WATER CANNER TO ENSURE A GOOD SEAL.

- FOLLOW CURRENT FOOD SAFETY PRACTICES.

- DON'T TAKE A CHANCE ON CONSUMING FOOD THAT MIGHT BE SPOILED. IF IN DOUBT, THROW IT OUT.

Single-Fruit Jams

We all have our favorite jam. Whether yours is strawberry or raspberry, cherry or peach, we can agree that there is nothing like well-made jam with a good set and pleasing balance of sweetness that lets the pure fruit taste shine through. You'll find all the classics here, some using the traditional long-boil method and others with added pectin that require minimal cooking.

APRICOT JAM

LEAVE THE SKINS ON WHEN MAKING APRICOT JAM — THEY ADD TO THE COLOR AND FLAVOR. LOOK FOR APRICOTS THAT ARE TENDER BUT NOT TOO SOFT AND HAVE A GOOD FRAGRANCE.

8 CUPS	SLICED OR CHOPPED APRICOTS (ABOUT 5 LBS/2.5 KG)	2 L
4½ CUPS	GRANULATED SUGAR	1.125 L

PLACE APRICOTS IN A LARGE, DEEP, HEAVY-BOTTOMED POT. ADD SUGAR IN A STEADY STREAM, STIRRING CONSTANTLY. HEAT OVER MEDIUM HEAT, STIRRING CONSTANTLY TO DISSOLVE SUGAR. INCREASE HEAT TO HIGH AND BRING TO A FULL BOIL, STIRRING CONSTANTLY. REDUCE HEAT TO MEDIUM-HIGH AND BOIL RAPIDLY, STIRRING OFTEN AND REDUCING HEAT FURTHER AS MIXTURE THICKENS, FOR 20 TO 25 MINUTES OR UNTIL THICKENED. TEST FOR SETTING POINT (SEE PAGE 24). REMOVE FROM HEAT AND SKIM OFF ANY FOAM.

LADLE INTO STERILIZED JARS TO WITHIN $\frac{1}{4}$ INCH (0.5 CM) OF RIM; WIPE RIMS. APPLY PREPARED LIDS AND RINGS; TIGHTEN RINGS JUST UNTIL FINGERTIP-TIGHT. PROCESS JARS IN A BOILING WATER CANNER FOR 10 MINUTES (SEE PAGE 27). TRANSFER JARS TO A TOWEL-LINED SURFACE AND LET REST AT ROOM TEMPERATURE UNTIL SET. CHECK SEALS; REFRIGERATE ANY UNSEALED JARS FOR UP TO 3 WEEKS. MAKES ABOUT FIVE 8-OUNCE (250 ML) JARS.

TIP: CHOOSE FIRM, RIPE OR SLIGHTLY UNDERRIPE APRICOTS. DO NOT PEEL, BUT DO DISCARD PITS. THE SKINS ADD FLAVOR, COLOR AND TEXTURE TO JAMS AND CONSERVES. DO NOT FREEZE APRICOTS FOR PRESERVING, AS THEY WOULD NEED TO BE PEELED AND HAVE JUICE, SUGAR OR SYRUP ADDED.

NOTE: THE KERNELS FOUND INSIDE APRICOT PITS WERE ONCE INCLUDED IN JAM RECIPES, BUT ARE NO LONGER CONSIDERED SAFE, AS THEY CONTAIN A TOXIC COMPOUND.

VARIATIONS

SPICED APRICOT JAM: STIR IN $\frac{3}{4}$ TSP (3 ML) GROUND CINNAMON AND $\frac{1}{4}$ TSP (1 ML) GROUND NUTMEG WITH THE SUGAR.

APRICOT JAM WITH LIQUEUR: STIR IN 3 TBSP (45 ML) APRICOT BRANDY OR AMARETTO AFTER SKIMMING OFF ANY FOAM.

RECIPE SUGGESTION: USE TO MAKE RUM- AND LIME-GLAZED PORK RIBS, PAGE 274.

BLACKBERRY JAM

BLACKBERRIES HAVE AN ABUNDANCE OF NATURAL PECTIN, SO THIS JAM WILL SET WELL. IT IS DARK, WITH A RICH BERRY TASTE AND SOFT SPREAD.

8 CUPS	BLACKBERRIES (ABOUT 2 LBS/1 KG)	2 L
1/2 CUP	WATER	125 ML
1/4 CUP	LEMON JUICE	60 ML
4 CUPS	GRANULATED SUGAR	1 L

IN A LARGE, DEEP, HEAVY-BOTTOMED POT, COMBINE BLACKBERRIES, WATER AND LEMON JUICE. BRING TO A BOIL OVER HIGH HEAT. REDUCE HEAT AND SIMMER, STIRRING OCCASIONALLY, FOR 5 MINUTES. BRING TO A FULL BOIL OVER HIGH HEAT, STIRRING CONSTANTLY. ADD SUGAR IN A STEADY STREAM, STIRRING CONSTANTLY. RETURN TO A FULL BOIL, STIRRING CONSTANTLY TO DISSOLVE SUGAR. REDUCE HEAT TO MEDIUM-HIGH AND BOIL RAPIDLY, STIRRING OFTEN AND REDUCING HEAT FURTHER AS MIXTURE THICKENS, FOR 12 TO 15 MINUTES OR UNTIL THICKENED. TEST FOR SETTING POINT (SEE PAGE 24). REMOVE FROM HEAT AND SKIM OFF ANY FOAM.

LADLE INTO STERILIZED JARS TO WITHIN 1/4 INCH (0.5 CM) OF RIM; WIPE RIMS. APPLY PREPARED LIDS AND RINGS; TIGHTEN RINGS JUST UNTIL FINGERTIP-TIGHT. PROCESS JARS IN A BOILING WATER CANNER FOR 10 MINUTES (SEE PAGE 27). TRANSFER JARS TO A TOWEL-LINED SURFACE AND LET REST AT ROOM TEMPERATURE UNTIL SET. CHECK SEALS; REFRIGERATE ANY UNSEALED JARS FOR UP TO 3 WEEKS. MAKES ABOUT FIVE 8-OUNCE (250 ML) JARS.

BLACK CURRANT JAM

TRY THIS CLASSIC JAM IN BLACK CURRANT
LINZER SLICES (PAGE 286).

6 CUPS	BLACK CURRANTS, BEARDS REMOVED (SEE BOX, PAGE 81)	1.5 L
4 CUPS	WATER	1 L
6 CUPS	GRANULATED SUGAR	1.5 L

IN A LARGE, DEEP, HEAVY-BOTTOMED POT, COMBINE CURRANTS AND WATER. BRING TO A BOIL OVER HIGH HEAT. REDUCE HEAT AND SIMMER, STIRRING OCCASIONALLY, FOR 15 MINUTES OR UNTIL SOFTENED. USE A POTATO MASHER TO CRUSH CURRANTS, IF DESIRED. BRING TO A FULL BOIL OVER HIGH HEAT, STIRRING CONSTANTLY. ADD SUGAR IN A STEADY STREAM, STIRRING CONSTANTLY. RETURN TO A FULL BOIL, STIRRING CONSTANTLY TO DISSOLVE SUGAR. REDUCE HEAT TO MEDIUM-HIGH AND BOIL RAPIDLY, STIRRING OFTEN AND REDUCING HEAT FURTHER AS MIXTURE THICKENS, FOR 6 TO 10 MINUTES OR UNTIL THICKENED. TEST FOR SETTING POINT (SEE PAGE 24). REMOVE FROM HEAT AND SKIM OFF ANY FOAM.

LADLE INTO STERILIZED JARS TO WITHIN 1/4 INCH (0.5 CM) OF RIM; WIPE RIMS. APPLY PREPARED LIDS AND RINGS; TIGHTEN RINGS JUST UNTIL FINGERTIP-TIGHT. PROCESS JARS IN A BOILING WATER CANNER FOR 10 MINUTES (SEE PAGE 27). TRANSFER JARS TO A TOWEL-LINED SURFACE AND LET REST AT ROOM TEMPERATURE UNTIL SET. CHECK SEALS; REFRIGERATE ANY UNSEALED JARS FOR UP TO 3 WEEKS. MAKES ABOUT SEVEN 8-OUNCE (250 ML) JARS.

BLUEBERRY JAM

THIS RECIPE CAN BE MADE WITH CULTIVATED BLUEBERRIES, BUT THE INTENSE FLAVOR OF WILD ONES MAKES THIS AN EXTRA-SPECIAL JAM.

3 CUPS	WILD BLUEBERRIES	750 ML
1/4 CUP	WATER	60 ML
1 TBSP	LEMON JUICE	15 ML
3 1/2 CUPS	GRANULATED SUGAR	875 ML
1	POUCH (3 OZ/85 ML) LIQUID PECTIN	1

IN A LARGE, DEEP, HEAVY-BOTTOMED POT, COMBINE BLUEBERRIES, WATER AND LEMON JUICE. BRING TO A BOIL OVER HIGH HEAT. REDUCE HEAT AND SIMMER, COVERED, FOR 3 MINUTES. USE A POTATO MASHER TO CRUSH BLUEBERRIES. BRING TO A FULL BOIL OVER HIGH HEAT, STIRRING CONSTANTLY. ADD SUGAR IN A STEADY STREAM, STIRRING CONSTANTLY. RETURN TO A FULL BOIL, STIRRING CONSTANTLY TO DISSOLVE SUGAR. IMMEDIATELY STIR IN PECTIN; RETURN TO A FULL BOIL. BOIL HARD FOR 1 MINUTE, STIRRING CONSTANTLY. REMOVE FROM HEAT AND SKIM OFF ANY FOAM.

LADLE INTO STERILIZED JARS TO WITHIN 1/4 INCH (0.5 CM) OF RIM; WIPE RIMS. APPLY PREPARED LIDS AND RINGS; TIGHTEN RINGS JUST UNTIL FINGERTIP-TIGHT. PROCESS JARS IN A BOILING WATER CANNER FOR 10 MINUTES (SEE PAGE 27). TRANSFER JARS TO A TOWEL-LINED SURFACE AND LET REST AT ROOM TEMPERATURE UNTIL SET. CHECK SEALS; REFRIGERATE ANY UNSEALED JARS FOR UP TO 3 WEEKS. MAKES ABOUT FOUR 8-OUNCE (250 ML) JARS.

BOYSENBERRY JAM

BOYSENBERRIES, A CROSS BETWEEN BLACKBERRIES, RASPBERRIES AND LOGANBERRIES, HAVE THE SHAPE OF LARGE RASPBERRIES, A DARK PURPLE COLOR AND A RICH SWEET-TART FLAVOR. THEY MAKE AN EXQUISITE JAM.

| 7 CUPS | BOYSENBERRIES | 1.75 L |
| 4 CUPS | GRANULATED SUGAR | 1 L |

PLACE BOYSENBERRIES IN A LARGE, DEEP, HEAVY-BOTTOMED POT. BRING TO A BOIL OVER HIGH HEAT, STIRRING OCCASIONALLY. REDUCE HEAT AND SIMMER, STIRRING OFTEN, FOR ABOUT 3 MINUTES OR UNTIL BERRIES BEGIN TO RELEASE SOME JUICE. BRING TO A BOIL OVER HIGH HEAT, STIRRING CONSTANTLY. ADD SUGAR IN A STEADY STREAM, STIRRING CONSTANTLY. RETURN TO A BOIL, STIRRING CONSTANTLY TO DISSOLVE SUGAR. REDUCE HEAT TO MEDIUM-HIGH AND BOIL RAPIDLY, STIRRING OFTEN AND REDUCING HEAT FURTHER AS MIXTURE THICKENS, FOR 8 TO 12 MINUTES OR UNTIL THICKENED. TEST FOR SETTING POINT (SEE PAGE 24). REMOVE FROM HEAT AND SKIM OFF ANY FOAM.

LADLE INTO STERILIZED JARS TO WITHIN 1/4 INCH (0.5 CM) OF RIM; WIPE RIMS. APPLY PREPARED LIDS AND RINGS; TIGHTEN RINGS JUST UNTIL FINGERTIP-TIGHT. PROCESS JARS IN A BOILING WATER CANNER FOR 10 MINUTES (SEE PAGE 27). TRANSFER JARS TO A TOWEL-LINED SURFACE AND LET REST AT ROOM TEMPERATURE UNTIL SET. CHECK SEALS; REFRIGERATE ANY UNSEALED JARS FOR UP TO 3 WEEKS. MAKES ABOUT FIVE 8-OUNCE (250 ML) JARS.

SOUR CHERRY JAM

SOUR CHERRIES MAKE A DELICIOUS, SLIGHTLY TART JAM.

4 CUPS	FINELY CHOPPED PITTED SOUR (TART) CHERRIES	1 L
1 TBSP	LEMON JUICE	15 ML
1	PACKAGE (1.75 OZ/49 OR 57 G) POWDERED PECTIN	1
4½ CUPS	GRANULATED SUGAR	1.125 L

IN A LARGE, DEEP, HEAVY-BOTTOMED POT, COMBINE CHERRIES AND LEMON JUICE. STIR IN PECTIN UNTIL DISSOLVED. BRING TO A FULL BOIL OVER HIGH HEAT, STIRRING CONSTANTLY. ADD SUGAR IN A STEADY STREAM, STIRRING CONSTANTLY. RETURN TO A FULL BOIL, STIRRING CONSTANTLY TO DISSOLVE SUGAR. BOIL HARD FOR 1 MINUTE. REMOVE FROM HEAT AND SKIM OFF ANY FOAM. STIR FOR 5 TO 8 MINUTES TO PREVENT FLOATING FRUIT.

LADLE INTO STERILIZED JARS TO WITHIN ¼ INCH (0.5 CM) OF RIM; WIPE RIMS. APPLY PREPARED LIDS AND RINGS; TIGHTEN RINGS JUST UNTIL FINGERTIP-TIGHT. PROCESS JARS IN A BOILING WATER CANNER FOR 10 MINUTES (SEE PAGE 27). TRANSFER JARS TO A TOWEL-LINED SURFACE AND LET REST AT ROOM TEMPERATURE UNTIL SET. CHECK SEALS; REFRIGERATE ANY UNSEALED JARS FOR UP TO 3 WEEKS. MAKES ABOUT FIVE 8-OUNCE (250 ML) JARS.

TIP: YOU CAN USE A FOOD PROCESSOR TO CHOP CHERRIES; JUST MAKE SURE ALL OF THE PITS ARE REMOVED,

THEN PULSE A FEW TIMES, SCRAPE DOWN THE SIDES AND PULSE AGAIN. DO NOT PURÉE.

NOTE: MOST SOUR (TART) CHERRIES GROWN IN NORTH AMERICA ARE THE MONTMORENCY VARIETY, NAMED AFTER A VALLEY IN FRANCE WHERE THEY ORIGINATED. THEY ARE GROWN IN MICHIGAN AND WISCONSIN, AND IN THE NIAGARA REGION OF ONTARIO, CANADA.

RECIPE SUGGESTION: USE TO FILL SMALL BAKED TART SHELLS AND ADD A DOLLOP OF WHIPPED CREAM. OR SPREAD ON CRÊPES AND ROLL UP.

THE IMPORTANCE OF SUGAR IN PRESERVING

SUGAR HAS TWO MAIN ROLES IN PRESERVING. ONE IS TO CREATE A GOOD SET, OR GEL, FOR JAMS, JELLIES AND MARMALADES, AND THE OTHER IS TO ENSURE QUALITY OVER LONG STORAGE. IT ALSO CONTRIBUTES TO THE FLAVOR BALANCE, BALANCING THE ACIDITY SO THE PRODUCT IS NOT TOO SOUR TO EAT. UNLESS A RECIPE SPECIFIES THAT A CHANGE IS POSSIBLE, YOU SHOULD NEVER REDUCE OR INCREASE THE AMOUNT OF SUGAR CALLED FOR, AS YOU'LL RISK AN UNSUCCESSFUL SET AND A POOR-QUALITY PRESERVE.

SWEET CHERRY JAM

USE DARK RED SWEET CHERRIES SUCH AS BING FOR THIS RECIPE. RAINIER CHERRIES (A BING AND VAN CHERRY CROSS WITH A CREAMY YELLOW FLESH AND A BRIGHT RED BLUSH) MAY ALSO BE USED.

4 CUPS	FINELY CHOPPED PITTED SWEET CHERRIES	1 L
1/4 CUP	LEMON JUICE	60 ML
1	PACKAGE (1.75 OZ/49 OR 57 G) POWDERED PECTIN	1
4 CUPS	GRANULATED SUGAR	1 L

IN A LARGE, DEEP, HEAVY-BOTTOMED POT, COMBINE CHERRIES AND LEMON JUICE. STIR IN PECTIN UNTIL DISSOLVED. BRING TO A FULL BOIL OVER HIGH HEAT, STIRRING CONSTANTLY. ADD SUGAR IN A STEADY STREAM, STIRRING CONSTANTLY. RETURN TO A FULL BOIL, STIRRING CONSTANTLY TO DISSOLVE SUGAR. BOIL HARD FOR 1 MINUTE. REMOVE FROM HEAT AND SKIM OFF ANY FOAM.

LADLE INTO STERILIZED JARS TO WITHIN 1/4 INCH (0.5 CM) OF RIM; WIPE RIMS. APPLY PREPARED LIDS AND RINGS; TIGHTEN RINGS JUST UNTIL FINGERTIP-TIGHT. PROCESS JARS IN A BOILING WATER CANNER FOR 10 MINUTES (SEE PAGE 27). TRANSFER JARS TO A TOWEL-LINED SURFACE AND LET REST AT ROOM TEMPERATURE UNTIL SET. CHECK SEALS; REFRIGERATE ANY UNSEALED JARS FOR UP TO 3 WEEKS. MAKES ABOUT FIVE 8-OUNCE (250 ML) JARS.

TIP: IF USING FROZEN FRUIT, MEASURE WHILE STILL FROZEN AND LET THAW BEFORE ADDING TO THE POT.

VARIATIONS

SWEET CHERRY JAM WITH BALSAMIC VINEGAR: REPLACE THE LEMON JUICE WITH BALSAMIC VINEGAR.

SWEET CHERRY JAM WITH LIQUEUR: STIR IN $1/4$ CUP (60 ML) CHERRY BRANDY OR KIRSCH AFTER SKIMMING OFF ANY FOAM.

SWEET CHERRY JAM WITH VANILLA: SPLIT 1 VANILLA BEAN LENGTHWISE AND SCRAPE OUT SEEDS WITH A PARING KNIFE. ADD BEAN AND SEEDS TO POT AFTER STIRRING IN PECTIN. REMOVE BEAN BEFORE LADLING JAM INTO JARS.

SPICED SWEET CHERRY JAM: ADD $1/2$ TSP (2 ML) GROUND CINNAMON WITH THE SUGAR.

RECIPE SUGGESTION: THIS JAM IS A GREAT CHOICE TO STIR INTO PLAIN YOGURT OR TO TOP A CHEESECAKE.

A MORNING WITHOUT COFFEE IS LIKE – SLEEP.

GINGER JAM

WHY SETTLE FOR GINGER WHEN YOU CAN HAVE DOUBLE GINGER! THE SMALL BITS OF SWEET CRYSTALLIZED GINGER ADD INTERESTING FLAVOR BITES.

2 1/2 CUPS	ALL-NATURAL APPLE JUICE	625 ML
1/4 CUP	FINELY GRATED GINGERROOT	60 ML
1/2 CUP	FINELY CHOPPED CRYSTALLIZED GINGER	125 ML
2 TBSP	LEMON JUICE	30 ML
3 1/2 CUPS	GRANULATED SUGAR	875 ML
1	POUCH (3 OZ/85 ML) LIQUID PECTIN	1

IN A LARGE, DEEP, HEAVY-BOTTOMED POT, COMBINE APPLE JUICE AND GRATED GINGER. BRING TO A BOIL OVER HIGH HEAT. REDUCE HEAT AND SIMMER, COVERED, FOR 10 MINUTES. STIR IN CRYSTALLIZED GINGER AND LEMON JUICE. ADD SUGAR IN A STEADY STREAM, STIRRING CONSTANTLY. BRING TO A FULL BOIL OVER HIGH HEAT, STIRRING CONSTANTLY TO DISSOLVE SUGAR. IMMEDIATELY STIR IN PECTIN; RETURN TO A FULL BOIL. BOIL HARD FOR 1 MINUTE, STIRRING CONSTANTLY. REMOVE FROM HEAT AND SKIM OFF ANY FOAM. STIR FOR 5 TO 8 MINUTES TO PREVENT FLOATING GINGER.

LADLE INTO STERILIZED JARS TO WITHIN 1/4 INCH (0.5 CM) OF RIM; WIPE RIMS. APPLY PREPARED LIDS AND RINGS; TIGHTEN RINGS JUST UNTIL FINGERTIP-TIGHT. PROCESS JARS IN A BOILING WATER CANNER FOR 10 MINUTES (SEE PAGE 27). TRANSFER JARS TO A TOWEL-LINED SURFACE AND LET REST AT ROOM TEMPERATURE UNTIL SET. CHECK SEALS; REFRIGERATE ANY UNSEALED

JARS FOR UP TO 3 WEEKS. MAKES ABOUT FOUR 8-OUNCE (250 ML) JARS.

TIP: SUPERMARKETS NOW CARRY ALL-NATURAL APPLE JUICE, WHICH IS UNFILTERED AND LOOKS MORE LIKE APPLE CIDER, THOUGH IT MAY NOT BE AS TART. SHAKE BEFORE USING.

TIP: WHEN FILLING JARS, IT'S IMPORTANT TO LEAVE SUFFICIENT HEADSPACE BETWEEN THE TOP OF THE FOOD AND THE TOP OF THE JAR TO GET A GOOD VACUUM SEAL.

ABOUT CRYSTALLIZED GINGER

CRYSTALLIZED AND CANDIED GINGER ARE THE SAME THING: GINGER THAT HAS BEEN PRESERVED BY COOKING IN A SUGAR SYRUP, THEN COATING WITH GRANULATED SUGAR. IT IS AVAILABLE IN SUPERMARKETS AND BULK STORES, AND COMES IN SLICES OR PIECES. PRESERVED GINGER IN SYRUP COMES IN SMALL JARS AND MAY BE FOUND AT SPECIALTY FOOD STORES.

MANGO JAM

MANGOS ARE MUCH MORE AVAILABLE AND AFFORDABLE THAN EVER BEFORE, ESPECIALLY FRAGRANT ATAULFO MANGOS, WHICH USED TO BE AVAILABLE ONLY IN ETHNIC MARKETS. BUY THEM BY THE CASE WHEN IN SEASON, AS IT IS MORE ECONOMICAL.

4 CUPS	FINELY CHOPPED MANGOS	1 L
1/4 CUP	LEMON JUICE	60 ML
1/2 TSP	GROUND CINNAMON	2 ML
1/2 TSP	GROUND CARDAMOM	2 ML
3 1/2 CUPS	GRANULATED SUGAR	875 ML
2 CUPS	PACKED BROWN SUGAR	500 ML
2	POUCHES (EACH 3 OZ/85 ML) LIQUID PECTIN	2

IN A LARGE, DEEP, HEAVY-BOTTOMED POT, COMBINE MANGOS, LEMON JUICE, CINNAMON AND CARDAMOM. BRING TO A FULL BOIL OVER HIGH HEAT, STIRRING CONSTANTLY. ADD GRANULATED SUGAR IN A STEADY STREAM, STIRRING CONSTANTLY. STIR IN BROWN SUGAR. RETURN TO A FULL BOIL, STIRRING CONSTANTLY TO DISSOLVE SUGAR. IMMEDIATELY STIR IN PECTIN; RETURN TO A FULL BOIL. BOIL HARD FOR 1 MINUTE, STIRRING CONSTANTLY. REMOVE FROM HEAT AND SKIM OFF ANY FOAM. STIR FOR 5 TO 8 MINUTES TO PREVENT FLOATING FRUIT.

LADLE INTO STERILIZED JARS TO WITHIN 1/4 INCH (0.5 CM) OF RIM; WIPE RIMS. APPLY PREPARED LIDS AND RINGS; TIGHTEN RINGS JUST UNTIL FINGERTIP-TIGHT. PROCESS JARS IN A BOILING WATER CANNER FOR 10 MINUTES (SEE PAGE 27). TRANSFER JARS TO A TOWEL-LINED SURFACE AND LET REST AT ROOM

TEMPERATURE UNTIL SET. CHECK SEALS; REFRIGERATE ANY UNSEALED JARS FOR UP TO 3 WEEKS. MAKES ABOUT FIVE 8-OUNCE (250 ML) JARS.

TIP: FOR INFORMATION ON PREPARING MANGOS, SEE BOX, PAGE 265.

TIP: ONE LARGE REGULAR MANGO YIELDS ABOUT 1 CUP (250 ML) CHOPPED; AN ATAULFO MANGO YIELDS ABOUT $\frac{3}{4}$ CUP (175 ML) CHOPPED.

VARIATION

MANGO MINT JAM: OMIT THE SPICES AND BROWN SUGAR. INCREASE THE GRANULATED SUGAR TO $5\frac{1}{2}$ CUPS (1.375 L). STIR IN $\frac{1}{4}$ CUP (60 ML) FINELY CHOPPED FRESH MINT LEAVES (SPEARMINT OR ORANGE MINT) AFTER ADDING THE PECTIN.

ABOUT MANGOS

MANGOS ARE FRAGRANT AND JUICY WHEN RIPE. THEY ARE GROWN IN TROPICAL REGIONS SUCH AS INDIA (ALPHONSO MANGOS), THE WEST INDIES, MEXICO (ATAULFO MANGOS), FLORIDA AND HAWAII. ATAULFO MANGOS (ALSO CALLED CHAMPAGNE MANGOS) ARE ALMOST FIBERLESS WITH A BUTTERY FLESH AND THIN PIT.

NECTARINE JAM

THE PEEL OF THE NECTARINE ADDS TO THE OVERALL FLAVOR OF THE JAM, AND IT TAKES LESS TIME, AS YOU SAVE THE STEP OF PEELING.

4 CUPS	FINELY CHOPPED UNPEELED NECTARINES	1 L
3 TBSP	LEMON JUICE	45 ML
1	PACKAGE (1.75 OZ/49 OR 57 G) POWDERED PECTIN	1
4½ CUPS	GRANULATED SUGAR	1.125 L

IN A LARGE, DEEP, HEAVY-BOTTOMED POT, COMBINE NECTARINES AND LEMON JUICE. STIR IN PECTIN UNTIL DISSOLVED. BRING TO A FULL BOIL OVER HIGH HEAT, STIRRING CONSTANTLY. ADD SUGAR IN A STEADY STREAM, STIRRING CONSTANTLY. RETURN TO A FULL BOIL, STIRRING CONSTANTLY TO DISSOLVE SUGAR. BOIL HARD FOR 1 MINUTE. REMOVE FROM HEAT AND SKIM OFF ANY FOAM. STIR FOR 5 TO 8 MINUTES TO PREVENT FLOATING FRUIT.

LADLE INTO STERILIZED JARS TO WITHIN ¼ INCH (0.5 CM) OF RIM; WIPE RIMS. APPLY PREPARED LIDS AND RINGS; TIGHTEN RINGS JUST UNTIL FINGERTIP-TIGHT. PROCESS JARS IN A BOILING WATER CANNER FOR 10 MINUTES (SEE PAGE 27). TRANSFER JARS TO A TOWEL-LINED SURFACE AND LET REST AT ROOM TEMPERATURE UNTIL SET. CHECK SEALS; REFRIGERATE ANY UNSEALED JARS FOR UP TO 3 WEEKS. MAKES ABOUT FIVE 8-OUNCE (250 ML) JARS.

FREE WINE — TOMORROW.

SPICED PEACH JAM

HERE'S AN APPEALING AMBER-COLORED JAM WITH A HINT OF SPICE. SPREAD ON BUTTERED TOASTED ENGLISH MUFFINS FOR A MID-AFTERNOON TREAT.

8 CUPS	CHOPPED PEELED PEACHES (SEE BOX, PAGE 87)	2 L
7 CUPS	GRANULATED SUGAR	1.75 L
2 TSP	GROUND CINNAMON	10 ML
1/2 TSP	GROUND NUTMEG	2 ML
1 TBSP	LEMON JUICE	15 ML

IN A LARGE, DEEP HEAVY-BOTTOMED POT, MASH PEACHES (A POTATO MASHER WORKS WELL). STIR IN SUGAR, CINNAMON, NUTMEG AND LEMON JUICE. BRING TO A BOIL OVER MEDIUM-HIGH HEAT, STIRRING CONSTANTLY. REDUCE HEAT AND SIMMER, STIRRING FREQUENTLY, FOR ABOUT 45 MINUTES OR UNTIL THICK ENOUGH TO MOUND ON A SPOON. REMOVE FROM HEAT AND SKIM OFF ANY FOAM.

LADLE INTO STERILIZED JARS TO WITHIN 1/4 INCH (0.5 CM) OF RIM; WIPE RIMS. APPLY PREPARED LIDS AND RINGS; TIGHTEN RINGS JUST UNTIL FINGERTIP-TIGHT. PROCESS JARS IN A BOILING WATER CANNER FOR 10 MINUTES (SEE PAGE 27). TRANSFER JARS TO A TOWEL-LINED SURFACE AND LET REST AT ROOM TEMPERATURE UNTIL SET. CHECK SEALS; REFRIGERATE ANY UNSEALED JARS FOR UP TO 3 WEEKS. MAKES ABOUT SIX 8-OUNCE (250 ML) JARS.

RECIPE SUGGESTIONS: BRUSH ON GRILLED PORK TENDERLOIN A FEW MINUTES BEFORE THE END OF COOKING TIME. OR USE TO MAKE PEACHY CHEESE DIP (PAGE 266) OR STICKY BAKED CHICKEN (PAGE 276).

PEAR JAM

BARTLETT PEARS ARE A GOOD CHOICE FOR THIS AMAZING DARK AND DELICIOUS JAM. MAKE SURE THE PEARS ARE TENDER BUT NOT TOO SOFT OR THEY WILL BE DIFFICULT TO PEEL.

4 CUPS	FINELY CHOPPED PEELED PEARS	1 L
1/4 CUP	LEMON JUICE	60 ML
1	PACKAGE (1.75 OZ/49 OR 57 G) POWDERED PECTIN	1
3 CUPS	GRANULATED SUGAR	750 ML
2 CUPS	PACKED BROWN SUGAR	500 ML
1/2 TSP	GROUND CINNAMON	2 ML

IN A LARGE, DEEP, HEAVY-BOTTOMED POT, COMBINE PEARS AND LEMON JUICE. STIR IN PECTIN UNTIL DISSOLVED. BRING TO A FULL BOIL OVER HIGH HEAT, STIRRING CONSTANTLY. ADD GRANULATED SUGAR IN A STEADY STREAM, STIRRING CONSTANTLY. STIR IN BROWN SUGAR AND CINNAMON. RETURN TO A FULL BOIL, STIRRING CONSTANTLY TO DISSOLVE SUGAR. BOIL HARD FOR 1 MINUTE. REMOVE FROM HEAT AND SKIM OFF ANY FOAM. STIR FOR 5 TO 8 MINUTES TO PREVENT FLOATING FRUIT.

LADLE INTO STERILIZED JARS TO WITHIN 1/4 INCH (0.5 CM) OF RIM; WIPE RIMS. APPLY PREPARED LIDS AND RINGS; TIGHTEN RINGS JUST UNTIL FINGERTIP-TIGHT. PROCESS JARS IN A BOILING WATER CANNER FOR 10 MINUTES (SEE PAGE 27). TRANSFER JARS TO A TOWEL-LINED SURFACE AND LET REST AT ROOM TEMPERATURE UNTIL SET. CHECK SEALS; REFRIGERATE ANY UNSEALED

CONTINUED ON PAGE 55...

Apricot Jam (page 38) and Traditional Strawberry Jam (page 66)

Sour Cherry Jam (page 44)

Bumbleberry Jam (page 70)

Kiwi, Pineapple and Orange Jam (page 84)

JARS FOR UP TO 3 WEEKS. MAKES ABOUT FIVE 8-OUNCE (250 ML) JARS.

TIP: LEMON JUICE (THE AMOUNT IN THE RECIPE) OR A SMALL AMOUNT OF ASCORBIC ACID COLOR-KEEPER (SUCH AS FRUIT-FRESH; SEE BELOW) WILL PREVENT CUT PEARS FROM BROWNING. AS YOU CHOP PEARS, SPRINKLE A BIT OVER AND STIR IN.

TIP: THE BEST, SAFEST WAY TO LIFT JARS OUT OF THE CANNER IS WITH A JAR LIFTER, SPECIALIZED TONGS COATED WITH SILICONE AND DESIGNED TO FIT AROUND THE NECKS OF JARS.

PREVENTING BROWNING

FRUIT-FRESH IS AN ASCORBIC ACID COLOR-KEEPER THAT PREVENTS THE NATURAL ENZYMATIC BROWNING OF FRUIT, ESPECIALLY APPLES, BANANAS AND PEARS. USE ACCORDING TO PACKAGE DIRECTIONS, EITHER DIRECTLY ON FRUIT OR DISSOLVED IN WATER.

DAMSON PLUM JAM

DAMSON PLUMS ARE EXCELLENT FOR JAMS.
WHEN THEY COOK, THE SKIN PEELS BACK AND
THE FLESH SOFTENS TO RELEASE THE PIT. LOOK
FOR THESE PLUMS AT FARMERS' MARKETS IN
LATE AUGUST TO EARLY SEPTEMBER.

7 CUPS	DAMSON PLUMS	1.75 ML
2½ CUPS	WATER	625 ML
5½ CUPS	GRANULATED SUGAR	1.375 ML

IN A LARGE, DEEP, HEAVY-BOTTOMED POT, COMBINE
PLUMS AND WATER. BRING TO A BOIL OVER HIGH HEAT.
REDUCE HEAT AND BOIL GENTLY FOR 15 MINUTES, STIRRING
OCCASIONALLY. USE A SLOTTED SPOON TO REMOVE PITS
(WHICH HAVE BECOME LOOSENED FROM FRUIT) AND PLACE
THEM IN A COLANDER OVER A LARGE BOWL. SHAKE TO
DRAIN EXTRA PULP AND SKINS FROM PITS; ADD BACK
TO POT AND DISCARD PITS. ADD SUGAR IN A STEADY
STREAM, STIRRING CONSTANTLY. BRING TO A BOIL
OVER HIGH HEAT, STIRRING CONSTANTLY TO DISSOLVE
SUGAR. REDUCE HEAT TO MEDIUM-HIGH AND BOIL RAPIDLY,
STIRRING OFTEN AND REDUCING HEAT FURTHER AS
MIXTURE THICKENS, FOR 8 TO 12 MINUTES OR UNTIL
THICKENED. TEST FOR SETTING POINT (SEE PAGE 24).
REMOVE FROM HEAT AND SKIM OFF ANY FOAM.

LADLE INTO STERILIZED JARS TO WITHIN ¼ INCH
(0.5 CM) OF RIM; WIPE RIMS. APPLY PREPARED LIDS
AND RINGS; TIGHTEN RINGS JUST UNTIL FINGERTIP-
TIGHT. PROCESS JARS IN A BOILING WATER CANNER
FOR 10 MINUTES (SEE PAGE 27). TRANSFER JARS TO

A TOWEL-LINED SURFACE AND LET REST AT ROOM TEMPERATURE UNTIL SET. CHECK SEALS; REFRIGERATE ANY UNSEALED JARS FOR UP TO 3 WEEKS. MAKES ABOUT SIX 8-OUNCE (250 ML) JARS.

TIP: WHEN FILLING JARS, IT'S IMPORTANT TO LEAVE SUFFICIENT HEADSPACE BETWEEN THE TOP OF THE FOOD AND THE TOP OF THE JAR TO GET A GOOD VACUUM SEAL.

NOTE: DO NOT CONFUSE DAMSON PLUMS WITH ITALIAN PLUMS, WHICH ARE IN SEASON AROUND THE SAME TIME. DAMSONS ARE SMALL AND DARK PURPLE, VERY TART AND THEIR PIT IS DIFFICULT TO REMOVE, SO ARE LEFT IN UNTIL JAM STARTS TO COOK. ITALIAN PLUMS ARE LARGER AND PURPLISH-BLACK, AND ARE FREESTONE. THEY ARE SWEETER, SO ARE WONDERFUL FOR EATING RAW AND FOR BAKING WITH.

THIRTY-FIVE IS WHEN YOU FINALLY GET YOUR HEAD TOGETHER AND YOUR BODY STARTS FALLING APART.

RED OR BLACK PLUM JAM

THE DEEP BURGUNDY COLOR OF THIS JAM
COMES FROM PEELS THAT ARE LEFT ON.

9 CUPS	CHOPPED PITTED FIRM RED OR BLACK PLUMS	2.25 L
1/4 CUP	LEMON JUICE	60 ML
6 CUPS	GRANULATED SUGAR	1.5 L

PLACE PLUMS IN A LARGE, DEEP, HEAVY-BOTTOMED POT. STIR IN LEMON JUICE. ADD SUGAR IN A STEADY STREAM, STIRRING CONSTANTLY. HEAT OVER MEDIUM HEAT, STIRRING CONSTANTLY TO DISSOLVE SUGAR. INCREASE HEAT TO HIGH AND BRING TO A FULL BOIL, STIRRING CONSTANTLY. REDUCE HEAT TO MEDIUM-HIGH AND BOIL RAPIDLY, STIRRING OFTEN AND REDUCING HEAT FURTHER AS MIXTURE THICKENS, FOR 20 TO 22 MINUTES OR UNTIL THICKENED. TEST FOR SETTING POINT (SEE PAGE 24). REMOVE FROM HEAT AND SKIM OFF ANY FOAM.

LADLE INTO STERILIZED JARS TO WITHIN 1/4 INCH (0.5 CM) OF RIM; WIPE RIMS. APPLY PREPARED LIDS AND RINGS; TIGHTEN RINGS JUST UNTIL FINGERTIP-TIGHT. PROCESS JARS IN A BOILING WATER CANNER FOR 10 MINUTES (SEE PAGE 27). TRANSFER JARS TO A TOWEL-LINED SURFACE AND LET REST AT ROOM TEMPERATURE UNTIL SET. CHECK SEALS; REFRIGERATE ANY UNSEALED JARS FOR UP TO 3 WEEKS. MAKES ABOUT SIX 8-OUNCE (250 ML) JARS.

NOTE: THERE ARE MANY VARIETIES OF PLUMS AVAILABLE, INCLUDING PLUMCOTS, A CROSS BETWEEN A PLUM AND AN APRICOT. THEY CAN ALSO BE USED HERE.

TRADITIONAL RASPBERRY JAM

GO TO PICK-YOUR-OWN FARMS TO GET THE BEST
QUALITY AND PRICE FOR RASPBERRIES, OR PICK THEM
UP IN SEASON AT LOCAL FARMERS' MARKETS.

| 9 CUPS | RASPBERRIES | 2.25 L |
| 4½ CUPS | GRANULATED SUGAR | 1.125 L |

PLACE RASPBERRIES IN A LARGE, DEEP, HEAVY-BOTTOMED
POT. ADD SUGAR IN A STEADY STREAM, STIRRING
CONSTANTLY. HEAT OVER MEDIUM HEAT, STIRRING
CONSTANTLY TO DISSOLVE SUGAR. INCREASE HEAT TO
HIGH AND BRING TO A FULL BOIL, STIRRING CONSTANTLY.
REDUCE HEAT TO MEDIUM- HIGH AND BOIL RAPIDLY,
STIRRING OFTEN AND REDUCING HEAT FURTHER AS
MIXTURE THICKENS, FOR 10 TO 12 MINUTES OR UNTIL
THICKENED. TEST FOR SETTING POINT (SEE PAGE 24).
REMOVE FROM HEAT AND SKIM OFF ANY FOAM.

LADLE INTO STERILIZED JARS TO WITHIN ¼ INCH
(0.5 CM) OF RIM; WIPE RIMS. APPLY PREPARED LIDS
AND RINGS; TIGHTEN RINGS JUST UNTIL FINGERTIP-
TIGHT. PROCESS JARS IN A BOILING WATER CANNER FOR
10 MINUTES (SEE PAGE 27). TRANSFER JARS TO A TOWEL-
LINED SURFACE AND LET REST AT ROOM TEMPERATURE
UNTIL SET. CHECK SEALS; REFRIGERATE ANY UNSEALED
JARS FOR UP TO 3 WEEKS. MAKES ABOUT SIX 8-OUNCE
(250 ML) JARS.

TIP: TO FREEZE BERRIES, WASH AND PLACE IN A SINGLE
LAYER ON A BAKING SHEET. ONCE FROZEN, MEASURE AND
PLACE IN FREEZER BAGS OR CONTAINERS, LABELED WITH
THE AMOUNT.

SHORTCUT RASPBERRY JAM

THE ADDITION OF COMMERCIAL PECTIN REDUCES THE COOKING TIME GREATLY, AND THERE'S NO NEED TO TEST FOR THE SETTING POINT. JAM RETAINS A BETTER COLOR AND FLAVOR.

9 CUPS	RASPBERRIES	2.25 L
4 3/4 CUPS	GRANULATED SUGAR	1.175 L
1	POUCH (3 OZ/85 ML) LIQUID PECTIN	1

PLACE RASPBERRIES IN A LARGE, DEEP, HEAVY-BOTTOMED POT; CRUSH WITH A POTATO MASHER. ADD SUGAR IN A STEADY STREAM, STIRRING CONSTANTLY. BRING TO A FULL BOIL OVER HIGH HEAT, STIRRING CONSTANTLY. IMMEDIATELY STIR IN PECTIN; RETURN TO A FULL BOIL. BOIL HARD FOR 1 MINUTE, STIRRING CONSTANTLY. REMOVE FROM HEAT AND SKIM OFF ANY FOAM.

LADLE INTO STERILIZED JARS TO WITHIN 1/4 INCH (0.5 CM) OF RIM; WIPE RIMS. APPLY PREPARED LIDS AND RINGS; TIGHTEN RINGS JUST UNTIL FINGERTIP-TIGHT. PROCESS JARS IN A BOILING WATER CANNER FOR 10 MINUTES (SEE PAGE 27). TRANSFER JARS TO A TOWEL-LINED SURFACE AND LET REST AT ROOM TEMPERATURE UNTIL SET. CHECK SEALS; REFRIGERATE ANY UNSEALED JARS FOR UP TO 3 WEEKS. *MAKES ABOUT FOUR 8-OUNCE (250 ML) JARS.*

TIP: WHEN USING FROZEN FRUIT, MEASURE WHOLE BERRIES BEFORE THAWING. LET THAW SLIGHTLY BEFORE ADDING TO THE POT.

TIP: WHEN FILLING JARS, IT'S IMPORTANT TO LEAVE SUFFICIENT HEADSPACE BETWEEN THE TOP OF THE FOOD AND THE TOP OF THE JAR TO GET A GOOD VACUUM SEAL.

VARIATIONS

SEEDLESS RASPBERRY JAM: COOK RASPBERRIES FOR 5 MINUTES AFTER ADDING SUGAR. LET FOAM SUBSIDE, THEN STRAIN THROUGH A FINE-MESH SIEVE INTO A LARGE BOWL. IF DESIRED, STRAIN MIXTURE A SECOND TIME, STIRRING GENTLY WITH A SPATULA; DO NOT PUSH FIRMLY OR TOO MANY SEEDS WILL GO THROUGH. RETURN TO A CLEAN POT.

BLACK RASPBERRY JAM: USE BLACK RASPBERRIES IN PLACE OF RED ONES.

RECIPE SUGGESTION: USE IN PLACE OF STRAWBERRY JAM TO MAKE CHOCOLATE STRAWBERRY TORTE (PAGE 284).

I FINALLY FIGURED OUT WHAT I WANT TO BE WHEN I GET OLDER: YOUNGER.

RHUBARB JAM

RHUBARB IS TYPICALLY ENJOYED AS A FRUIT BUT IS ACTUALLY A PERENNIAL VEGETABLE. IN WINTER MONTHS, LOOK FOR GREENHOUSE RHUBARB, WHICH HAS A LOVELY RED-PINK COLOR.

6 CUPS	DICED RHUBARB ($1/2$-INCH/1 CM PIECES)	1.5 L
3/4 CUP	WATER	175 ML
1	PACKAGE (1.75 OZ/49 OR 57 G) POWDERED PECTIN	1
5 CUPS	GRANULATED SUGAR	1.25 L

IN A LARGE, DEEP, HEAVY-BOTTOMED POT, COMBINE RHUBARB AND WATER. BRING TO A BOIL OVER HIGH HEAT. REDUCE HEAT AND SIMMER, COVERED, FOR ABOUT 2 MINUTES OR UNTIL RHUBARB IS TENDER. STIR IN PECTIN UNTIL DISSOLVED. BRING TO A FULL BOIL OVER HIGH HEAT, STIRRING CONSTANTLY. ADD SUGAR IN A STEADY STREAM, STIRRING CONSTANTLY. RETURN TO A FULL BOIL, STIRRING CONSTANTLY TO DISSOLVE SUGAR. BOIL HARD FOR 1 MINUTE. REMOVE FROM HEAT AND SKIM OFF ANY FOAM.

LADLE INTO STERILIZED JARS TO WITHIN $1/4$ INCH (0.5 CM) OF RIM; WIPE RIMS. APPLY PREPARED LIDS AND RINGS; TIGHTEN RINGS JUST UNTIL FINGERTIP-TIGHT. PROCESS JARS IN BOILING WATER CANNER FOR 10 MINUTES (SEE PAGE 27). TRANSFER JARS TO A TOWEL-LINED SURFACE AND LET REST AT ROOM TEMPERATURE UNTIL SET. CHECK SEALS; REFRIGERATE ANY UNSEALED JARS FOR UP TO 3 WEEKS. MAKES ABOUT SIX 8-OUNCE (250 ML) JARS.

TIP: THIS RECIPE CAN ALSO BE MADE WITH FROZEN RHUBARB.

TIP: THE BEST, SAFEST WAY TO LIFT JARS OUT OF THE CANNER IS WITH A JAR LIFTER, SPECIALIZED TONGS COATED WITH SILICONE AND DESIGNED TO FIT AROUND THE NECKS OF JARS.

VARIATIONS

RHUBARB JAM WITH MINT: ADD $1/4$ CUP (60 ML) FINELY CHOPPED FRESH MINT AFTER STIRRING IN THE SUGAR.

RHUBARB JAM WITH GINGER: ADD I TBSP (15 ML) FINELY GRATED GINGERROOT TO THE RHUBARB BEFORE COOKING.

RHUBARB JAM WITH ROSE WATER: ADD I TBSP (15 ML) ROSE WATER AFTER SKIMMING OFF THE FOAM.

PORT: A FINE RED WINE
SERVED ON THE LEFT SIDE OF THE BOAT.

SASKATOON BERRY JAM

THESE DARK PURPLE BERRIES WITH LARGE SEEDS HAVE A DISTINCTIVE TASTE YOU DON'T FORGET. THE SHRUB/SMALL TREE, NATIVE TO NORTH AMERICA, IS A MEMBER OF THE APPLE FAMILY AND IS ALSO KNOWN AS SERVICEBERRY, JUNEBERRY AND SHAD BUSH.

6 CUPS	SASKATOON BERRIES	1.5 L
3 TBSP	LEMON JUICE	45 ML
5 CUPS	GRANULATED SUGAR	1.25 L
1 TSP	GROUND CINNAMON	5 ML
2	POUCHES (EACH 3 OZ/85 ML) LIQUID PECTIN	2

IN A LARGE, DEEP, HEAVY-BOTTOMED POT, COMBINE BERRIES AND LEMON JUICE; CRUSH WITH A POTATO MASHER. BRING TO A BOIL OVER HIGH HEAT, STIRRING CONSTANTLY. REDUCE HEAT AND SIMMER, COVERED, FOR 15 MINUTES OR UNTIL BERRIES ARE SOFTENED. BRING TO A FULL BOIL OVER HIGH HEAT, STIRRING CONSTANTLY. ADD SUGAR IN A STEADY STREAM, STIRRING CONSTANTLY. STIR IN CINNAMON. RETURN TO A FULL BOIL, STIRRING CONSTANTLY TO DISSOLVE SUGAR. IMMEDIATELY STIR IN PECTIN; RETURN TO A FULL BOIL. BOIL HARD FOR 1 MINUTE, STIRRING CONSTANTLY. REMOVE FROM HEAT AND SKIM OFF ANY FOAM. STIR FOR 5 TO 8 MINUTES TO PREVENT FLOATING FRUIT.

LADLE INTO STERILIZED JARS TO WITHIN 1/4 INCH (0.5 CM) OF RIM. WIPE RIMS AND APPLY PREPARED LIDS AND RINGS; TIGHTEN RINGS JUST UNTIL FINGERTIP-TIGHT. PROCESS JARS IN A BOILING WATER CANNER FOR

10 MINUTES (SEE PAGE 27). TRANSFER JARS TO A TOWEL-LINED SURFACE AND LET REST AT ROOM TEMPERATURE UNTIL SET. CHECK SEALS; REFRIGERATE ANY UNSEALED JARS FOR UP TO 3 WEEKS. MAKES ABOUT SIX 8-OUNCE (250 ML) JARS.

RECIPE SUGGESTION: WARM THIS JAM, DILUTE IT WITH A LITTLE WATER OR ORANGE JUICE AND SERVE OVER PANCAKES OR WAFFLES.

SUBSTITUTING REGIONAL BERRIES

THERE ARE MANY REGIONAL BERRIES THAT ARE TERRIFIC FOR PRESERVES AND MAY BE SUBSTITUTED IN RECIPES. KEEP AN EYE OUT FOR BERRIES THAT ARE NATIVE TO YOUR AREA, AND MAKE GOOD USE OF THEM WHEN THEY'RE IN SEASON.

TRADITIONAL STRAWBERRY JAM

STRAWBERRY JAM IS ONE OF THE MOST POPULAR PRESERVES TO MAKE, ESPECIALLY WHEN LOCAL FRUIT IS IN SEASON. THIS RECIPE USES THE LONG-BOIL METHOD, WITH NO ADDED PECTIN.

6 CUPS	CRUSHED STRAWBERRIES	1.5 L
3 TBSP	LEMON JUICE	45 ML
5 CUPS	GRANULATED SUGAR	1.25 L

IN A LARGE, HEAVY-BOTTOMED POT, COMBINE STRAWBERRIES AND LEMON JUICE. BRING TO A BOIL OVER HIGH HEAT, STIRRING CONSTANTLY. ADD SUGAR IN A STEADY STREAM, STIRRING CONSTANTLY. BRING TO A FULL BOIL, STIRRING CONSTANTLY TO DISSOLVE SUGAR. REDUCE HEAT TO MEDIUM-HIGH AND BOIL RAPIDLY, STIRRING OFTEN AND REDUCING HEAT FURTHER AS MIXTURE THICKENS, FOR 20 TO 22 MINUTES OR UNTIL THICKENED. TEST FOR SETTING POINT (SEE PAGE 24). REMOVE FROM HEAT AND SKIM OFF ANY FOAM. STIR FOR 5 TO 8 MINUTES TO PREVENT FLOATING FRUIT.

LADLE INTO STERILIZED JARS TO WITHIN $\frac{1}{4}$ INCH (0.5 CM) OF RIM; WIPE RIMS. APPLY PREPARED LIDS AND RINGS; TIGHTEN RINGS JUST UNTIL FINGERTIP-TIGHT. PROCESS JARS IN BOILING WATER CANNER (SEE PAGE 27) FOR 10 MINUTES. TRANSFER JARS TO A TOWEL-LINED SURFACE AND LET REST AT ROOM TEMPERATURE UNTIL SET. CHECK SEALS; REFRIGERATE ANY UNSEALED JARS FOR UP TO 3 WEEKS. MAKES ABOUT FIVE 8-OUNCE (250 ML) JARS.

SHORTCUT STRAWBERRY JAM

ADDING COMMERCIAL PECTIN REDUCES
THE COOKING TIME, AND THE JAM HAS A
BRIGHTER COLOR AND BETTER FLAVOR.

3½ CUPS	CRUSHED STRAWBERRIES	875 ML
¼ CUP	LEMON JUICE	60 ML
7 CUPS	GRANULATED SUGAR	1.75 L
1	POUCH (3 OZ/85 ML) LIQUID PECTIN	1

IN A LARGE, DEEP, HEAVY-BOTTOMED POT, COMBINE
STRAWBERRIES AND LEMON JUICE. ADD SUGAR IN A
STEADY STREAM, STIRRING CONSTANTLY. BRING TO
A FULL BOIL OVER HIGH HEAT, STIRRING CONSTANTLY
TO DISSOLVE SUGAR. IMMEDIATELY STIR IN PECTIN;
RETURN TO A FULL BOIL. BOIL HARD FOR 1 MINUTE,
STIRRING CONSTANTLY. REMOVE FROM HEAT AND SKIM
OFF ANY FOAM. STIR FOR 5 TO 8 MINUTES TO PREVENT
FLOATING FRUIT.

LADLE INTO STERILIZED JARS TO WITHIN ¼ INCH
(0.5 CM) OF RIM; WIPE RIMS. APPLY PREPARED LIDS
AND RINGS; TIGHTEN RINGS JUST UNTIL FINGERTIP-
TIGHT. PROCESS JARS IN A BOILING WATER CANNER FOR
10 MINUTES (SEE PAGE 27). TRANSFER JARS TO A TOWEL-
LINED SURFACE AND LET REST AT ROOM TEMPERATURE
UNTIL SET. CHECK SEALS; REFRIGERATE ANY UNSEALED
JARS FOR UP TO 3 WEEKS. MAKES ABOUT SEVEN 8-OUNCE
(250 ML) JARS.

TIP: IF YOU LEAVE THE LEMON JUICE OUT OF STRAWBERRY
JAM, IT WILL NOT SET — STRAWBERRIES ARE NOT HIGH
ENOUGH IN ACID.

Mixed-Fruit Jams

Create unique tastes with interesting combinations of fruits. Fruits with lower pectin are matched up with fruits high in pectin to give a good set. Whether you use two fruits or a bevy of berries, you are sure to find new favorites. Have fun picking your own berries or tree fruits, and even rhubarb, to make jam in season, or to freeze for jam-making when they're not as readily available.

APPLE BERRY JAM

THIS SOFT-SPREADING JAM IS IDEAL TO MAKE WHEN YOU HAVE LITTLE BITS OF FRUIT LEFT OVER AND THERE'S NOT ENOUGH FOR ANY ONE JAM.

2	LARGE APPLES, PEELED AND GRATED OR FINELY CHOPPED	2
2 CUPS	CRUSHED STRAWBERRIES	500 ML
2 CUPS	RASPBERRIES	500 ML
2 CUPS	RED CURRANTS OR GOOSEBERRIES, BEARDS REMOVED (SEE BOX, PAGE 83)	500 ML
2 TBSP	LEMON JUICE	30 ML
5 CUPS	GRANULATED SUGAR	1.25 L

IN A LARGE, DEEP, HEAVY-BOTTOMED POT, COMBINE APPLES, STRAWBERRIES, RASPBERRIES, RED CURRANTS AND LEMON JUICE. BRING TO A BOIL OVER HIGH HEAT, STIRRING OCCASIONALLY. REDUCE HEAT AND SIMMER, STIRRING OCCASIONALLY, FOR ABOUT 7 MINUTES OR UNTIL

SOFTENED. ADD SUGAR IN A STEADY STREAM, STIRRING
CONSTANTLY. INCREASE HEAT TO HIGH AND BRING TO A
FULL BOIL, STIRRING CONSTANTLY TO DISSOLVE SUGAR.
REDUCE HEAT TO MEDIUM-HIGH AND BOIL HARD, STIRRING
OFTEN AND REDUCING HEAT FURTHER AS MIXTURE
THICKENS, FOR 12 TO 15 MINUTES OR UNTIL THICKENED.
TEST FOR SETTING POINT (SEE PAGE 24). REMOVE FROM
HEAT AND SKIM OFF ANY FOAM.

LADLE INTO STERILIZED JARS TO WITHIN $\frac{1}{4}$ INCH
(0.5 CM) OF RIM; WIPE RIMS. APPLY PREPARED LIDS
AND RINGS; TIGHTEN RINGS JUST UNTIL FINGERTIP-
TIGHT. PROCESS JARS IN A BOILING WATER CANNER FOR
10 MINUTES (SEE PAGE 27). TRANSFER JARS TO A TOWEL-
LINED SURFACE AND LET REST AT ROOM TEMPERATURE
UNTIL SET. CHECK SEALS; REFRIGERATE ANY UNSEALED
JARS FOR UP TO 3 WEEKS. MAKES ABOUT SIX 8-OUNCE
(250 ML) JARS.

TIP: GRATING THE APPLES INSTEAD OF CHOPPING THEM
WILL SAVE YOU TIME WHEN MAKING THIS RECIPE.

BUMBLEBERRY JAM

BUMBLEBERRY, OR JUMBLEBERRY, IS A MIX OF
BERRIES AND OTHER FRUITS, SUCH AS RHUBARB
OR APPLES. WONDERFUL IN PIES AND CRISPS,
IT'S ALSO A GREAT JAM COMBO.

I CUP	CRUSHED STRAWBERRIES	250 ML
I CUP	RASPBERRIES	250 ML
I CUP	BLUEBERRIES	250 ML
I CUP	BLACKBERRIES	250 ML
I CUP	CHOPPED RHUBARB (1/2-INCH/1 CM PIECES)	250 ML
5 CUPS	GRANULATED SUGAR	1.25 L
I	POUCH (3 OZ/85 ML) LIQUID PECTIN	I

IN A LARGE, DEEP, HEAVY-BOTTOMED POT, COMBINE
BERRIES AND RHUBARB. BRING TO A BOIL OVER HIGH
HEAT, STIRRING CONSTANTLY. REDUCE HEAT AND
SIMMER FOR ABOUT 10 MINUTES OR UNTIL RHUBARB IS
SOFTENED. ADD SUGAR IN A STEADY STREAM, STIRRING
CONSTANTLY. INCREASE HEAT TO HIGH AND BRING TO A
FULL BOIL, STIRRING CONSTANTLY TO DISSOLVE SUGAR.
IMMEDIATELY STIR IN PECTIN; RETURN TO A FULL BOIL.
BOIL HARD FOR I MINUTE, STIRRING CONSTANTLY. REMOVE
FROM HEAT AND SKIM OFF ANY FOAM. STIR FOR 5 TO
8 MINUTES TO PREVENT FLOATING FRUIT.

LADLE INTO STERILIZED JARS TO WITHIN 1/4 INCH
(0.5 CM) OF RIM; WIPE RIMS. APPLY PREPARED LIDS
AND RINGS; TIGHTEN RINGS JUST UNTIL FINGERTIP-
TIGHT. PROCESS JARS IN A BOILING WATER CANNER
FOR 10 MINUTES (SEE PAGE 27). TRANSFER JARS TO

A TOWEL-LINED SURFACE AND LET REST AT ROOM TEMPERATURE UNTIL SET. CHECK SEALS; REFRIGERATE ANY UNSEALED JARS FOR UP TO 3 WEEKS. MAKES ABOUT FIVE 8-OUNCE (250 ML) JARS.

TIP: FREEZE PREMEASURED AMOUNTS OF CHOPPED RHUBARB AND IN-SEASON BERRIES SO YOU HAVE THEM ON HAND WHEN YOU HAVE MORE TIME TO MAKE JAM IN THE WINTER.

USING BERRIES IN PRESERVES

EITHER FRESH OR FROZEN BERRIES CAN BE USED FOR PRESERVES. FROZEN BERRIES WILL PRODUCE MORE JUICE WHEN THAWED, SO PRESERVES MAY NEED SLIGHTLY MORE COOKING TIME. IF USING FRESH BERRIES, CHOOSE FIRM, RIPE, DRY FRUIT. STORE FRESH BERRIES (EXCEPT CRANBERRIES; SEE BOX, PAGE 101) IN A SINGLE LAYER UNDER A PAPER TOWEL IN THE REFRIGERATOR, BUT DO NOT STORE THEM FOR TOO LONG BEFORE USING. WASH, RINSE AND DRAIN ALL BERRIES BEFORE USE. FOR STRAWBERRIES, REMOVE HULLS AND STEMS AFTER WASHING.

FIVE-BERRY JAM

A WONDERFUL BERRY BLEND WITH A DEEP BURGUNDY COLOR, A BIT OF TARTNESS AND UNDERTONES OF BLACK CURRANT, THIS IS A PERFECT RECIPE TO MAKE WHEN YOU HAVE SMALL AMOUNTS OF BERRIES.

2 CUPS	RASPBERRIES	500 ML
2 CUPS	BLACKBERRIES	500 ML
2 CUPS	BLACK CURRANTS, BEARDS REMOVED (SEE TIP, OPPOSITE)	500 ML
2 CUPS	RED CURRANTS	500 ML
2 CUPS	GOOSEBERRIES, BEARDS REMOVED	500 ML
5 CUPS	GRANULATED SUGAR	1.25 L

IN A LARGE, DEEP, HEAVY-BOTTOMED POT, COMBINE RASPBERRIES, BLACKBERRIES, BLACK CURRANTS, RED CURRANTS AND GOOSEBERRIES. BRING TO A BOIL OVER HIGH HEAT, STIRRING CONSTANTLY. REDUCE HEAT AND SIMMER FOR 5 MINUTES, STIRRING CONSTANTLY. ADD SUGAR IN A STEADY STREAM, STIRRING CONSTANTLY. INCREASE HEAT TO HIGH AND BRING TO A FULL BOIL, STIRRING CONSTANTLY TO DISSOLVE SUGAR. REDUCE HEAT TO MEDIUM-HIGH AND BOIL HARD, STIRRING OFTEN AND REDUCING HEAT FURTHER AS MIXTURE THICKENS, FOR 5 TO 8 MINUTES OR UNTIL THICKENED. TEST FOR SETTING POINT (SEE PAGE 24). REMOVE FROM HEAT AND SKIM OFF ANY FOAM.

LADLE INTO STERILIZED JARS TO WITHIN 1/4 INCH (0.5 CM) OF RIM; WIPE RIMS. APPLY PREPARED LIDS AND RINGS; TIGHTEN RINGS JUST UNTIL FINGERTIP-TIGHT. PROCESS JARS IN A BOILING WATER CANNER

FOR 10 MINUTES (SEE PAGE 27). TRANSFER JARS TO A TOWEL-LINED SURFACE AND LET REST AT ROOM TEMPERATURE UNTIL SET. CHECK SEALS; REFRIGERATE ANY UNSEALED JARS FOR UP TO 3 WEEKS. MAKES ABOUT SIX 8-OUNCE (250 ML) JARS.

TIP: THE BEARDS (BLOSSOM ENDS) OF THE BLACK CURRANTS AND GOOSEBERRIES MUST BE SNIPPED FROM THE ENDS BEFORE USE. A SMALL PAIR OF CURVED-BLADE MANICURE SCISSORS IS THE PERFECT TOOL FOR THIS TASK.

NOTE: GOOSEBERRIES AND CURRANTS ARE RELATED BOTANICALLY; HOWEVER, GOOSEBERRIES HAVE SPINES ON THEIR STEMS. GOOSEBERRY BUSHES CAN BE PRODUCTIVE FOR 15 TO 20 YEARS.

BY THE TIME YOU'RE OLD ENOUGH
TO KNOW YOUR WAY AROUND,
YOU'RE NOT GOING ANYWHERE.

BLUEBERRY AND ORANGE JAM

A LOVELY PAIRING OF FRUITS.
USE WILD BLUEBERRIES FOR THE BEST FLAVOR.

4	LARGE ORANGES	4
3 CUPS	BLUEBERRIES	750 ML
1/4 CUP	LEMON JUICE	60 ML
6 CUPS	GRANULATED SUGAR	1.5 L
2	POUCHES (EACH 3 OZ/85 ML) LIQUID PECTIN	2

USING A FINE GRATER, REMOVE 2 TBSP (30 ML) ORANGE RIND; SET ASIDE. PEEL AND SECTION ORANGES (SEE BOX, OPPOSITE), REMOVING ALL PITH, SEEDS AND MEMBRANES, AND CHOP THE FRUIT, RESERVING ANY JUICES.

PLACE BLUEBERRIES IN A LARGE, DEEP, HEAVY-BOTTOMED POT. USE A POTATO MASHER TO CRUSH ABOUT ONE-THIRD OF THE BERRIES TO RELEASE SOME OF THEIR JUICE. STIR IN ORANGE RIND, ORANGES WITH JUICE AND LEMON JUICE. BRING TO A BOIL OVER HIGH HEAT, STIRRING OCCASIONALLY. ADD SUGAR IN A STEADY STREAM, STIRRING CONSTANTLY. BRING TO A FULL BOIL OVER HIGH HEAT, STIRRING CONSTANTLY TO DISSOLVE SUGAR. IMMEDIATELY STIR IN PECTIN; RETURN TO A FULL BOIL. BOIL HARD FOR 1 MINUTE, STIRRING CONSTANTLY. REMOVE FROM HEAT AND SKIM OFF ANY FOAM.

LADLE INTO STERILIZED JARS TO WITHIN 1/4 INCH (0.5 CM) OF RIM; WIPE RIMS. APPLY PREPARED LIDS AND RINGS; TIGHTEN RINGS JUST UNTIL FINGERTIP-TIGHT. PROCESS JARS IN A BOILING WATER CANNER FOR

10 MINUTES (SEE PAGE 27). TRANSFER JARS TO A TOWEL-LINED SURFACE AND LET REST AT ROOM TEMPERATURE UNTIL SET. CHECK SEALS; REFRIGERATE ANY UNSEALED JARS FOR UP TO 3 WEEKS. MAKES ABOUT SIX 8-OUNCE (250 ML) JARS.

VARIATION
BLUEBERRY JAM: OMIT THE ORANGES, AND INCREASE THE BLUEBERRIES TO 4 CUPS (1 L).

HOW TO SECTION CITRUS FRUIT

SECTIONING MEANS REMOVING ALL UNWANTED ELEMENTS — SKIN, WHITE PITH AND MEMBRANES — FROM CITRUS FRUIT, LEAVING ONLY THE JUICY PARTS. USING A SMALL SERRATED KNIFE, TRIM THE TOP AND BOTTOM OFF THE FRUIT. SET ON A CUTTING BOARD, WITH ONE FLAT END DOWN, AND CUT OFF THE SKIN IN CURVED STRIPS, REMOVING AS MUCH OF THE WHITE PITH AS POSSIBLE. HOLDING THE FRUIT ON ITS SIDE, CAREFULLY INSERT THE TIP OF THE KNIFE BETWEEN THE RIGHT SIDE OF A SECTION OF FLESH AND THE MEMBRANE, THEN CUT ALONG THE MEMBRANE. REPEAT ON THE LEFT SIDE. LOOSEN THE SECTION WITH THE KNIFE AND REMOVE. CONTINUE REMOVING SECTIONS, FOLDING EMPTY MEMBRANES TO ONE SIDE LIKE PAGES OF A BOOK, UNTIL ALL THE FLESH IS REMOVED.

SWEET CHERRY AND PLUM JAM

USE BLACK (DEEP RED) SWEET CHERRIES AND BLACK
PLUMS FOR A DEEP (COLORED) AND DELICIOUS JAM!

1½ LBS	SWEET CHERRIES, SUCH AS BING, FINELY CHOPPED	750 G
1½ LBS	BLACK PLUMS, FINELY CHOPPED	750 G
3 TBSP	LEMON JUICE	45 ML
1	PACKAGE (1.75 OZ/49 OR 57 G) POWDERED PECTIN	1
6¼ CUPS	GRANULATED SUGAR	1.55 L
⅓ CUP	CHERRY BRANDY (OPTIONAL)	75 ML

IN A LARGE, DEEP, HEAVY-BOTTOMED POT, COMBINE
CHERRIES, PLUMS AND LEMON JUICE. STIR IN PECTIN
UNTIL DISSOLVED. BRING TO A BOIL OVER HIGH HEAT,
STIRRING CONSTANTLY. REDUCE HEAT AND SIMMER FOR
3 MINUTES, STIRRING OFTEN. ADD SUGAR IN A STEADY
STREAM, STIRRING CONSTANTLY. INCREASE HEAT TO
HIGH AND BRING TO A FULL BOIL, STIRRING CONSTANTLY
TO DISSOLVE SUGAR. BOIL HARD FOR 1 MINUTE. REMOVE
FROM HEAT AND SKIM OFF ANY FOAM. STIR IN CHERRY
BRANDY (IF USING.)

LADLE INTO STERILIZED JARS TO WITHIN ¼ INCH
(0.5 CM) OF RIM; WIPE RIMS. APPLY PREPARED LIDS
AND RINGS; TIGHTEN RINGS JUST UNTIL FINGERTIP-
TIGHT. PROCESS JARS IN A BOILING WATER CANNER FOR
10 MINUTES (SEE PAGE 27). TRANSFER JARS TO A TOWEL-
LINED SURFACE AND LET REST AT ROOM TEMPERATURE
UNTIL SET. CHECK SEALS; REFRIGERATE ANY UNSEALED
JARS FOR UP TO 3 WEEKS. MAKES ABOUT SEVEN 8-OUNCE
(250 ML) JARS.

TIP: YOU'LL NEED ABOUT 10 LARGE PLUMS FOR THIS RECIPE. TO REMOVE PITS FROM PLUMS, CUT IN HALF THROUGH THE STEM AND TWIST TO SEPARATE THE HALVES. REPEAT, CUTTING THE HALF THAT STILL HAS THE PIT IN HALF, THEN TWISTING THE STONE FROM THE CENTER. THIS TECHNIQUE HELPS A LOT WHEN THE PITS ARE TIGHTLY IMBEDDED IN SLIGHTLY UNDERRIPE FRUIT.

TIP: USE A FOOD PROCESSOR FITTED WITH A METAL BLADE TO FINELY CHOP THE CHERRIES AND THE PLUMS. CHOP EACH SEPARATELY, PULSING ON AND OFF, SCRAPING DOWN SIDES AND BEING SURE NOT TO PURÉE THEM. OR USE A KNIFE.

USING CHERRIES IN PRESERVES

BOTH SWEET AND SOUR (TART) CHERRIES MAY BE USED TO MAKE JAMS AND CONSERVES; USE SOUR (TART) CHERRIES FOR JELLY. CHOOSE FIRM, RIPE, GLOSSY FRUIT AND STORE IN THE REFRIGERATOR. BEFORE USE, REMOVE STEMS AND PITS. TO PIT CHERRIES, YOU CAN EITHER USE A CHERRY PITTER OR HALVE THE FRUIT AND REMOVE THE PIT WITH A PARING KNIFE. SOME CHERRIES COME PITTED, A BIG TIME-SAVER. PITTED CHERRIES CAN BE FROZEN USING THE SAME METHOD USED FOR BERRIES (SEE PAGE 129). IF YOU HAVE A LARGE AMOUNT OF CHERRIES (THEY SOMETIMES COME IN LARGE PAILS), YOU MAY WANT TO DIVIDE THEM INTO PREMEASURED QUANTITIES.

CRANBERRY AND RASPBERRY JAM

CRAN-RASPBERRY IS A POPULAR COMBINATION
OFTEN USED IN FRUIT DRINKS. A TOUCH OF ORANGE
GIVES A PLEASANT ACCENT.

3 CUPS	FRESH OR FROZEN CRANBERRIES	750 ML
3 CUPS	RASPBERRIES, MASHED	750 ML
6 1/2 CUPS	GRANULATED SUGAR	1.625 L
	FINELY GRATED ZEST AND JUICE OF 1 LARGE ORANGE	
2 TBSP	LEMON JUICE	30 ML
1	POUCH (3 OZ/85 ML) LIQUID PECTIN	1

IN A FOOD PROCESSOR, FINELY CHOP CRANBERRIES.
TRANSFER TO A DUTCH OVEN OR LARGE, HEAVY-
BOTTOMED POT. ADD RASPBERRIES, SUGAR, ORANGE ZEST,
ORANGE JUICE AND LEMON JUICE. BRING TO A BOIL OVER
MEDIUM-HIGH HEAT, STIRRING CONSTANTLY. BOIL HARD,
STIRRING CONSTANTLY, FOR 1 MINUTE. REMOVE FROM
HEAT AND STIR IN PECTIN. STIR AND SKIM FOR 5 MINUTES.

LADLE INTO STERILIZED JARS TO WITHIN 1/4 INCH
(0.5 CM) OF RIM; WIPE RIMS. APPLY PREPARED LIDS AND
RINGS; TIGHTEN RINGS JUST UNTIL FINGERTIP-TIGHT.
PROCESS JARS IN A BOILING WATER CANNER FOR
10 MINUTES (SEE PAGE 27). TRANSFER JARS TO A
TOWEL-LINED SURFACE AND LET REST AT ROOM
TEMPERATURE UNTIL SET. CHECK SEALS; REFRIGERATE
ANY UNSEALED JARS FOR UP TO 3 WEEKS. MAKES ABOUT
SIX 8-OUNCE (250 ML) JARS.

RECIPE SUGGESTION: USE AS A FILLING FOR A CHOCOLATE
LAYER CAKE, OR SPREAD ON A TURKEY, CHICKEN OR HAM
SANDWICH.

BLACK AND RED CURRANT JAM

THIS RECIPE COMBINES THE BEST OF
BOTH FRUITS AND RESULTS IN A DEEP RED COLOR.

4 CUPS	BLACK CURRANTS, BEARDS REMOVED	1 L
	(SEE BOX, PAGE 81)	
4 CUPS	RED CURRANTS	1 L
1/2 CUP	WATER	125 ML
4 1/2 CUPS	GRANULATED SUGAR	1.125 L

IN A LARGE, DEEP, HEAVY-BOTTOMED POT, COMBINE BLACK CURRANTS, RED CURRANTS AND WATER. BRING TO A BOIL OVER HIGH HEAT. REDUCE HEAT AND SIMMER, COVERED, STIRRING OCCASIONALLY, FOR 15 MINUTES OR UNTIL SOFTENED. USE A POTATO MASHER TO CRUSH CURRANTS, IF DESIRED. ADD SUGAR IN A STEADY STREAM, STIRRING CONSTANTLY. INCREASE HEAT TO HIGH AND BRING TO A FULL BOIL, STIRRING CONSTANTLY TO DISSOLVE SUGAR. REDUCE HEAT TO MEDIUM-HIGH AND BOIL HARD, STIRRING OFTEN AND REDUCING HEAT FURTHER AS MIXTURE THICKENS, FOR 10 TO 12 MINUTES OR UNTIL THICKENED. TEST FOR SETTING POINT (SEE PAGE 24). REMOVE FROM HEAT AND SKIM OFF ANY FOAM.

LADLE INTO STERILIZED JARS TO WITHIN 1/4 INCH (0.5 CM) OF RIM; WIPE RIMS. APPLY PREPARED LIDS AND RINGS; TIGHTEN RINGS JUST UNTIL FINGERTIP-TIGHT. PROCESS JARS IN A BOILING WATER CANNER FOR 10 MINUTES (SEE PAGE 27). TRANSFER JARS TO A TOWEL-LINED SURFACE AND LET REST AT ROOM TEMPERATURE UNTIL SET. CHECK SEALS; REFRIGERATE ANY UNSEALED JARS FOR UP TO 3 WEEKS. MAKES ABOUT FIVE 8-OUNCE (250 ML) JARS.

RED CURRANT AND ORANGE JAM

RED CURRANTS AND ORANGES
MAKE A TASTY PAIRING IN THIS VIBRANT JAM.

4	LARGE ORANGES	4
5 CUPS	RED CURRANTS	1.25 L
4 1/2 CUPS	GRANULATED SUGAR	1.125 L

USING A FINE GRATER, REMOVE 2 TBSP (30 ML) ORANGE RIND; SET ASIDE. PEEL AND SECTION ORANGES (SEE BOX, PAGE 75), REMOVING ALL PITH, SEEDS AND MEMBRANES, AND CHOP THE FRUIT, RESERVING ANY JUICES.

PLACE CURRANTS IN A LARGE, DEEP, HEAVY-BOTTOMED POT AND CRUSH WITH A POTATO MASHER. STIR IN ORANGE RIND AND ORANGES WITH JUICE. BRING TO A BOIL OVER HIGH HEAT, STIRRING CONSTANTLY. REDUCE HEAT AND SIMMER, COVERED, FOR 5 MINUTES. ADD SUGAR IN A STEADY STREAM, STIRRING CONSTANTLY. INCREASE HEAT TO HIGH AND BRING TO A FULL BOIL, STIRRING CONSTANTLY TO DISSOLVE SUGAR. REDUCE HEAT TO MEDIUM-HIGH AND BOIL HARD, STIRRING CONSTANTLY AND REDUCING HEAT FURTHER AS MIXTURE THICKENS, FOR 7 TO 10 MINUTES OR UNTIL THICKENED. TEST FOR SETTING POINT (SEE PAGE 24). REMOVE FROM HEAT AND SKIM OFF ANY FOAM.

LADLE INTO STERILIZED JARS TO WITHIN 1/4 INCH (0.5 CM) OF RIM; WIPE RIMS. APPLY PREPARED LIDS AND RINGS; TIGHTEN RINGS JUST UNTIL FINGERTIP-TIGHT. PROCESS JARS IN A BOILING WATER CANNER FOR 10 MINUTES (SEE PAGE 27). TRANSFER JARS TO

A TOWEL-LINED SURFACE AND LET REST AT ROOM TEMPERATURE UNTIL SET. CHECK SEALS; REFRIGERATE ANY UNSEALED JARS FOR UP TO 3 WEEKS. MAKES ABOUT FIVE 8-OUNCE (250 ML) JARS.

RECIPE SUGGESTION: HEAT JAM SLIGHTLY AND PRESS THROUGH A SIEVE TO REMOVE SEEDS. USE TO GLAZE A FRUIT FLAN OR TART, OR DRIZZLE OVER CHEESECAKE.

USING CURRANTS IN PRESERVES

RED AND BLACK CURRANTS ARE GREAT FOR JAMS OR JELLIES. CHOOSE FIRM, RIPE, DRY FRUIT. REMOVE FROM STEMS BEFORE USE. BLACK CURRANTS NEED THEIR "BEARDS" (BLOSSOM ENDS) SNIPPED FOR JAMS, BUT THAT STEP IS NOT NECESSARY FOR JELLIES. TO REMOVE BEARDS, USE SMALL SCISSORS, SUCH AS CURVED MANICURE SCISSORS (KEEP NEW ONES ASIDE JUST FOR THIS JOB), AND SNIP CLOSE TO THE FRUIT. FREEZE CURRANTS AS YOU WOULD BERRIES (SEE PAGE 129).

GOOSEBERRY AND ORANGE JAM

*ORANGES GIVE A PLEASANT FLAVOR BOOST
AND PERK UP THE COLOR OF THE GOOSEBERRIES.
THIS RECIPE MAY ALSO BE MADE WITH ANY
COLOR OF GOOSEBERRIES.*

2	LARGE ORANGES	2
5 CUPS	GREEN GOOSEBERRIES, BEARDS REMOVED (SEE BOX, OPPOSITE)	1.25 L
4 CUPS	GRANULATED SUGAR	1 L

USING A FINE GRATER, GRATE 1 TBSP (15 ML) ORANGE RIND; SET ASIDE. PEEL AND SECTION ORANGES (SEE BOX, PAGE 75), REMOVING ALL PITH, SEEDS AND MEMBRANES, AND CHOP THE FRUIT, RESERVING ANY JUICES.

IN A LARGE, DEEP, HEAVY-BOTTOMED POT, COMBINE ORANGE RIND, ORANGES WITH JUICE, AND GOOSEBERRIES. BRING TO A BOIL OVER HIGH HEAT, STIRRING CONSTANTLY. REDUCE HEAT AND SIMMER FOR 5 MINUTES OR UNTIL GOOSEBERRIES ARE SOFTENED. CRUSH ANY WHOLE BERRIES WITH BACK OF SPOON. ADD SUGAR IN A STEADY STREAM, STIRRING CONSTANTLY. INCREASE HEAT TO HIGH AND BRING TO A FULL BOIL, STIRRING CONSTANTLY TO DISSOLVE SUGAR. REDUCE HEAT TO MEDIUM-HIGH AND BOIL HARD, STIRRING OFTEN AND REDUCING HEAT FURTHER AS MIXTURE THICKENS, FOR 10 TO 12 MINUTES OR UNTIL THICKENED. TEST FOR SETTING POINT (SEE PAGE 24). REMOVE FROM HEAT AND SKIM OFF ANY FOAM.

LADLE INTO STERILIZED JARS TO WITHIN 1/4 INCH (0.5 CM) OF RIM; WIPE RIMS. APPLY PREPARED LIDS AND RINGS; TIGHTEN RINGS JUST UNTIL FINGERTIP-TIGHT.

PROCESS JARS IN A BOILING WATER CANNER FOR
10 MINUTES (SEE PAGE 27). TRANSFER JARS TO A TOWEL-
LINED SURFACE AND LET REST AT ROOM TEMPERATURE
UNTIL SET. CHECK SEALS; REFRIGERATE ANY UNSEALED
JARS FOR UP TO 3 WEEKS. MAKES ABOUT FOUR 8-OUNCE
(250 ML) JARS.

USING GOOSEBERRIES IN PRESERVES

CHOOSE FIRM, BRIGHTLY COLORED GREEN, RED OR WHITE
FRUIT. REMOVE "BEARDS" BY SNIPPING OFF THE BLOSSOM
ENDS USING SMALL SCISSORS, SUCH AS CURVED
MANICURE SCISSORS (KEEP NEW ONES ASIDE JUST FOR
THIS JOB). FREEZE AS YOU WOULD OTHER BERRIES (SEE
PAGE 59).

KIWI, PINEAPPLE AND ORANGE JAM

ENJOY A TASTY COMBINATION OF FRUITS IN THIS BEAUTIFUL LIGHT GREEN AND ORANGE JAM.

3	MEDIUM ORANGES	3
3 CUPS	FINELY CHOPPED KIWIFRUIT (ABOUT 8 LARGE)	750 ML
1	CAN (8 OZ/227 ML) OR 1 CUP (250 ML) CRUSHED PINEAPPLE, WITH JUICE	1
1/4 CUP	LIME JUICE	60 ML
1	PACKAGE (1.75 OZ/49 OR 57 G) POWDERED PECTIN	1
5 1/2 CUPS	GRANULATED SUGAR	1.375 L

PEEL AND SECTION ORANGES (SEE BOX, PAGE 75), REMOVING ALL PITH, SEEDS AND MEMBRANES, AND CHOP THE FRUIT, RESERVING ANY JUICES.

IN A LARGE, DEEP, HEAVY-BOTTOMED POT, COMBINE ORANGES WITH JUICE, KIWIS, PINEAPPLE WITH JUICE AND LIME JUICE. STIR IN PECTIN UNTIL DISSOLVED. BRING TO A FULL BOIL OVER HIGH HEAT, STIRRING CONSTANTLY. ADD SUGAR IN A STEADY STREAM, STIRRING CONSTANTLY. RETURN TO A FULL BOIL, STIRRING CONSTANTLY TO DISSOLVE SUGAR. BOIL HARD FOR 1 MINUTE. REMOVE FROM HEAT AND SKIM OFF ANY FOAM. STIR FOR 5 TO 8 MINUTES TO PREVENT FLOATING FRUIT.

LADLE INTO STERILIZED JARS TO WITHIN 1/4 INCH (0.5 CM) OF RIM; WIPE RIMS. APPLY PREPARED LIDS AND RINGS; TIGHTEN RINGS JUST UNTIL FINGERTIP-TIGHT. PROCESS JARS IN A BOILING WATER CANNER FOR

10 MINUTES (SEE PAGE 27). TRANSFER JARS TO A TOWEL-LINED SURFACE AND LET REST AT ROOM TEMPERATURE UNTIL SET. CHECK SEALS; REFRIGERATE ANY UNSEALED JARS FOR UP TO 3 WEEKS. MAKES ABOUT SIX 8-OUNCE (250 ML) JARS.

TIP: IF DESIRED, ADD 1 TBSP (15 ML) FINELY GRATED ORANGE RIND TO THIS RECIPE; GRATE BEFORE PEELING AND ADD WITH THE CHOPPED ORANGES.

RECIPE SUGGESTIONS: USE TO FILL A JELLY ROLL, OR STIR INTO WHIPPED CREAM TO TOP A GINGER CAKE.

USING KIWIFRUIT IN PRESERVES

EITHER GREEN OR GOLD KIWIFRUIT CAN BE USED IN PRESERVES. CHOOSE FIRM, RIPE FRUIT. ALWAYS PEEL KIWIFRUIT BEFORE CHOPPING IT.

PEACH AND RASPBERRY JAM

TRY THIS JAM STIRRED INTO PLAIN YOGURT.

3½ CUPS	CHOPPED PEELED PEACHES (SEE BOX, OPPOSITE)	875 ML
2 CUPS	RASPBERRIES	500 ML
¼ CUP	LEMON JUICE	60 ML
7 CUPS	GRANULATED SUGAR	1.75 L
2	POUCHES (EACH 3 OZ/85 ML) LIQUID PECTIN	2

IN A LARGE, DEEP, HEAVY-BOTTOMED POT, COMBINE PEACHES, RASPBERRIES AND LEMON JUICE. BRING TO A BOIL OVER HIGH HEAT, STIRRING CONSTANTLY. ADD SUGAR IN A STEADY STREAM, STIRRING CONSTANTLY. BRING TO A FULL BOIL, STIRRING CONSTANTLY TO DISSOLVE SUGAR. IMMEDIATELY STIR IN PECTIN; RETURN TO A FULL BOIL. BOIL HARD FOR 1 MINUTE, STIRRING CONSTANTLY. REMOVE FROM HEAT AND SKIM OFF ANY FOAM.

LADLE INTO STERILIZED JARS TO WITHIN ¼ INCH (0.5 CM) OF RIM; WIPE RIMS. APPLY PREPARED LIDS AND RINGS; TIGHTEN RINGS JUST UNTIL FINGERTIP-TIGHT. PROCESS JARS IN A BOILING WATER CANNER FOR 10 MINUTES (SEE PAGE 27). TRANSFER JARS TO A TOWEL-LINED SURFACE AND LET REST AT ROOM TEMPERATURE UNTIL SET. CHECK SEALS; REFRIGERATE ANY UNSEALED JARS FOR UP TO 3 WEEKS. *MAKES ABOUT SEVEN 8-OUNCE (250 ML) JARS.*

NOTE: THIS JAM IS A TAKEOFF OF THE PEACH MELBA DESSERT CREATED AROUND 1894 BY A FRENCH CHEF TO HONOR NELLIE MELBA, AN AUSTRALIAN SOPRANO WHO PERFORMED IN LONDON, ENGLAND.

SERVING SUGGESTION: SERVE OVER VANILLA OR CHOCOLATE ICE CREAM OR CHEESECAKE.

HOW TO PEEL PEACHES

BRING A MEDIUM POT OF WATER TO A BOIL OVER HIGH HEAT. PLACE PEACHES IN WATER TWO AT A TIME; BOIL FOR 20 TO 30 SECONDS. REMOVE PEACHES WITH A SLOTTED SPOON AND IMMEDIATELY IMMERSE IN A BOWL OF COLD WATER. REPEAT WITH REMAINING PEACHES. WHEN PEACHES ARE COOL ENOUGH TO HANDLE, SLIT DOWN THE SIDE OF THE PEEL WITH A PARING KNIFE AND SLIP OFF PEEL. CUT PEACHES IN HALF AND REMOVE PITS.

PINEAPPLE AND MANGO JAM

THIS JAM HAS A LOVELY TROPICAL FLAVOR.
USE ATAULFO MANGOS IF THEY ARE AVAILABLE,
AS THEIR FLAVOR AND TEXTURE ARE SUPERIOR.
IF DESIRED, REPLACE MANGOS WITH PAPAYA.

2 CUPS	FINELY CHOPPED FRESH PINEAPPLE (OR WELL-DRAINED CANNED CRUSHED PINEAPPLE)	500 ML
2 CUPS	FINELY CHOPPED MANGOS	500 ML
$\frac{1}{4}$ CUP	LIME JUICE	60 ML
$4\frac{1}{2}$ CUPS	GRANULATED SUGAR	1.125 L
1	POUCH (3 OZ/85 ML) LIQUID PECTIN	1
	GRENADINE OR AMBER RUM (OPTIONAL)	

IN A LARGE, DEEP, HEAVY-BOTTOMED POT, COMBINE PINEAPPLE, MANGOS AND LIME JUICE. BRING TO A BOIL OVER HIGH HEAT, STIRRING CONSTANTLY. REDUCE HEAT AND SIMMER, STIRRING OFTEN, FOR 6 TO 8 MINUTES OR UNTIL PINEAPPLE IS SOFTENED. IF DESIRED, USE AN IMMERSION BLENDER OR A POTATO MASHER TO BREAK UP ANY LARGE PIECES. ADD SUGAR IN A STEADY STREAM, STIRRING CONSTANTLY. INCREASE HEAT TO HIGH AND BRING TO A FULL BOIL, STIRRING CONSTANTLY TO DISSOLVE SUGAR. IMMEDIATELY STIR IN PECTIN; RETURN TO A FULL BOIL. BOIL HARD FOR 1 MINUTE, STIRRING CONSTANTLY. REMOVE FROM HEAT AND SKIM OFF ANY FOAM.

ADD ABOUT 2 TSP (10 ML) GRENADINE (IF USING) TO EACH JAR. LADLE JAM INTO STERILIZED JARS TO WITHIN $\frac{1}{4}$ INCH (0.5 CM) OF RIM; WIPE RIMS. APPLY PREPARED LIDS AND RINGS; TIGHTEN RINGS JUST UNTIL FINGERTIP-

TIGHT. PROCESS JARS IN A BOILING WATER CANNER FOR 10 MINUTES (SEE PAGE 27). TRANSFER JARS TO A TOWEL-LINED SURFACE AND LET REST AT ROOM TEMPERATURE UNTIL SET. CHECK SEALS; REFRIGERATE ANY UNSEALED JARS FOR UP TO 3 WEEKS. MAKES ABOUT FOUR 8-OUNCE (250 ML) JARS.

TIP: YOU'LL NEED ABOUT 4 ATAULFO MANGOS OR 2 REGULAR MANGOS FOR THIS RECIPE.

RECIPE SUGGESTIONS: USE JAM TO MAKE GLAZE FOR ROASTED HAM: MIX TOGETHER $\frac{1}{4}$ CUP (60 ML) JAM AND 1 TSP (5 ML) DIJON MUSTARD. OR USE TO MAKE RUM- AND LIME-GLAZED PORK RIBS (PAGE 274)

USING MANGOS IN PRESERVES

CHOOSE FIRM, RIPE FRUIT THAT GIVES SLIGHTLY WHEN PRESSED AND IS FRAGRANT. (ALTERNATIVELY, YOU CAN BUY UNDERRIPE MANGOS AND RIPEN THEM AT HOME IN A PAPER BAG AT ROOM TEMPERATURE.) ALWAYS PEEL MANGOS (SEE BOX, PAGE 265) AND REMOVE THE PIT. RIPE SWEET MANGOS HAVE A FRAGRANT AROMA, AND THE SKIN YIELDS SLIGHTLY TO PRESSURE WHEN GENTLY SQUEEZED. DO NOT USE MANGOS THAT ARE WRINKLED OR HAVE SOFT SPOTS. THERE ARE MANY VARIETIES OF SWEET MANGOS AVAILABLE, AND THEY ARE INTERCHANGEABLE. ATAULFO MANGOS, WHICH ARE GREAT FOR PRESERVES BECAUSE THEY HAVE A TENDER TEXTURE AND ARE LESS FIBROUS, ARE MORE AVAILABLE NOW. LOOK FOR FROZEN CHOPPED MANGOS AS WELL.

RASPBERRY AND BLUEBERRY JAM

THIS JAM IS A GREAT CHOICE TO STIR INTO
PLAIN YOGURT OR TO TOP A CHEESECAKE.

3 CUPS	RASPBERRIES	750 ML
2 CUPS	BLUEBERRIES	500 ML
2 TBSP	LEMON JUICE	30 ML
3¾ CUPS	GRANULATED SUGAR	925 ML

IN A LARGE, DEEP, HEAVY-BOTTOMED POT, COMBINE RASPBERRIES, BLUEBERRIES AND LEMON JUICE. USING A POTATO MASHER, CRUSH ABOUT HALF THE BERRIES TO RELEASE SOME OF THEIR JUICE. BRING TO A BOIL OVER HIGH HEAT, STIRRING CONSTANTLY. ADD SUGAR IN A STEADY STREAM, STIRRING CONSTANTLY. BRING TO A FULL BOIL, STIRRING CONSTANTLY TO DISSOLVE SUGAR. REDUCE HEAT TO MEDIUM-HIGH AND BOIL HARD, STIRRING OFTEN AND REDUCING HEAT FURTHER AS MIXTURE THICKENS, FOR 10 TO 12 MINUTES OR UNTIL THICKENED. TEST FOR SETTING POINT (SEE PAGE 24). REMOVE FROM HEAT AND SKIM OFF ANY FOAM.

LADLE INTO STERILIZED JARS TO WITHIN ¼ INCH (0.5 CM) OF RIM; WIPE RIMS. APPLY PREPARED LIDS AND RINGS; TIGHTEN RINGS JUST UNTIL FINGERTIP-TIGHT. PROCESS JARS IN A BOILING WATER CANNER FOR 10 MINUTES (SEE PAGE 27). TRANSFER JARS TO A TOWEL-LINED SURFACE AND LET REST AT ROOM TEMPERATURE UNTIL SET. CHECK SEALS; REFRIGERATE ANY UNSEALED JARS FOR UP TO 3 WEEKS. *MAKES ABOUT FOUR 8-OUNCE (250 ML) JARS.*

Raspberry and Plum Jam (page 91)

Cranberry Orange Marmalade (page 100)
and Honey Lemon Marmalade (page 102)

Carrot and Pineapple Marmalade (page 110)

Christmas Marmalade (page 114)

RASPBERRY AND PLUM JAM

PLUMS ADD DELICIOUS YUMMINESS TO THIS JAM, WHICH HAS HALF THE SEEDS OF REGULAR RASPBERRY JAM. IT CAN ALSO BE MADE WITH RED OR BLACK PLUMS, OR WITH PLUMCOTS (A CROSS OF PLUMS AND APRICOTS).

2 CUPS	RASPBERRIES	500 ML
2 CUPS	FINELY CHOPPED YELLOW OR RED PLUMS	500 ML
1/4 CUP	LEMON JUICE	60 ML
5 CUPS	GRANULATED SUGAR	1.25 L
1	POUCH (3 OZ/85 ML) LIQUID PECTIN	1

IN A LARGE, DEEP, HEAVY-BOTTOMED POT, COMBINE RASPBERRIES, PLUMS AND LEMON JUICE. BRING TO A BOIL OVER HIGH HEAT, STIRRING CONSTANTLY. ADD SUGAR IN A STEADY STREAM, STIRRING CONSTANTLY. BRING TO A FULL BOIL, STIRRING CONSTANTLY TO DISSOLVE SUGAR. IMMEDIATELY STIR IN PECTIN; RETURN TO A FULL BOIL. BOIL HARD FOR 1 MINUTE, STIRRING CONSTANTLY. REMOVE FROM HEAT AND SKIM OFF ANY FOAM. STIR FOR 5 TO 8 MINUTES TO PREVENT FLOATING FRUIT.

LADLE INTO STERILIZED JARS TO WITHIN 1/4 INCH (0.5 CM) OF RIM; WIPE RIMS. APPLY PREPARED LIDS AND RINGS; TIGHTEN RINGS JUST UNTIL FINGERTIP-TIGHT. PROCESS JARS IN A BOILING WATER CANNER FOR 10 MINUTES (SEE PAGE 27). TRANSFER JARS TO A TOWEL-LINED SURFACE AND LET REST AT ROOM TEMPERATURE UNTIL SET. CHECK SEALS; REFRIGERATE ANY UNSEALED JARS FOR UP TO 3 WEEKS. MAKES ABOUT SIX 8-OUNCE (250 ML) JARS.

STRAWBERRY AND KIWI JAM

STRAWBERRIES AND KIWIS HAVE COMPLEMENTARY
FLAVORS AND GIVE THIS JAM A NICE TEXTURE.

2 CUPS	CRUSHED STRAWBERRIES	500 ML
2 CUPS	FINELY CHOPPED KIWIFRUIT	500 ML
1	PACKAGE (1.75 OZ/49 OR 57 G) POWDERED PECTIN	1
3½ CUPS	GRANULATED SUGAR	875 ML

IN A LARGE, DEEP, HEAVY-BOTTOMED POT, COMBINE
STRAWBERRIES AND KIWIS. STIR IN PECTIN UNTIL
DISSOLVED. BRING TO A FULL BOIL OVER HIGH HEAT,
STIRRING CONSTANTLY. ADD SUGAR IN A STEADY STREAM,
STIRRING CONSTANTLY. RETURN TO A FULL BOIL, STIRRING
CONSTANTLY TO DISSOLVE SUGAR. BOIL HARD FOR
1 MINUTE. REMOVE FROM HEAT AND SKIM OFF ANY FOAM.
STIR FOR 5 TO 8 MINUTES TO PREVENT FLOATING FRUIT.

LADLE INTO STERILIZED JARS TO WITHIN ¼ INCH
(0.5 CM) OF RIM; WIPE RIMS. APPLY PREPARED LIDS
AND RINGS; TIGHTEN RINGS JUST UNTIL FINGERTIP-
TIGHT. PROCESS JARS IN A BOILING WATER CANNER FOR
10 MINUTES (SEE PAGE 27). TRANSFER JARS TO A TOWEL-
LINED SURFACE AND LET REST AT ROOM TEMPERATURE
UNTIL SET. CHECK SEALS; REFRIGERATE ANY UNSEALED
JARS FOR UP TO 3 WEEKS. MAKES ABOUT FIVE 8-OUNCE
(250 ML) JARS.

TIP: REMOVE THE PITHY CENTER CORE FROM
STRAWBERRIES BEFORE CRUSHING. IT HAS NO FLAVOR
AND A TOUGH TEXTURE. AFTER RINSING THE BERRIES,

PLACE A LARGE STRAW AT THE TAPERED END OF THE STRAWBERRY AND PUSH INTO FRUIT TOWARD THE STEM. THE GREEN CALYX AND THE CORE WILL POP OUT WITH MINIMAL STRAWBERRY WASTE.

TIP: ONE POUND (500 G) OF STRAWBERRIES EQUALS ABOUT $3\frac{3}{4}$ CUPS (925 ML) OF WHOLE MEDIUM BERRIES AND YIELDS ABOUT 3 CUPS (750 ML) SLICED BERRIES OR ABOUT $1\frac{1}{2}$ CUPS (375 ML) CRUSHED BERRIES.

TIP: WHEN FILLING JARS, IT'S IMPORTANT TO LEAVE SUFFICIENT HEADSPACE BETWEEN THE TOP OF THE FOOD AND THE TOP OF THE JAR TO GET A GOOD VACUUM SEAL.

RECIPE SUGGESTION: STIR THIS JAM INTO YOUR FAVORITE CHEESECAKE BATTER.

SERVING SUGGESTION: ENJOY THIS JAM WITH CREAM CHEESE AND BAGELS.

IF YOU CAN'T BE A GOOD EXAMPLE, THEN YOU'LL JUST HAVE TO BE A HORRIBLE WARNING.

STRAWBERRY AND RHUBARB JAM

THESE CLASSIC EARLY SUMMER COMPANIONS MAKE FABULOUS JAM. IF DESIRED, FREEZE CUT RHUBARB IN A PREMEASURED AMOUNT TO ADD DIRECTLY TO THE POT LATER ON.

4 CUPS	CHOPPED RHUBARB ($1/2$-INCH/1 CM PIECES)	1 L
3 CUPS	CHOPPED STRAWBERRIES	750 ML
$1/4$ CUP	LEMON JUICE	60 ML
$4 1/2$ CUPS	GRANULATED SUGAR	1.125 L

IN A LARGE, DEEP, HEAVY-BOTTOMED POT, COMBINE RHUBARB, STRAWBERRIES AND LEMON JUICE. BRING TO A BOIL OVER HIGH HEAT, STIRRING CONSTANTLY. ADD SUGAR IN A STEADY STREAM, STIRRING CONSTANTLY. BRING TO A FULL BOIL, STIRRING CONSTANTLY TO DISSOLVE SUGAR. REDUCE HEAT TO MEDIUM-HIGH AND BOIL HARD, STIRRING OFTEN AND REDUCING HEAT FURTHER AS MIXTURE THICKENS, FOR 20 TO 25 MINUTES OR UNTIL THICKENED. TEST FOR SETTING POINT (SEE PAGE 24). REMOVE FROM HEAT AND SKIM OFF ANY FOAM.

LADLE INTO STERILIZED JARS TO WITHIN $1/4$ INCH (0.5 CM) OF RIM; WIPE RIMS. APPLY PREPARED LIDS AND RINGS; TIGHTEN RINGS JUST UNTIL FINGERTIP-TIGHT. PROCESS JARS IN A BOILING WATER CANNER FOR 10 MINUTES (SEE PAGE 27). TRANSFER JARS TO A TOWEL-LINED SURFACE AND LET REST AT ROOM TEMPERATURE UNTIL SET. CHECK SEALS; REFRIGERATE ANY UNSEALED JARS FOR UP TO 3 WEEKS. MAKES ABOUT FOUR 8-OUNCE (250 ML) JARS.

TIP: ONE POUND (500 G) OF STRAWBERRIES EQUALS ABOUT 3¾ CUPS (925 ML) OF WHOLE MEDIUM BERRIES AND YIELDS ABOUT 3 CUPS (750 ML) SLICED BERRIES OR ABOUT 1½ CUPS (375 ML) CRUSHED BERRIES.

TIP: THE BEST, SAFEST WAY TO LIFT JARS OUT OF THE CANNER IS WITH A JAR LIFTER, SPECIALIZED TONGS COATED WITH SILICONE AND DESIGNED TO FIT AROUND THE NECKS OF JARS.

VARIATION: IF DESIRED, ADD 3 TBSP (45 ML) FINELY GRATED ORANGE RIND.

RECIPE SUGGESTIONS: STIR INTO VANILLA YOGURT OR A VANILLA SMOOTHIE, OR DOLLOP ON TOP OF COFFEECAKE BATTER BEFORE BAKING.

USING RHUBARB IN PRESERVES

CHOOSE FIRM STALKS THAT ARE NOT TOO LARGE (LARGE STALKS BECOME WOODY). FOR PRESERVES, RHUBARB IS USUALLY CUT INTO ½-INCH (1 CM) PIECES. TO FREEZE, PLACE CHOPPED PIECES IN A FREEZER BAG.

Marmalades

What defines a marmalade is the use of one or more citrus fruits, or citrus fruits in combination with other fruits or vegetables. Rich in natural pectin, the fruit rind and pulp/juice are cooked with sugar to create a gel. The rind may be thick and long or very fine and short and adds a touch of bitter-tart. Citrus rind must be washed well with soapy water and rinsed thoroughly. Marmalades sometimes take a while to set, especially those without added pectin. Let jars rest, undisturbed, for about a week.

SEVILLE ORANGE MARMALADE

SEVILLE ORANGES ARE HIGHER IN PECTIN THAN SWEET ORANGES, MAKING THEM IDEAL FOR MARMALADES.

6	LARGE SEVILLE ORANGES	6
	WATER	
	GRANULATED SUGAR	

CUT ORANGES IN HALF AND SQUEEZE OUT JUICE. REMOVE SEEDS AND PLACE IN A SQUARE OF SEVERAL LAYERS OF CHEESECLOTH. CUT ORANGES IN HALF AGAIN. SCRAPE MEMBRANES FROM PEELS AND ADD TO CHEESECLOTH; TIE WITH STRING. SLICE PEEL VERY THINLY. MEASURE THE VOLUME OF JUICE AND PEEL; YOU SHOULD GET ABOUT 6 CUPS (1.5 L).

PLACE IN A DUTCH OVEN OR A LARGE, HEAVY-BOTTOMED POT. ADD AN EQUAL VOLUME OF WATER. PLACE CHEESECLOTH BAG IN CENTER OF POT AND BRING TO A BOIL OVER HIGH HEAT. REDUCE HEAT AND SIMMER, STIRRING OCCASIONALLY AND SQUEEZING CHEESECLOTH BAG, FOR ABOUT 2 HOURS OR UNTIL PEEL IS VERY SOFT.

MEASURE PEEL AND LIQUID, SQUEEZING CHEESECLOTH BAG; DISCARD BAG. STIR IN AN EQUAL VOLUME OF SUGAR. BRING TO A BOIL OVER MEDIUM HEAT, STIRRING CONSTANTLY TO DISSOLVE SUGAR. BOIL RAPIDLY, STIRRING OFTEN, FOR 10 TO 15 MINUTES OR UNTIL MARMALADE THICKENS. TEST FOR THE SETTING POINT (SEE PAGE 24). REMOVE FROM HEAT AND SKIM OFF ANY FOAM. STIR FOR 5 TO 8 MINUTES TO PREVENT RIND FROM FLOATING.

LADLE INTO STERILIZED JARS TO WITHIN $1/4$ INCH (0.5 CM) OF RIM; WIPE RIMS. APPLY PREPARED LIDS AND RINGS; TIGHTEN RINGS JUST UNTIL FINGERTIP-TIGHT. PROCESS JARS IN A BOILING WATER CANNER FOR 10 MINUTES (SEE PAGE 27). TRANSFER JARS TO A TOWEL-LINED SURFACE AND LET REST AT ROOM TEMPERATURE UNTIL SET. CHECK SEALS; REFRIGERATE ANY UNSEALED JARS FOR UP TO 3 WEEKS. THIS MARMALADE IS BEST SERVED AFTER RESTING FOR 1 WEEK. MAKES ABOUT SEVEN 8-OUNCE (250 ML) JARS.

NOTE: SEVILLE ORANGES, GROWN IN THE MEDITERRANEAN, ARE BITTER AND NOT EATEN FRESH.

VARIATION: ADD ABOUT 1 TSP (5 ML) ORANGE LIQUEUR OR WHISKEY TO EACH JAR BEFORE FILLING WITH MARMALADE.

BLOOD ORANGE MARMALADE

LOOK FOR BLOOD ORANGES IN STORES FROM DECEMBER TO MAY. THEIR FLESH IS DEEP RED WITH SOME ORANGE, AND THERE IS ALSO SOMETIMES RED IN THE RIND, WHICH GIVES THIS MARMALADE A DEEP RED COLOR AND UNIQUE BERRY-LIKE FLAVOR.

12 to 14	MEDIUM BLOOD ORANGES	12 to 14
1 1/2 CUPS	WATER	375 ML
3 TBSP	LEMON JUICE	45 ML
1	PACKAGE (1.75 OZ/49 OR 57 G) POWDERED PECTIN	1
5 CUPS	GRANULATED SUGAR	1.25 L

USING A PARING KNIFE, REMOVE PEEL FROM SEVERAL OF THE ORANGES IN LARGE STRIPS, TAKING SOME OF THE WHITE PITH IF DESIRED; THINLY SLICE TO MAKE 3/4 CUP (175 ML). IN A SMALL SAUCEPAN, COMBINE PEEL AND WATER. BRING TO A FULL BOIL OVER HIGH HEAT. REDUCE HEAT AND SIMMER, COVERED, FOR 15 TO 20 MINUTES OR UNTIL PEEL IS SOFTENED. SET ASIDE.

REMOVE AND DISCARD REMAINING PEEL AND PITH FROM ORANGES. FINELY CHOP ORANGES, DISCARDING SEEDS. MEASURE TO MAKE 3 CUPS (750 ML), INCLUDING JUICES.

IN A DUTCH OVEN OR A LARGE, HEAVY-BOTTOMED POT, COMBINE CHOPPED ORANGES AND LEMON JUICE. ADD COOKED PEEL WITH LIQUID. BRING TO A BOIL OVER HIGH HEAT; REDUCE HEAT AND SIMMER FOR 5 MINUTES. STIR IN PECTIN UNTIL DISSOLVED. BRING TO A FULL BOIL OVER HIGH HEAT, STIRRING CONSTANTLY. ADD SUGAR IN

A STEADY STREAM, STIRRING CONSTANTLY. RETURN TO A FULL BOIL, STIRRING CONSTANTLY TO DISSOLVE SUGAR. BOIL HARD FOR 1 MINUTE. REMOVE FROM HEAT AND SKIM OFF ANY FOAM. STIR FOR 5 TO 8 MINUTES TO PREVENT RIND FROM FLOATING.

LADLE INTO STERILIZED JARS TO WITHIN $\frac{1}{4}$ INCH (0.5 CM) OF RIM; WIPE RIMS. APPLY PREPARED LIDS AND RINGS; TIGHTEN RINGS JUST UNTIL FINGERTIP-TIGHT. PROCESS JARS IN A BOILING WATER CANNER FOR 10 MINUTES (SEE PAGE 27). TRANSFER JARS TO A TOWEL-LINED SURFACE AND LET REST AT ROOM TEMPERATURE UNTIL SET. CHECK SEALS; REFRIGERATE ANY UNSEALED JARS FOR UP TO 3 WEEKS. THIS MARMALADE IS BEST SERVED AFTER RESTING FOR 1 WEEK. MAKES ABOUT SIX 8-OUNCE (250 ML) JARS.

RECIPE SUGGESTIONS: USE MARMALADES IN PLACE OF SUGAR TO SWEETEN A GRAPEFRUIT HALF: SPREAD ON CUT HALF AND MICROWAVE UNTIL WARM. OR USE TO MAKE JOLLY GOOD BREAD AND BUTTER PUDDING (PAGE 288).

I WAS ALWAYS TAUGHT TO RESPECT MY ELDERS, BUT IT KEEPS GETTING HARDER TO FIND ONE.

CRANBERRY ORANGE MARMALADE

THIS CLASSIC TASTE COMBINATION PRODUCES A DEEP RED MARMALADE WITH LOTS OF ORANGE RIND.

4	MEDIUM SEEDLESS ORANGES (APPROX.)	4
I CUP	WATER	250 ML
$2\frac{1}{4}$ CUPS	CRANBERRY COCKTAIL	550 ML
3 TBSP	LEMON JUICE	45 ML
$3\frac{1}{2}$ CUPS	GRANULATED SUGAR	875 ML
I CUP	COARSELY CHOPPED CRANBERRIES	250 ML

CUT ORANGES IN HALF AND SQUEEZE OUT JUICE; MEASURE $2\frac{2}{3}$ CUPS (650 ML) JUICE. CUT ORANGES IN HALF AGAIN. SCRAPE MEMBRANES FROM PEELS AND DISCARD. THINLY SLICE PEEL; MEASURE $\frac{3}{4}$ CUP (175 ML).

IN A DUTCH OVEN OR A LARGE, HEAVY-BOTTOMED POT, COMBINE ORANGE JUICE, PEEL AND WATER. BRING TO A BOIL OVER HIGH HEAT. REDUCE HEAT AND SIMMER, COVERED, FOR ABOUT 20 MINUTES OR UNTIL PEEL IS SOFTENED. STIR IN CRANBERRY COCKTAIL AND LEMON JUICE. ADD SUGAR IN A STEADY STREAM, STIRRING CONSTANTLY. HEAT OVER MEDIUM HEAT, STIRRING CONSTANTLY TO DISSOLVE SUGAR. INCREASE HEAT TO HIGH AND BRING TO A FULL BOIL, STIRRING CONSTANTLY. BOIL RAPIDLY FOR 5 MINUTES, STIRRING OFTEN. STIR IN CRANBERRIES; COOK, STIRRING OFTEN, FOR 5 TO 10 MINUTES OR UNTIL MARMALADE THICKENS. TEST FOR SETTING POINT (SEE PAGE 24). REMOVE FROM HEAT AND SKIM OFF ANY FOAM. STIR FOR 5 TO 8 MINUTES TO PREVENT RIND FROM FLOATING.

LADLE INTO STERILIZED JARS TO WITHIN $\frac{1}{4}$ INCH (0.5 CM) OF RIM; WIPE RIMS. APPLY PREPARED LIDS AND RINGS; TIGHTEN RINGS JUST UNTIL FINGERTIP-TIGHT. PROCESS JARS IN A BOILING WATER CANNER FOR 10 MINUTES (SEE PAGE 27). TRANSFER JARS TO A TOWEL-LINED SURFACE AND LET REST AT ROOM TEMPERATURE UNTIL SET. CHECK SEALS; REFRIGERATE ANY UNSEALED JARS FOR UP TO 3 WEEKS. THIS MARMALADE IS BEST SERVED AFTER RESTING FOR 1 WEEK. MAKES ABOUT FIVE 8-OUNCE (250 ML) JARS.

TIP: BE SURE TO STIR THE SUGAR IN WELL, SO IT DISSOLVES COMPLETELY, OR CRYSTALS WILL FORM IN THE MARMALADE.

RECIPE SUGGESTIONS: USE TO GLAZE CHICKEN AND TURKEY, OR ADD SOME TO A SANDWICH.

USING CRANBERRIES IN PRESERVES

CHOOSE FIRM, RIPE, RED FRUIT. FREEZE WHEN IN SEASON (SEPTEMBER/OCTOBER) BY PLACING BAGS OF WHOLE BERRIES INSIDE A FREEZER BAG TO KEEP THEM FROM DRYING OUT.

HONEY LEMON MARMALADE

THIS GOLDEN-COLORED JELLY WITH FINELY
SLICED RIND HAS A NICE BALANCE OF TART AND SWEET.

6	LARGE LEMONS	6
1½ CUPS	WATER	375 ML
2¾ CUPS	GRANULATED SUGAR	675 ML
1½ CUPS	LIQUID HONEY	375 ML
1	POUCH (3 OZ/85 ML) LIQUID PECTIN	1

USING A VEGETABLE PEELER, REMOVE RIND FROM SEVERAL
OF THE LEMONS IN WIDE STRIPS; THINLY SLICE TO MAKE
¾ CUP (175 ML). IN A SMALL SAUCEPAN, COMBINE RIND
AND WATER. BRING TO A BOIL OVER HIGH HEAT. REDUCE
HEAT AND SIMMER, COVERED, FOR 15 TO 20 MINUTES OR
UNTIL RIND IS SOFTENED. SET ASIDE.

REMOVE REMAINING PEEL AND PITH FROM LEMONS.
FINELY CHOP LEMONS, DISCARDING SEEDS AND ANY
CONNECTIVE MEMBRANES. PLACE IN A 4-CUP (1 L)
MEASURE WITH ANY JUICE. SQUEEZE ANY JUICE FROM
PEEL INTO THE MEASURE; DISCARD PEEL. ADD COOKED
RIND WITH LIQUID AND ENOUGH WATER TO MAKE 3 CUPS
(750 ML) TOTAL.

IN A DUTCH OVEN OR A LARGE, HEAVY-BOTTOMED
POT, COMBINE LEMON MIXTURE AND SUGAR. BRING TO
A FULL BOIL OVER HIGH HEAT, STIRRING CONSTANTLY
TO DISSOLVE SUGAR. STIR IN HONEY. RETURN TO A FULL
BOIL, STIRRING CONSTANTLY. IMMEDIATELY STIR IN
PECTIN; RETURN TO A FULL BOIL. BOIL HARD FOR 1 MINUTE,
STIRRING CONSTANTLY. REMOVE FROM HEAT AND SKIM

OFF ANY FOAM. STIR FOR 5 TO 8 MINUTES TO PREVENT RIND FROM FLOATING.

LADLE INTO STERILIZED JARS TO WITHIN $\frac{1}{4}$ INCH (0.5 CM) OF RIM; WIPE RIMS. APPLY PREPARED LIDS AND RINGS; TIGHTEN RINGS JUST UNTIL FINGERTIP-TIGHT. PROCESS JARS IN A BOILING WATER CANNER FOR 10 MINUTES (SEE PAGE 27). TRANSFER JARS TO A TOWEL-LINED SURFACE AND LET REST AT ROOM TEMPERATURE UNTIL SET. CHECK SEALS; REFRIGERATE ANY UNSEALED JARS FOR UP TO 3 WEEKS. THIS MARMALADE IS BEST SERVED AFTER RESTING FOR 1 WEEK. MAKES ABOUT FIVE 8-OUNCE (250 ML) JARS.

TIP: THIS MIXTURE WILL BOIL UP VERY HIGH, SO MAKE SURE TO USE A DEEP POT. REDUCE HEAT TO MEDIUM-HIGH IF NECESSARY.

SERVING SUGGESTION: STIR A SPOONFUL OR TWO INTO HOT TEA WHEN YOU HAVE A COLD.

VARIATION
LEMON MARMALADE: REPLACE THE HONEY WITH GRANULATED SUGAR (TOTAL SUGAR EQUAL TO $4\frac{1}{4}$ CUPS/1.05 L).

THAT DAY WAS A TOTAL WASTE OF MAKEUP.

LEMON, ORANGE AND
PINK GRAPEFRUIT MARMALADE

*A CLASSIC FRUIT TRIO MARMALADE WITH A
DEEP ORANGE COLOR AND INTENSE CITRUS FLAVOR.*

4	MEDIUM LEMONS	4
3	LARGE ORANGES	3
2	SMALL PINK GRAPEFRUIT	2
4 CUPS	WATER	1 L
7 1/2 CUPS	GRANULATED SUGAR	1.875 L

USING A VEGETABLE PEELER, REMOVE RIND FROM LEMONS, ORANGES AND GRAPEFRUIT IN WIDE STRIPS; THINLY SLICE AND PACK TO MAKE 3 CUPS (750 ML) TOTAL. LINE A LARGE STRAINER WITH SEVERAL LAYERS OF CHEESECLOTH AND PLACE OVER A MEDIUM BOWL. CUT LEMONS, ORANGES AND GRAPEFRUIT IN HALF AND SQUEEZE OUT JUICE; POUR JUICE THROUGH CHEESECLOTH TO CATCH THE SEEDS. MEASURE JUICE TO MAKE 3 CUPS (750 ML). PLACE SQUEEZED FRUIT HALVES IN CHEESECLOTH WITH SEEDS; TIE SECURELY WITH STRING.

IN A DUTCH OVEN OR A LARGE, HEAVY-BOTTOMED POT, COMBINE RIND, JUICE, WATER AND CHEESECLOTH BAG. BRING TO A FULL BOIL OVER HIGH HEAT. REDUCE HEAT AND SIMMER, COVERED, FOR 25 TO 30 MINUTES OR UNTIL RIND IS SOFTENED. SQUEEZE LIQUID FROM CHEESECLOTH BAG INTO POT; DISCARD BAG. ADD SUGAR IN A STEADY STREAM, STIRRING CONSTANTLY. HEAT OVER MEDIUM HEAT, STIRRING CONSTANTLY TO DISSOLVE SUGAR. INCREASE HEAT TO HIGH AND BRING TO A FULL BOIL, STIRRING

CONSTANTLY. BOIL RAPIDLY, UNCOVERED, STIRRING OFTEN, FOR 20 TO 25 MINUTES OR UNTIL MARMALADE THICKENS. TEST FOR SETTING POINT (SEE PAGE 24). REMOVE FROM HEAT AND SKIM OFF ANY FOAM. STIR FOR 5 TO 8 MINUTES TO PREVENT RIND FROM FLOATING.

LADLE INTO STERILIZED JARS TO WITHIN $\frac{1}{4}$ INCH (0.5 CM) OF RIM; WIPE RIMS. APPLY PREPARED LIDS AND RINGS; TIGHTEN RINGS JUST UNTIL FINGERTIP-TIGHT. PROCESS JARS IN A BOILING WATER CANNER (SEE PAGE 27) FOR 10 MINUTES. TRANSFER JARS TO A TOWEL-LINED SURFACE AND LET REST AT ROOM TEMPERATURE UNTIL SET. CHECK SEALS; REFRIGERATE ANY UNSEALED JARS FOR UP TO 3 WEEKS. THIS MARMALADE IS BEST SERVED AFTER RESTING FOR 1 WEEK. MAKES ABOUT SEVEN 8-OUNCE (250 ML) JARS.

TIP: TRY MAKING THIS RECIPE WITH CARA CARA ORANGES OR TANGELOS. YOU MAY ALSO USE RED GRAPEFRUIT, IF DESIRED. CARA CARA ORANGES ARE RED-FLESHED AND ARE GROWN IN SOUTH AFRICA, VENEZUELA AND CALIFORNIA. TANGELOS ARE A CROSS BETWEEN A TANGERINE AND EITHER A GRAPEFRUIT OR A POMELO.

PARENTS FOR SALE: BUY ONE, GET ONE FREE.

LIME MARMALADE

*THIS MOUTH-PUCKERING MARMALADE HAS THE
TARTNESS OF A BRITISH-STYLE MARMALADE.*

10 to 12	LARGE LIMES	10 to 12
4 CUPS	WATER	1 L
5 CUPS	GRANULATED SUGAR	1.25 ML

USING A VEGETABLE PEELER, REMOVE RIND FROM LIMES
IN WIDE STRIPS; THINLY SLICE TO MAKE 1½ CUPS (375 ML).
CUT LIMES IN HALF AND SQUEEZE OUT JUICE; MEASURE
TO MAKE 2 CUPS (500 ML). DISCARD ANY REMAINING PEEL,
PITH AND SEEDS. IN A MEDIUM SAUCEPAN, COMBINE
RIND, JUICE AND WATER. BRING TO A BOIL OVER HIGH
HEAT. REDUCE HEAT AND SIMMER, COVERED, FOR 15 TO
20 MINUTES OR UNTIL RIND IS SOFTENED.

TRANSFER RIND WITH LIQUID TO A DUTCH OVEN OR A
LARGE, HEAVY-BOTTOMED POT. ADD SUGAR IN A STEADY
STREAM, STIRRING CONSTANTLY. HEAT OVER MEDIUM
HEAT, STIRRING CONSTANTLY TO DISSOLVE SUGAR.
INCREASE HEAT TO HIGH AND BRING TO A FULL BOIL,
STIRRING CONSTANTLY. BOIL RAPIDLY, STIRRING OFTEN,
FOR 15 TO 20 MINUTES OR UNTIL MARMALADE THICKENS.
TEST FOR SETTING POINT (SEE PAGE 24). REMOVE
FROM HEAT AND SKIM OFF ANY FOAM. STIR FOR 5 TO
8 MINUTES TO PREVENT RIND FROM FLOATING.

LADLE INTO STERILIZED JARS TO WITHIN ¼ INCH
(0.5 CM) OF RIM; WIPE RIMS. APPLY PREPARED LIDS
AND RINGS; TIGHTEN RINGS JUST UNTIL FINGERTIP-
TIGHT. PROCESS JARS IN A BOILING WATER CANNER

FOR 10 MINUTES (SEE PAGE 27). TRANSFER JARS TO A TOWEL-LINED SURFACE AND LET REST AT ROOM TEMPERATURE UNTIL SET. CHECK SEALS; REFRIGERATE ANY UNSEALED JARS FOR UP TO 3 WEEKS. THIS MARMALADE IS BEST SERVED AFTER RESTING FOR 1 WEEK. MAKES ABOUT FIVE 8-OUNCE (250 ML) JARS.

TIP: TO SUIT YOUR OWN TASTE, THICKNESS OF PEEL CAN BE CHANGED TO EXTRA-FINE RIND OR THICK.

TIP: WHEN FILLING JARS, IT'S IMPORTANT TO LEAVE SUFFICIENT HEADSPACE BETWEEN THE TOP OF THE FOOD AND THE TOP OF THE JAR TO GET A GOOD VACUUM SEAL.

RECIPE SUGGESTION: ADD THIS MARMALADE TO WHIPPED CREAM, THEN USE IT TO FILL SMALL TARTS. TOP WITH SMALL RASPBERRIES OR BLUEBERRIES OR A SLICE OF STRAWBERRY.

A BACHELOR IS A MAN WHO NEVER MADE THE SAME MISTAKE ONCE. — PHYLLIS DILLER

ZUCCHINI ORANGE MARMALADE

*THIS SURPRISING MARMALADE
IS EASY TO MAKE YEAR-ROUND AND HAS
AN INTENSE, FRESH ORANGE FLAVOR.*

	FINELY GRATED RIND OF 4 LARGE SEEDLESS ORANGES	
2 CUPS	ORANGE JUICE	500 ML
4 CUPS	LIGHTLY PACKED SHREDDED ZUCCHINI	1 L
7 CUPS	GRANULATED SUGAR	1.75 L
1/4 CUP	LEMON JUICE	60 ML
2	POUCHES (EACH 3 OZ/85 ML) LIQUID PECTIN	2

IN A SMALL SAUCEPAN, COMBINE ORANGE RIND AND JUICE. BRING TO A SIMMER OVER HIGH HEAT. REDUCE HEAT AND SIMMER, COVERED, FOR 10 MINUTES OR UNTIL RIND IS SOFTENED. SET ASIDE.

IN A DUTCH OVEN OR A LARGE, HEAVY-BOTTOMED POT OVER MEDIUM HEAT, COOK ZUCCHINI, STIRRING FREQUENTLY, FOR 5 MINUTES OR UNTIL SOFTENED (WATER WILL COME OUT OF ZUCCHINI AS IT BEGINS TO COOK). ADD SUGAR IN A STEADY STREAM, STIRRING CONSTANTLY. STIR IN LEMON JUICE AND COOKED ORANGE RIND AND JUICE. BRING TO A FULL BOIL OVER HIGH HEAT, STIRRING CONSTANTLY TO DISSOLVE SUGAR. IMMEDIATELY STIR IN PECTIN; RETURN TO A FULL BOIL. BOIL HARD FOR 1 MINUTE, STIRRING CONSTANTLY. REMOVE FROM HEAT AND SKIM OFF ANY FOAM. STIR FOR 5 TO 8 MINUTES TO PREVENT RIND AND ZUCCHINI FROM FLOATING.

LADLE INTO STERILIZED JARS TO WITHIN ¼ INCH (0.5 CM) OF RIM; WIPE RIMS. APPLY PREPARED LIDS AND RINGS; TIGHTEN RINGS JUST UNTIL FINGERTIP-TIGHT. PROCESS JARS IN A BOILING WATER CANNER (SEE PAGE 27) FOR 10 MINUTES. TRANSFER JARS TO A TOWEL-LINED SURFACE AND LET REST AT ROOM TEMPERATURE UNTIL SET. CHECK SEALS; REFRIGERATE ANY UNSEALED JARS FOR UP TO 3 WEEKS. MAKES ABOUT FIVE 8-OUNCE (250 ML) JARS.

NOTE: ZUCCHINI IS MOST OFTEN COOKED AS A VEGETABLE BUT IS BOTANICALLY A FRUIT. IT IS A SUMMER SQUASH, RELATED TO CUCUMBERS, MELONS AND OTHER VARIETIES OF SQUASH.

USING ZUCCHINI IN PRESERVES

FOR BEST RESULTS WHEN MAKING MARMALADE OR PICKLING, USE SMALL OR MEDIUM ZUCCHINI. LARGER ZUCCHINI CAN BE USED FOR RELISHES AS LONG AS THEY ARE NOT SOFT AND SPONGY. YOU MAY WANT TO REMOVE THE SEED PORTION FROM LARGER ZUCCHINI IF IT IS SOFT. FRESH ZUCCHINI HAS SHINY, SMOOTH SKIN AND NO SIGNS OF DECAY OR SOFT SPOTS. TO CLEAN ZUCCHINI, GENTLY RUB IT WITH A CLEAN WAFFLE-WEAVE DISHCLOTH. ALWAYS TRIM OFF THE STEM AND BLOSSOM ENDS BEFORE USING.

CARROT AND PINEAPPLE MARMALADE

A TASTY MARMALADE WITH A LOVELY GOLDEN COLOR. GREAT ON BRAN MUFFINS.

6 CUPS	CHOPPED CARROTS (ABOUT 2 LBS/1 KG)	1.5 L
3	LEMONS, CHOPPED, PEEL AND ALL	3
3	ORANGES, CHOPPED, PEEL AND ALL	3
1	CAN (14 OZ/398 ML) CRUSHED PINEAPPLE, WITH JUICE	1
6 CUPS	GRANULATED SUGAR	1.5 L

FINELY GRIND CARROTS AND FRUITS IN A FOOD PROCESSOR OR GRINDER. PLACE IN A DUTCH OVEN OR A LARGE, HEAVY-BOTTOMED POT. STIR IN SUGAR; LET STAND OVERNIGHT OR FOR AT LEAST 8 HOURS.

BRING TO A BOIL OVER MEDIUM HEAT, STIRRING CONSTANTLY TO DISSOLVE SUGAR. BOIL RAPIDLY, STIRRING OFTEN, FOR 10 TO 15 MINUTES OR UNTIL MARMALADE THICKENS. TEST FOR THE SETTING POINT (SEE PAGE 24). REMOVE FROM HEAT AND SKIM OFF ANY FOAM. STIR FOR 5 TO 8 MINUTES TO PREVENT RIND FROM FLOATING.

LADLE INTO STERILIZED JARS TO WITHIN 1/4 INCH (0.5 CM) OF RIM; WIPE RIMS. APPLY PREPARED LIDS AND RINGS; TIGHTEN RINGS JUST UNTIL FINGERTIP-TIGHT. PROCESS JARS IN A BOILING WATER CANNER FOR 10 MINUTES (SEE PAGE 27). TRANSFER JARS TO A TOWEL-LINED SURFACE AND LET REST AT ROOM TEMPERATURE UNTIL SET. CHECK SEALS; REFRIGERATE ANY UNSEALED JARS FOR UP TO 3 WEEKS. *MAKES ABOUT SEVEN 8-OUNCE (250 ML) JARS.*

TIP: IF YOU WISH, GRATE THE CARROTS AND FINELY CHOP THE LEMONS AND ORANGES.

TIP: WHEN FILLING JARS, IT'S IMPORTANT TO LEAVE SUFFICIENT HEADSPACE BETWEEN THE TOP OF THE FOOD AND THE TOP OF THE JAR TO GET A GOOD VACUUM SEAL.

RECIPE SUGGESTION: USE AS A GLAZE FOR HAM OR PORK CHOPS.

USING CITRUS FRUIT IN PRESERVES

CHOOSE FIRM, DEEP-COLORED, GLOSSY FRUIT WITH BLEMISH-FREE RINDS. THE FRUIT SHOULD BE HEAVY FOR ITS SIZE. STORE IN THE REFRIGERATOR IN PERFORATED PLASTIC OR MESH BAGS IN THE CRISPER DRAWER. BEFORE USING CITRUS FRUIT FOR MARMALADES, SCRUB RINDS WELL WITH SOAPY WATER AND RINSE. DO NOT FREEZE CITRUS FRUIT TO USE FOR PRESERVING. ANY EXTRA JUICE CAN BE FROZEN IN ICE CUBE TRAYS, THEN TRANSFERRED TO FREEZER BAGS AND USED FOR OTHER RECIPES.

GREEN TOMATO MARMALADE

MAKE THIS IN THE FALL BEFORE FROST, WHEN YOU STILL HAVE GREEN TOMATOES IN THE GARDEN.

10 to 14	GREEN TOMATOES	10 to 14
5½ CUPS	GRANULATED SUGAR	1.375 L
2	LEMONS	2

FINELY CHOP TOMATOES AND PLACE IN A LARGE BOWL. STIR IN SUGAR; LET STAND OVERNIGHT OR FOR AT LEAST 8 HOURS.

COARSELY CHOP THE LEMONS, RIND AND ALL, AND REMOVE SEEDS. TRANSFER TOMATO MIXTURE TO A DUTCH OVEN OR A LARGE, HEAVY-BOTTOMED POT. STIR IN LEMONS. BRING TO A BOIL OVER HIGH HEAT, STIRRING TO DISSOLVE SUGAR. REDUCE HEAT AND SIMMER FOR 45 TO 50 MINUTES OR UNTIL THICK. TEST FOR THE SETTING POINT (SEE PAGE 24). REMOVE FROM HEAT AND SKIM OFF ANY FOAM. STIR FOR 5 TO 8 MINUTES TO PREVENT RIND FROM FLOATING.

LADLE INTO STERILIZED JARS TO WITHIN ¼ INCH (0.5 CM) OF RIM; WIPE RIMS. APPLY PREPARED LIDS AND RINGS; TIGHTEN RINGS JUST UNTIL FINGERTIP-TIGHT. PROCESS JARS IN A BOILING WATER CANNER FOR 10 MINUTES (SEE PAGE 27). TRANSFER JARS TO A TOWEL-LINED SURFACE AND LET REST AT ROOM TEMPERATURE UNTIL SET. CHECK SEALS; REFRIGERATE ANY UNSEALED JARS FOR UP TO 3 WEEKS. MAKES ABOUT SIX 8-OUNCE (250 ML) JARS.

TIP: YOU WILL NEED ABOUT 3 LBS (1.5 KG) GREEN TOMATOES FOR THIS RECIPE.

TIP: WHEN FILLING JARS, IT'S IMPORTANT TO LEAVE SUFFICIENT HEADSPACE BETWEEN THE TOP OF THE FOOD AND THE TOP OF THE JAR TO GET A GOOD VACUUM SEAL.

TIP: THE BEST, SAFEST WAY TO LIFT JARS OUT OF THE CANNER IS WITH A JAR LIFTER, SPECIALIZED TONGS COATED WITH SILICONE AND DESIGNED TO FIT AROUND THE NECKS OF JARS.

VARIATIONS

GREEN TOMATO GINGER JAM: ADD 3 TBSP (45 ML) FINELY CHOPPED CANDIED GINGER WITH THE LEMONS.

GREEN TOMATO JALAPEÑO JAM: ADD 2 TBSP (30 ML) FINELY CHOPPED JALAPEÑO PEPPERS (OR TO TASTE) WITH THE LEMONS.

THE REASON THAT WOMEN DON'T PLAY FOOTBALL IS BECAUSE 11 OF THEM WOULD NEVER WEAR THE SAME OUTFIT IN PUBLIC. – PHYLLIS DILLER

CHRISTMAS MARMALADE

THIS IS A GREAT RECIPE TO MAKE
FOR CHRISTMAS OR HOSTESS GIFTS.

3	MEDIUM ORANGES	3
2	LEMONS	2
1½ CUPS	COLD WATER	375 ML
2/3 CUP	FINELY CHOPPED CANDIED GINGER	150 ML
6 CUPS	SUGAR	1.5 L
½ CUP	CHOPPED DRAINED BOTTLED MARASCHINO CHERRIES	125 ML
1	POUCH (85 ML) LIQUID PECTIN	1

HALVE ORANGES AND LEMONS THROUGH THE STEM END. PLACE CUT SIDE DOWN ON BOARD; SLICE PAPER THIN. DISCARD ANY SEEDS. PLACE FRUIT IN A DUTCH OVEN OR A LARGE, HEAVY-BOTTOMED POT. ADD WATER AND BRING TO A BOIL OVER HIGH HEAT. REDUCE HEAT, COVER AND SIMMER FOR ABOUT 30 MINUTES OR UNTIL RINDS ARE TENDER AND TRANSPARENT. STIR OCCASIONALLY.

DRAIN GINGER, RESERVING THE SYRUP. FINELY CHOP GINGER. STIR CHOPPED GINGER, GINGER SYRUP, SUGAR AND CHERRIES INTO ORANGE-LEMON MIXTURE. BRING TO A FULL ROLLING BOIL, OVER HIGH HEAT, STIRRING CONSTANTLY. BOIL HARD FOR 1 MINUTE. REMOVE FROM HEAT AND STIR IN PECTIN. CONTINUE STIRRING AND SKIMMING FOR 5 TO 8 MINUTES TO PREVENT RIND FROM FLOATING.

LADLE INTO STERILIZED JARS TO WITHIN ¼ INCH (0.5 CM) OF RIM; WIPE RIMS. APPLY PREPARED LIDS AND RINGS; TIGHTEN RINGS JUST UNTIL FINGERTIP-TIGHT.

PROCESS JARS IN A BOILING WATER CANNER FOR 10 MINUTES (SEE PAGE 27). TRANSFER JARS TO A TOWEL-LINED SURFACE AND LET REST AT ROOM TEMPERATURE UNTIL SET. CHECK SEALS; REFRIGERATE ANY UNSEALED JARS FOR UP TO 3 WEEKS. MAKES ABOUT SEVEN 8-OUNCE (250 ML) JARS.

TIP: DECORATE JARS WITH FABRIC OR PLACE THEM IN A GIFT BAG FROM THE DOLLAR STORE. YOU CAN ALSO PLACE ONE IN A CLEAR PLASTIC BAG FROM A CRAFT OR BULK FOOD STORE AND ADD AN ANTIQUE SILVER SPOON. TIE WITH RIBBON.

USING SUGAR IN PRESERVES

USE ONLY REAL SUGAR FOR PRESERVES. SUGAR SUBSTITUTES ARE NOT SUITABLE UNLESS A RECIPE HAS BEEN SPECIFICALLY CREATED FOR THEIR USE. GRANULATED SUGAR AND BROWN SUGAR CAN BE USED INTERCHANGEABLY IN A RECIPE; HOWEVER, THE RESULTING FLAVOR WILL BE SLIGHTLY DIFFERENT. USE LIGHT BROWN (GOLDEN YELLOW) SUGAR FOR A DELICATE MOLASSES FLAVOR OR DARK BROWN SUGAR FOR A DEEPER FLAVOR.

Jellies

Jellies are sparkling, clear gels made with fruit juice (strained after cooking), wine or liqueurs, herb-infused liquids, or hot peppers, cooked with sugar. Some have added pectin, some don't. Jellies hold their shape but are tender enough to spread and will quiver when jiggled. They can be sweet or savory, with bits of pepper, garlic or herbs suspended in the gel.

Note: Do not squeeze a jelly bag (when one is called for in a recipe) or the jelly will be cloudy. See page 23 for information on how to use a jelly bag.

BLACK CURRANT JELLY

BLACK CURRANTS HAVE PLENTY OF NATURAL PECTIN, WHICH GIVES THIS JELLY A GOOD SET. USE IT TO MAKE GLAZED ROAST PORK LOIN (PAGE 272).

4 LBS	BLACK CURRANTS	2 KG
3 CUPS	WATER	750 ML
4 CUPS	GRANULATED SUGAR	1 L

IN A LARGE, DEEP, HEAVY-BOTTOMED POT, COMBINE CURRANTS AND WATER. BRING TO A BOIL OVER HIGH HEAT. REDUCE HEAT AND SIMMER, COVERED, FOR 8 TO 10 MINUTES OR UNTIL CURRANTS ARE SOFTENED. USE A POTATO MASHER TO FURTHER BREAK DOWN CURRANTS AND RELEASE JUICE. POUR INTO PREPARED JELLY BAG AND LET DRIP OVERNIGHT, WITHOUT SQUEEZING (SEE PAGE 23).

MEASURE EXACTLY 4 CUPS (1 L) OF LIQUID (ADD WATER IF THERE'S NOT ENOUGH LIQUID); POUR INTO THE CLEANED POT. BRING TO A FULL BOIL OVER HIGH HEAT, STIRRING CONSTANTLY. ADD SUGAR IN A STEADY STREAM, STIRRING CONSTANTLY. RETURN TO A FULL BOIL, STIRRING CONSTANTLY TO DISSOLVE SUGAR. BOIL, WITHOUT STIRRING, REDUCING HEAT A BIT IF IT STARTS TO BOIL OVER, FOR 5 TO 8 MINUTES OR UNTIL SETTING POINT IS REACHED (SEE PAGE 24). REMOVE FROM HEAT AND SKIM OFF ANY FOAM.

LADLE QUICKLY INTO STERILIZED JARS TO WITHIN $1/4$ INCH (0.5 CM) OF RIM; WIPE RIMS. APPLY PREPARED LIDS AND RINGS; TIGHTEN JUST UNTIL FINGERTIP-TIGHT. PROCESS JARS IN A BOILING WATER CANNER FOR 10 MINUTES (SEE PAGE 27). TRANSFER JARS TO A TOWEL-LINED SURFACE AND LET REST AT ROOM TEMPERATURE UNTIL SET. CHECK SEALS; REFRIGERATE ANY UNSEALED JARS FOR UP TO 3 WEEKS. MAKES ABOUT FOUR 8-OUNCE (250 ML) JARS.

NOTE: BLACK CURRANTS HAVE A LITTLE "BEARD" ON THE BLOSSOM END THAT MUST BE SNIPPED OFF FOR JAM, BUT THAT STEP IS UNNECESSARY WHEN YOU'RE MAKING JELLY.

NOTE: BLACK CURRANTS ARE A VERY RICH SOURCE OF VITAMIN C, SECOND ONLY TO ROSE HIPS. EVEN AFTER COOKING, THEY RETAIN HIGH LEVELS OF VITAMIN C. THEY ARE ALSO RICH IN ANTHOCYANINS AND OTHER IMPORTANT MINERALS, SUCH AS POTASSIUM.

RED CURRANT JELLY

RED CURRANTS MAKE A BRIGHT RED JELLY WITH A LOVELY FLAVOR. THIS RECIPE IS GREAT TO MAKE WHEN YOU HAVE AN ABUNDANT SUPPLY OF RED CURRANTS. YOU CAN ALSO FREEZE THE FRUIT OR THE JUICE FOR JELLY-MAKING AT A LATER DATE.

12 CUPS	RED CURRANTS	3 L
6 CUPS	WATER	1.5 L
6 CUPS	GRANULATED SUGAR	1.5 L

IN A LARGE, DEEP, HEAVY-BOTTOMED POT, COMBINE CURRANTS AND WATER. BRING TO A BOIL OVER HIGH HEAT. REDUCE HEAT AND SIMMER FOR 10 MINUTES OR UNTIL CURRANTS ARE SOFTENED. USE A POTATO MASHER TO FURTHER BREAK DOWN CURRANTS; SIMMER FOR 5 MINUTES. POUR INTO PREPARED JELLY BAG AND LET DRIP OVERNIGHT, WITHOUT SQUEEZING (SEE PAGE 23).

MEASURE EXACTLY 6 CUPS (1.5 L) OF LIQUID (ADD WATER IF THERE'S NOT ENOUGH LIQUID); POUR INTO THE CLEANED POT. BRING TO A FULL BOIL OVER HIGH HEAT, STIRRING CONSTANTLY. ADD SUGAR IN A STEADY STREAM, STIRRING CONSTANTLY. RETURN TO A FULL BOIL, STIRRING CONSTANTLY TO DISSOLVE SUGAR. BOIL, WITHOUT STIRRING, REDUCING HEAT A BIT IF IT STARTS TO BOIL OVER, FOR 5 TO 8 MINUTES OR UNTIL SETTING POINT IS REACHED (SEE PAGE 24). REMOVE FROM HEAT AND SKIM OFF ANY FOAM.

LADLE QUICKLY INTO STERILIZED JARS TO WITHIN 1/4 INCH (0.5 CM) OF RIM; WIPE RIMS. APPLY PREPARED

LIDS AND RINGS; TIGHTEN JUST UNTIL FINGERTIP-TIGHT. PROCESS JARS IN A BOILING WATER CANNER FOR 10 MINUTES (SEE PAGE 27). TRANSFER JARS TO A TOWEL-LINED SURFACE AND LET REST AT ROOM TEMPERATURE UNTIL SET. CHECK SEALS; REFRIGERATE ANY UNSEALED JARS FOR UP TO 3 WEEKS. MAKES ABOUT SEVEN 8-OUNCE (250 ML) JARS.

TIP: YOU'LL NEED ABOUT 3$\frac{1}{2}$ LBS (1.75 KG) OF CURRANTS FOR THIS RECIPE.

RECIPE SUGGESTIONS: THIN THE JELLY BY ADDING A LITTLE WATER, ORANGE JUICE OR LIQUEUR, AND SPOON OVER CHEESECAKE OR USE TO GLAZE A FRUIT FLAN. OR USE IT TO MAKE LEG OF LAMB WITH RED CURRANT SAUCE (PAGE 271) OR IN PLACE OF RASPBERRY JAM IN FRESH RASPBERRY HAZELNUT TART (PAGE 282).

NOWADAYS, YOU NEED 15 PHONE NUMBERS
TO REACH YOUR FAMILY OF THREE.

BLACKBERRY PLUM JELLY

THIS DARK JELLY HAS A VERY RICH, INTENSE FLAVOR.

3 LBS	PLUMS	1.5 KG
3 CUPS	BLACKBERRIES	750 ML
1	SMALL LEMON	1
3 CUPS	WATER	750 ML
5 CUPS	GRANULATED SUGAR	1.25 L

HALVE PLUMS AND REMOVE PITS. CUT EACH PLUM INTO 8 WEDGES. IN A LARGE, DEEP, HEAVY-BOTTOMED POT, COMBINE PLUMS AND BLACKBERRIES. CUT LEMON INTO WEDGES. SQUEEZE JUICE INTO POT; PLACE SQUEEZED WEDGES IN POT. STIR IN WATER. BRING TO A BOIL OVER HIGH HEAT. REDUCE HEAT AND SIMMER, COVERED, FOR 10 MINUTES OR UNTIL FRUIT IS SOFTENED. USE A POTATO MASHER TO FURTHER BREAK DOWN FRUIT; SIMMER, COVERED, FOR 5 MINUTES. POUR INTO PREPARED JELLY BAG AND LET DRIP OVERNIGHT, WITHOUT SQUEEZING (SEE PAGE 23).

MEASURE EXACTLY 6 CUPS (1.5 L) OF LIQUID (ADD WATER IF THERE'S NOT ENOUGH LIQUID); POUR INTO CLEAN POT. BRING TO A FULL BOIL OVER HIGH HEAT, STIRRING CONSTANTLY. ADD SUGAR IN A STEADY STREAM, STIRRING CONSTANTLY. RETURN TO A FULL BOIL, STIRRING CONSTANTLY TO DISSOLVE SUGAR. BOIL, WITHOUT STIRRING, REDUCING HEAT A BIT IF IT STARTS TO BOIL OVER, FOR 14 TO 16 MINUTES OR UNTIL SETTING POINT IS REACHED (SEE PAGE 24). REMOVE FROM HEAT AND SKIM OFF ANY FOAM.

LADLE QUICKLY INTO STERILIZED JARS TO WITHIN $\frac{1}{4}$ INCH (0.5 CM) OF RIM; WIPE RIMS. APPLY PREPARED LIDS AND RINGS; TIGHTEN JUST UNTIL FINGERTIP-TIGHT. PROCESS JARS IN A BOILING WATER CANNER FOR 10 MINUTES (SEE PAGE 27). TRANSFER JARS TO A TOWEL-LINED SURFACE AND LET REST AT ROOM TEMPERATURE UNTIL SET. CHECK SEALS; REFRIGERATE ANY UNSEALED JARS FOR UP TO 3 WEEKS. MAKES ABOUT FIVE 8-OUNCE (250 ML) JARS.

TIP: BE CAREFUL WHEN POURING THE LIQUID INTO THE JELLY BAG — IT CAN STAIN (CLOTHES, COUNTER, ETC.).

NOTE: THIS JELLY MIXTURE MAY BOIL OVER IF THE POT IS NOT DEEP ENOUGH. IF THE FROTH RISES TO THE TOP OF THE POT DURING COOKING, REDUCE THE HEAT TO PREVENT IT FROM BOILING OVER.

RECIPE SUGGESTION: HEAT WITH AN EQUAL AMOUNT OF MAPLE SYRUP, WHISKING TO BLEND, AND SERVE AS A SAUCE OVER PANCAKES OR WAFFLES.

THE DIFFERENCE BETWEEN A BAD HAIRCUT
AND A GOOD HAIRCUT IS TIME.

CRABAPPLE JELLY

THIS DEEP RED JELLY CAN BE USED
TO GLAZE MEATS OR FRUIT FLANS, OR SPREAD
ON FRESH-BAKED SCONES OR MUFFINS.

14 CUPS	CRABAPPLES	3.5 L
6 CUPS	WATER	1.5 L
4½ CUPS	GRANULATED SUGAR	1.125 L

CUT CRABAPPLES IN HALF THROUGH STEM, AND REMOVE
STEM AND BLOSSOM ENDS. IN A LARGE, DEEP, HEAVY-
BOTTOMED POT, COMBINE CRABAPPLES AND WATER. BRING
TO A BOIL OVER HIGH HEAT. REDUCE HEAT AND BOIL
GENTLY FOR 15 MINUTES OR UNTIL CRABAPPLES ARE
SOFTENED. USE A POTATO MASHER TO FURTHER BREAK
DOWN APPLES; BOIL GENTLY FOR 5 MINUTES. POUR INTO
PREPARED JELLY BAG AND LET DRIP OVERNIGHT, WITHOUT
SQUEEZING (SEE PAGE 23).

MEASURE EXACTLY 6 CUPS (1.5 L) OF LIQUID (ADD
WATER IF THERE'S NOT ENOUGH LIQUID); POUR INTO
THE CLEANED POT. BRING TO A FULL BOIL OVER HIGH
HEAT, STIRRING CONSTANTLY. ADD SUGAR IN A STEADY
STREAM, STIRRING CONSTANTLY. RETURN TO A FULL
BOIL, STIRRING CONSTANTLY TO DISSOLVE SUGAR. BOIL,
WITHOUT STIRRING, REDUCING HEAT A BIT IF IT STARTS
TO BOIL OVER, FOR 8 TO 12 MINUTES OR UNTIL SETTING
POINT IS REACHED (SEE PAGE 24). REMOVE FROM HEAT
AND SKIM OFF ANY FOAM.

LADLE QUICKLY INTO STERILIZED JARS TO WITHIN
¼ INCH (0.5 CM) OF RIM; WIPE RIMS. APPLY PREPARED
LIDS AND RINGS; TIGHTEN JUST UNTIL FINGERTIP-

TIGHT. PROCESS JARS IN A BOILING WATER CANNER FOR 10 MINUTES (SEE PAGE 27). TRANSFER JARS TO A TOWEL-LINED SURFACE AND LET REST AT ROOM TEMPERATURE UNTIL SET. CHECK SEALS; REFRIGERATE ANY UNSEALED JARS FOR UP TO 3 WEEKS. MAKES ABOUT SIX 8-OUNCE (250 ML) JARS.

TIP: BE CAREFUL WHEN POURING THE LIQUID INTO THE JELLY BAG — IT CAN STAIN (CLOTHES, COUNTER, ETC.).

NOTE: DO NOT SEAL JELLIES WITH PARAFFIN WAX. THIS PRACTICE IS NO LONGER CONSIDERED SAFE. PROCESS IN A BOILING WATER CANNER FOR A VALID SEAL. DO NOT INVERT JARS AFTER SEALING.

USING CRABAPPLES IN PRESERVES

CRABAPPLES MAKE EXCELLENT JELLY. REMOVE THE STEMS AND BLOSSOM ENDS. DO NOT PEEL OR REMOVE CORES.

CRANBERRY PORT JELLY

WITH ADDED PECTIN, THIS RUBY-COLORED,
LIGHTLY SPICED JELLY NEEDS LITTLE COOKING TIME.
IT IS GOOD WITH ANY GAME MEAT OR CHICKEN.
ALSO TRY IT ON BISCUITS OR TOAST.

7 CUPS	GRANULATED SUGAR	1.75 L
3 CUPS	CRANBERRY COCKTAIL	750 ML
1/4 TSP	GROUND CLOVES	1 ML
1/4 TSP	GROUND CINNAMON	1 ML
I CUP	PORT WINE	250 ML
2	POUCHES (EACH 3 OZ/85 ML) LIQUID PECTIN	2

IN A LARGE, DEEP, HEAVY-BOTTOMED POT, COMBINE
SUGAR, CRANBERRY COCKTAIL, CLOVES AND CINNAMON.
OVER HIGH HEAT, STIRRING CONSTANTLY, BRING TO A
FULL ROLLING BOIL THAT CANNOT BE STIRRED DOWN. STIR
IN WINE AND PECTIN. BOIL HARD, STIRRING CONSTANTLY,
FOR I MINUTE. REMOVE FROM HEAT AND QUICKLY SKIM
OFF FOAM.

LADLE QUICKLY INTO STERILIZED JARS TO WITHIN
1/4 INCH (0.5 CM) OF RIM; WIPE RIMS. APPLY PREPARED
LIDS AND RINGS; TIGHTEN JUST UNTIL FINGERTIP-
TIGHT. PROCESS JARS IN A BOILING WATER CANNER FOR
10 MINUTES (SEE PAGE 27). TRANSFER JARS TO A TOWEL-
LINED SURFACE AND LET REST AT ROOM TEMPERATURE
UNTIL SET. CHECK SEALS; REFRIGERATE ANY UNSEALED
JARS FOR UP TO 3 WEEKS. *MAKES ABOUT FOUR 8-OUNCE*
(250 ML) JARS.

TIP: THE BEST, SAFEST WAY TO LIFT JARS OUT OF THE CANNER IS WITH A JAR LIFTER, SPECIALIZED TONGS COATED WITH SILICONE AND DESIGNED TO FIT AROUND THE NECKS OF JARS.

NOTE: SOME BRANDS OF LIQUID PECTIN SUGGEST THAT YOU ADD IT AFTER BOILING THE JUICE AND SUGAR MIXTURE FOR 1 MINUTE. FOLLOW THE INSTRUCTIONS ON THE PECTIN PACKAGE YOU ARE USING WHEN MAKING THIS RECIPE.

RECIPE SUGGESTION: USE THIS JELLY TO MAKE TURKEY, BRIE AND CRANBERRY PANINI (PAGE 277).

USING SPICES IN PRESERVES

WHOLE SPICES, SUCH AS BAY LEAVES, CINNAMON STICKS, MUSTARD SEEDS, CELERY SEEDS, CLOVES AND ALLSPICE, CAN BE LEFT IN THE PICKLING LIQUID OR, WHEN A CLEAR LIQUID IS DESIRED, CAN BE TIED IN A SPICE BAG MADE OF CHEESECLOTH, THEN DISCARDED AFTER THEIR FLAVOR HAS INFUSED THE LIQUID. GROUND SPICES ARE SOMETIMES USED FOR A MORE EVEN DISTRIBUTION OF FLAVOR. FOR BOTH WHOLE AND GROUND SPICES, USE GOOD-QUALITY DRIED PRODUCTS THAT ARE FRAGRANT AND HAVE NO SIGNS OF MOLD OR DIRT.

CONCORD GRAPE JELLY

THIS IS THE TRADITIONAL GRAPE JELLY
OF PEANUT BUTTER AND JELLY SANDWICHES.
LOOK FOR THESE DEEP BLUISH-PURPLE GRAPES
AT FARMERS' MARKETS IN SEPTEMBER.

14 CUPS	STEMMED CONCORD GRAPES	3.5 L
1	TART APPLE, STEM AND BLOSSOM ENDS REMOVED, SLICED	1
2 CUPS	WATER	500 ML
3¾ CUPS	GRANULATED SUGAR	925 ML

IN A LARGE, DEEP, HEAVY-BOTTOMED POT, COMBINE GRAPES, APPLE AND WATER. BRING TO A FULL BOIL OVER HIGH HEAT. REDUCE HEAT TO MEDIUM-HIGH AND BOIL FOR 8 MINUTES OR UNTIL FRUIT IS SOFTENED. USE A POTATO MASHER TO FURTHER BREAK DOWN FRUIT; BOIL FOR 2 MINUTES. POUR INTO PREPARED JELLY BAG AND LET DRIP OVERNIGHT, WITHOUT SQUEEZING (SEE PAGE 23). REFRIGERATE LIQUID FOR 24 HOURS TO ALLOW GRANULES FORMED BY TARTARIC ACID TO SETTLE TO BOTTOM.

MEASURE EXACTLY 5 CUPS (1.25 L) OF LIQUID, BEING CAREFUL NOT TO INCLUDE ANY OF THE GRANULES (ADD WATER IF THERE'S NOT ENOUGH LIQUID); POUR INTO THE CLEANED POT. BRING TO A FULL BOIL OVER HIGH HEAT, STIRRING CONSTANTLY. ADD SUGAR IN A STEADY STREAM, STIRRING CONSTANTLY. RETURN TO A FULL BOIL, STIRRING CONSTANTLY TO DISSOLVE SUGAR. BOIL, WITHOUT STIRRING, REDUCING HEAT A BIT IF IT STARTS TO BOIL OVER, FOR 15 TO 20 MINUTES OR UNTIL SETTING POINT IS REACHED (SEE PAGE 24). REMOVE FROM HEAT AND SKIM OFF ANY FOAM.

CONTINUED ON PAGE 127...

Blackberry Plum Jelly (page 120)

Red and Green Pepper Jelly (page 134)

Apple Rum Raisin Conserve (page 146)

Pineapple, Mango and Papaya Conserve (page 152)

LADLE QUICKLY INTO STERILIZED JARS TO WITHIN 1/4 INCH (0.5 CM) OF RIM; WIPE RIMS. APPLY PREPARED LIDS AND RINGS; TIGHTEN JUST UNTIL FINGERTIP-TIGHT. PROCESS JARS IN A BOILING WATER CANNER FOR 10 MINUTES (SEE PAGE 27). TRANSFER JARS TO A TOWEL-LINED SURFACE AND LET REST AT ROOM TEMPERATURE UNTIL SET. CHECK SEALS; REFRIGERATE ANY UNSEALED JARS FOR UP TO 3 WEEKS. MAKES ABOUT FOUR 8-OUNCE (250 ML) JARS.

TIP: YOU'LL NEED ABOUT 5 1/2 LBS (2.75 KG) OF GRAPES FOR THIS RECIPE.

NOTE: TARTARIC ACID (FOUND IN GRAPES, BANANAS, MANGOS AND OTHER FRUIT) FORMS GRANULES AFTER THE FRUIT IS COOKED THAT CAN CAUSE JELLY TO CRYSTALLIZE AFTER IT SETS. BE SURE TO LET THE LIQUID SETTLE FOR 24 HOURS.

USING GRAPES IN PRESERVES

CONCORD GRAPES ARE THE MOST POPULAR CHOICE FOR JELLIES, BUT OTHER GRAPES CAN ALSO BE USED, SUCH AS CORONATION GRAPES. CHOOSE FIRM GRAPES AND REMOVE STEMS BEFORE COOKING. USE WHOLE GRAPES TO MAKE JUICE FOR JELLY.

RASPBERRY JELLY

THIS CLASSIC RECIPE WILL ALSO WORK FOR
BLACKBERRIES, BOYSENBERRIES OR LOGANBERRIES.
JELLIES ARE A GREAT WAY TO PRESERVE THESE
BERRIES AND ELIMINATE THE SEEDS.

10 CUPS	RASPBERRIES	2.5 L
2 CUPS	WATER	500 ML
3 TBSP	STRAINED LEMON JUICE (SEE TIP, OPPOSITE)	45 ML
1	PACKAGE (1.75 OZ/49 OR 57 G) POWDERED PECTIN	1
5¾ CUPS	GRANULATED SUGAR	1.425 L

IN A LARGE, DEEP, HEAVY-BOTTOMED POT, COMBINE
RASPBERRIES AND WATER. BRING TO A BOIL OVER
HIGH HEAT. REDUCE HEAT AND SIMMER, COVERED, FOR
5 MINUTES. USE A POTATO MASHER TO FURTHER BREAK
DOWN BERRIES. POUR INTO PREPARED JELLY BAG AND LET
DRIP OVERNIGHT, WITHOUT SQUEEZING (SEE PAGE 23).

MEASURE EXACTLY 4 CUPS (1 L) OF LIQUID (ADD WATER
IF THERE'S NOT ENOUGH LIQUID); POUR INTO CLEAN
POT. STIR IN LEMON JUICE. STIR IN PECTIN UNTIL
DISSOLVED. BRING TO A FULL BOIL OVER HIGH HEAT,
STIRRING CONSTANTLY. ADD SUGAR IN A STEADY STREAM,
STIRRING CONSTANTLY. RETURN TO A FULL BOIL, STIRRING
CONSTANTLY TO DISSOLVE SUGAR. BOIL HARD FOR
1 MINUTE. REMOVE FROM HEAT AND SKIM OFF ANY FOAM.

LADLE QUICKLY INTO STERILIZED JARS TO WITHIN
¼ INCH (0.5 CM) OF RIM; WIPE RIMS. APPLY PREPARED

LIDS AND RINGS; TIGHTEN JUST UNTIL FINGERTIP-
TIGHT. PROCESS JARS IN A BOILING WATER CANNER FOR
10 MINUTES (SEE PAGE 27). TRANSFER JARS TO A TOWEL-
LINED SURFACE AND LET REST AT ROOM TEMPERATURE
UNTIL SET. CHECK SEALS; REFRIGERATE ANY UNSEALED
JARS FOR UP TO 3 WEEKS. MAKES ABOUT SIX 8-OUNCE
(250 ML) JARS.

TIP: IF YOU WANT TO USE FROZEN BERRIES, YOU'LL
NEED ABOUT $2\frac{1}{2}$ LBS (1.25 KG) FROZEN UNSWEETENED
WHOLE RASPBERRIES.

TIP: TO ENSURE CLEAR JELLY, ALWAYS USE FRESHLY
SQUEEZED LEMON OR LIME JUICE THAT HAS BEEN
STRAINED.

RECIPE SUGGESTION: USE TO MAKE FRESH RASPBERRY
HAZELNUT TART (PAGE 282).

HOW TO FREEZE BERRIES

FIRST WASH THE BERRIES AND DRY WELL ON PAPER
TOWELS. LAY WHOLE BERRIES IN A SINGLE LAYER ON A
BAKING SHEET, FREEZE COMPLETELY, THEN TRANSFER
TO FREEZER BAGS OR CONTAINERS.

MINT JELLY

THIS IS A CLASSIC MINT JELLY, TYPICALLY
SERVED WITH ROASTED LAMB. IF DESIRED, ADD SOME
CHOPPED MINT LEAVES TO THE FINAL JELLY
AFTER REMOVING IT FROM THE HEAT.

2 1/2 CUPS	WATER	625 ML
2 CUPS	LOOSELY PACKED WHOLE MINT LEAVES	500 ML
3/4 CUP	CIDER VINEGAR	175 ML
1	PACKAGE (1.75 OZ/49 OR 57 G) POWDERED PECTIN	1
4 CUPS	GRANULATED SUGAR	1 L
1/2 CUP	FINELY CHOPPED MINT LEAVES (OPTIONAL)	125 ML
	GREEN FOOD COLORING (OPTIONAL)	

IN A LARGE, DEEP, HEAVY-BOTTOMED POT, COMBINE
WATER AND WHOLE MINT LEAVES. BRING TO A BOIL OVER
HIGH HEAT. REDUCE HEAT AND SIMMER, COVERED, FOR
15 MINUTES. STRAIN OVER A BOWL, SQUEEZING LEAVES;
RESERVE LIQUID AND DISCARD LEAVES.

MEASURE EXACTLY 2 CUPS (500 ML) OF LIQUID (ADD
WATER IF THERE'S NOT ENOUGH LIQUID); POUR INTO
THE CLEANED POT. STIR IN VINEGAR. STIR IN PECTIN
UNTIL DISSOLVED. BRING TO A FULL BOIL OVER HIGH
HEAT, STIRRING CONSTANTLY. ADD SUGAR IN A STEADY
STREAM, STIRRING CONSTANTLY. RETURN TO A FULL
BOIL, STIRRING CONSTANTLY TO DISSOLVE SUGAR. BOIL
HARD FOR 1 MINUTE. REMOVE FROM HEAT AND SKIM OFF
ANY FOAM. STIR IN FINELY CHOPPED MINT LEAVES AND

FOOD COLORING (IF USING). STIR FOR 5 TO 8 MINUTES TO PREVENT FLOATING MINT LEAVES.

LADLE INTO STERILIZED JARS TO WITHIN $1/4$ INCH (0.5 CM) OF RIM; WIPE RIMS. APPLY PREPARED LIDS AND RINGS; TIGHTEN JUST UNTIL FINGERTIP-TIGHT. PROCESS JARS IN A BOILING WATER CANNER FOR 10 MINUTES (SEE PAGE 27). TRANSFER JARS TO A TOWEL-LINED SURFACE AND LET REST AT ROOM TEMPERATURE UNTIL SET. CHECK SEALS; REFRIGERATE ANY UNSEALED JARS FOR UP TO 3 WEEKS. MAKES ABOUT FOUR 8-OUNCE (250 ML) JARS OR EIGHT 4-OUNCE (125 ML) JARS.

TIP: CHOOSE FROM THE MANY MINTS AVAILABLE, SUCH AS SPEARMINT (THE MOST COMMON MINT YOU'LL FIND IN GROCERY STORES), PEPPERMINT, APPLE MINT, PINEAPPLE MINT, LEMON MINT, ORANGE MINT — EVEN CHOCOLATE MINT.

Q: I CAN WHEN I CAN AND WHEN I CAN'T
I FREEZE. WHO AM I?
A: SOMEONE WHO PRESERVES.

MISS SCARLETT'S WINE CORDIAL JELLY

A PRETTY, LAYERED JELLY — PERFECT FOR CHRISTMAS GIFTING. SERVE WITH GAME OR FOWL.

6 CUPS	GRANULATED SUGAR	1.5 L
4 CUPS	DRY WHITE WINE	1 L
2	POUCHES (EACH 3 OZ/85 ML) LIQUID PECTIN	2
1/4 CUP	ORANGE LIQUEUR	60 ML
1/4 CUP	CRÈME DE CASSIS	60 ML
	RED FOOD COLORING	
1/4 CUP	GREEN CRÈME DE MENTHE	60 ML

IN A LARGE POT, BRING SUGAR AND WINE TO A SLOW BOIL OVER HIGH HEAT, STIRRING CONSTANTLY. ADD PECTIN AND BRING BACK TO A BOIL; BOIL HARD FOR 1 MINUTE. REMOVE FROM HEAT AND SKIM OFF ANY FOAM. POUR INTO THREE BOWLS, ABOUT 2 1/2 CUPS (625 ML) EACH. ADD ORANGE LIQUEUR TO ONE BOWL, CRÈME DE CASSIS AND A FEW DROPS OF RED FOOD COLORING TO THE SECOND BOWL, AND CRÈME DE MENTHE TO THE THIRD BOWL.

POUR ONE COLOR INTO BOTTOM THIRD OF EACH STERILIZED JAR AND LET COOL FOR 20 MINUTES — BE PATIENT. CAREFULLY ADD SECOND LAYER TO EACH JAR AND LET SET, THEN FILL EACH WITH THE THIRD LAYER, TO WITHIN 1/4 INCH (0.5 CM) OF RIM; WIPE RIMS. APPLY PREPARED LIDS AND RINGS; TIGHTEN JUST UNTIL FINGERTIP-TIGHT. PROCESS JARS IN A BOILING WATER CANNER FOR 10 MINUTES (SEE PAGE 27). TRANSFER JARS TO A TOWEL-LINED SURFACE AND LET REST AT ROOM

TEMPERATURE UNTIL SET. CHECK SEALS; REFRIGERATE ANY UNSEALED JARS FOR UP TO 3 WEEKS. MAKES ABOUT SIX 8-OUNCE (250 ML) JARS.

NOTE: YOU MAY HAVE TO REHEAT THE SECOND- AND THIRD-LAYER MIXTURES SLIGHTLY IN ORDER TO POUR THEM PROPERLY, AS THEY MAY BEGIN TO SET. YOU CAN DO THIS IN A LARGE GLASS MEASURE IN THE MICROWAVE, OR IN A MEDIUM SAUCEPAN.

TIP: WHEN FILLING JARS, IT'S IMPORTANT TO LEAVE SUFFICIENT HEADSPACE BETWEEN THE TOP OF THE FOOD AND THE TOP OF THE JAR TO GET A GOOD VACUUM SEAL.

TIP: THE BEST, SAFEST WAY TO LIFT JARS OUT OF THE CANNER IS WITH A JAR LIFTER, SPECIALIZED TONGS COATED WITH SILICONE AND DESIGNED TO FIT AROUND THE NECKS OF JARS.

TRANQUILIZERS WORK ONLY IF YOU
FOLLOW THE ADVICE ON THE BOTTLE:
KEEP AWAY FROM CHILDREN.
— PHYLLIS DILLER

RED AND GREEN PEPPER JELLY

THIS ATTRACTIVE JELLY HAS SUSPENDED BITS OF RED AND GREEN BELL PEPPER (IT CAN ALSO BE MADE WITH ALL RED OR ALL GREEN PEPPERS). HOT PEPPER JELLIES ARE VERY POPULAR AND MAKE GREAT HOLIDAY OR HOST/HOSTESS GIFTS.

1 CUP	FINELY CHOPPED RED BELL PEPPERS	250 ML
1 CUP	FINELY CHOPPED GREEN BELL PEPPERS	250 ML
1 OR 2	JALAPEÑO PEPPERS, MINCED (OPTIONAL)	1 OR 2
1 1/2 CUPS	CIDER VINEGAR	375 ML
1/2 TSP	HOT PEPPER SAUCE (OR 1/4 TSP/1 ML HOT PEPPER FLAKES)	2 ML
6 1/2 CUPS	GRANULATED SUGAR	1.625 L
2	POUCHES (3 OZ/85 ML EACH) LIQUID PECTIN	2

IN A LARGE, DEEP, HEAVY-BOTTOMED POT, COMBINE RED PEPPERS, GREEN PEPPERS, JALAPEÑO PEPPERS (IF USING), VINEGAR, HOT PEPPER SAUCE AND SUGAR. BRING TO A BOIL OVER MEDIUM HEAT, STIRRING CONSTANTLY. REDUCE HEAT AND BOIL GENTLY FOR 5 MINUTES. REMOVE FROM HEAT AND LET STAND FOR 20 MINUTES, STIRRING OCCASIONALLY. BRING TO A FULL BOIL OVER HIGH HEAT, STIRRING CONSTANTLY. IMMEDIATELY STIR IN PECTIN; RETURN TO A FULL BOIL. BOIL HARD FOR 1 MINUTE, STIRRING CONSTANTLY. REMOVE FROM HEAT AND SKIM OFF ANY FOAM. STIR FOR 5 TO 8 MINUTES TO PREVENT FLOATING PEPPERS.

LADLE INTO PREPARED JARS TO WITHIN 1/4 INCH (0.5 CM) OF RIM; WIPE RIMS. APPLY PREPARED LIDS AND

RINGS; TIGHTEN JUST UNTIL FINGERTIP-TIGHT. PROCESS JARS IN A BOILING WATER CANNER FOR 10 MINUTES (SEE PAGE 27). TRANSFER JARS TO A TOWEL-LINED SURFACE AND LET REST AT ROOM TEMPERATURE UNTIL SET. CHECK SEALS; REFRIGERATE ANY UNSEALED JARS FOR UP TO 3 WEEKS. MAKES ABOUT FIVE 8-OUNCE (250 ML) JARS.

TIP: TO TEST FOR FLOATING PEPPERS, FILL ONE JAR; LET REST FOR 1 MINUTE. IF PEPPERS START TO FLOAT UPWARD, POUR JELLY BACK INTO POT AND KEEP STIRRING; BEGIN AGAIN WITH A NEW STERILIZED JAR.

SERVING SUGGESTION: SERVE OVER CREAM CHEESE ON CRACKERS.

USING BELL PEPPERS IN PRESERVES

RED, YELLOW, GREEN OR ORANGE BELL PEPPERS ADD COLOR AND TASTE TO JELLIES, CHUTNEYS, RELISHES AND SALSAS. GREEN BELL PEPPERS HAVE THEIR OWN UNIQUE FLAVOR; DO NOT SUBSTITUTE THEM FOR OTHER COLORS UNLESS THE RECIPE SPECIFIES THAT YOU CAN DO SO. RED, ORANGE AND YELLOW BELL PEPPERS CAN BE USED INTERCHANGEABLY. STORE PEPPERS IN A PLASTIC BAG IN THE REFRIGERATOR CRISPER. BEFORE CHOPPING, TRIM OFF THE STEM END AND REMOVE ALL SEEDS AND MEMBRANES.

JALAPEÑO PEPPER JELLY

THIS IS ONE OF OUR CHRISTMAS EXCHANGE FAVORITES — MEN LOVE IT!

6	JALAPEÑO PEPPERS, WITH SEEDS, FINELY CHOPPED (OR TWO 4-OZ/ 114 ML CANS)	6
3	GREEN BELL PEPPERS, SEEDED AND FINELY CHOPPED	3
6½ CUPS	GRANULATED SUGAR	1.625 L
½ to 1 TSP	CAYENNE PEPPER	2 to 5 ML
1½ CUPS	WHITE VINEGAR	375 ML
2	POUCHES (EACH 3 OZ/85 ML) LIQUID PECTIN	2
4 to 6 DROPS	GREEN FOOD COLORING	4 to 6 DROPS

IN A LARGE, DEEP, HEAVY-BOTTOMED POT, COMBINE JALAPEÑOS, GREEN PEPPERS, SUGAR, CAYENNE AND VINEGAR. COOK OVER MEDIUM-HIGH HEAT, STIRRING FREQUENTLY, UNTIL MIXTURE BEGINS TO BOIL. BOIL FOR 10 MINUTES, STIRRING CONSTANTLY. ADD PECTIN AND BOIL FOR 1 MINUTE LONGER, WITHOUT STIRRING. REMOVE FROM HEAT AND SKIM OFF ANY FOAM. STIR FOR 5 TO 8 MINUTES TO PREVENT FLOATING PEPPERS.

LADLE INTO PREPARED JARS TO WITHIN ¼ INCH (0.5 CM) OF RIM; WIPE RIMS. APPLY PREPARED LIDS AND RINGS; TIGHTEN JUST UNTIL FINGERTIP-TIGHT. PROCESS JARS IN A BOILING WATER CANNER FOR 10 MINUTES (SEE PAGE 27). TRANSFER JARS TO A TOWEL-LINED SURFACE AND LET REST AT ROOM TEMPERATURE UNTIL SET. CHECK

SEALS; REFRIGERATE ANY UNSEALED JARS FOR UP TO 3 WEEKS. MAKES ABOUT SEVEN 4-OUNCE (125) ML JARS.

TIP: IF JELLY DOES NOT SET, RETURN TO POT, BRING TO A BOIL, ADD 1 POUCH (3 OZ/85 ML) LIQUID PECTIN AND BOIL FOR 1 MINUTE. THEN PROCESS AGAIN.

TIP: THE BEST, SAFEST WAY TO LIFT JARS OUT OF THE CANNER IS WITH A JAR LIFTER, SPECIALIZED TONGS COATED WITH SILICONE AND DESIGNED TO FIT AROUND THE NECKS OF JARS.

SERVING SUGGESTION: SERVE ON CRACKERS (KAVLI FLATBREAD IS BEST), WITH SOFT CREAM CHEESE.

THE SCOVILLE SCALE

THE SCOVILLE SCALE, NAMED AFTER THE PHARMACIST WHO DEVELOPED IT, IS USED TO MEASURE THE HEAT OF A PEPPER. THE HIGHER THE SCOVILLE RATING, THE HOTTER THE HEAT. FOR EXAMPLE, A BELL PEPPER HAS A RATING OF 0, A JALAPEÑO SCORES BETWEEN 5,000 AND 10,000, AND A HABANERO CAN BE ANYWHERE FROM 100,000 TO 500,000 SCOVILLE UNITS!

CRANBERRY HOT PEPPER JELLY

BRUSH THIS VIBRANT JELLY OVER
GRILLED CHICKEN OR SALMON, WHISK IT INTO A
VINAIGRETTE OR USE IT TO GIVE A TANGY TWIST
TO A PEANUT BUTTER AND JELLY SANDWICH.

4	JALAPEÑO PEPPERS, SEEDED AND FINELY CHOPPED	4
2	RED BELL PEPPERS, FINELY CHOPPED	2
1/2 CUP	COLD WATER	125 ML
1/2 CUP	CIDER VINEGAR	125 ML
6 CUPS	GRANULATED SUGAR	1.5 L
1 1/2 CUPS	FROZEN CRANBERRY CONCENTRATE, THAWED	375 ML
1	POUCH (3 OZ/85 ML) LIQUID PECTIN	1

IN A LARGE, DEEP, HEAVY-BOTTOMED POT, COMBINE
JALAPEÑOS, RED PEPPERS, COLD WATER AND VINEGAR.
BRING TO A BOIL OVER MEDIUM-HIGH HEAT, STIRRING
OFTEN. REDUCE HEAT AND SIMMER, COVERED, FOR
10 MINUTES. TRANSFER TO A COARSE-MESH SIEVE SET
OVER A BOWL AND EXTRACT AS MUCH LIQUID AS POSSIBLE
BY PRESSING THE MIXTURE WITH THE BACK OF A LARGE
SPOON. RINSE OUT THE SIEVE AND LINE WITH DAMPENED
CHEESECLOTH (OR USE A DAMPENED JELLY BAG). STRAIN
THE LIQUID AGAIN.

TRANSFER STRAINED LIQUID TO A CLEAN LARGE
POT. ADD SUGAR AND CRANBERRY CONCENTRATE. OVER
HIGH HEAT, STIRRING CONSTANTLY, BRING TO A FULL
ROLLING BOIL THAT CANNOT BE STIRRED DOWN. STIR IN
PECTIN. BOIL HARD, STIRRING CONSTANTLY, FOR 1 MINUTE.

REMOVE FROM HEAT AND SKIM OFF ANY FOAM. STIR FOR 5 TO 8 MINUTES TO PREVENT FLOATING PEPPERS.

LADLE INTO PREPARED JARS TO WITHIN $\frac{1}{4}$ INCH (0.5 CM) OF RIM; WIPE RIMS. APPLY PREPARED LIDS AND RINGS; TIGHTEN JUST UNTIL FINGERTIP-TIGHT. PROCESS JARS IN A BOILING WATER CANNER FOR 10 MINUTES (SEE PAGE 27). TRANSFER JARS TO A TOWEL-LINED SURFACE AND LET REST AT ROOM TEMPERATURE UNTIL SET. CHECK SEALS; REFRIGERATE ANY UNSEALED JARS FOR UP TO 3 WEEKS. MAKES ABOUT FOUR 8-OUNCE (250 ML) JARS.

TIP: WHEN FILLING JARS, IT'S IMPORTANT TO LEAVE SUFFICIENT HEADSPACE BETWEEN THE TOP OF THE FOOD AND THE TOP OF THE JAR TO GET A GOOD VACUUM SEAL.

USING DRIED HOT PEPPERS IN PRESERVES

HOT PEPPER FLAKES, DRIED CHILE PEPPERS AND CRUSHED RED CHILES ARE ALL DRIED HOT PEPPERS. THEY CAN BE USED IN PLACE OF FRESH CHILE PEPPERS TO MAKE HOT PEPPER JELLY AND CHUTNEY. YOU CAN ALSO USE HOT PEPPER SAUCE TO TURN UP THE HEAT.

GARLIC JELLY

THIS JELLY IS A GREAT CONDIMENT FOR CHICKEN, BEEF OR PORK, OR IT CAN BE USED TO DEGLAZE THE PAN — JUST ADD WINE TO CREATE A TASTY SAUCE.

2 CUPS	UNSWEETENED APPLE JUICE, WHITE WINE OR WATER	500 ML
I CUP	CIDER VINEGAR OR WHITE WINE VINEGAR	250 ML
1/4 CUP	FINELY MINCED GARLIC	60 ML
4 CUPS	GRANULATED SUGAR	I L
I	POUCH (3 OZ/85 ML) LIQUID PECTIN	I

IN A LARGE, DEEP, HEAVY-BOTTOMED POT, COMBINE APPLE JUICE, VINEGAR AND GARLIC. BRING TO A BOIL OVER HIGH HEAT. REDUCE HEAT AND SIMMER, COVERED, FOR 5 MINUTES. MEASURE EXACTLY $2\frac{1}{2}$ CUPS (625 ML) OF LIQUID (ADDING WATER IF THERE'S NOT ENOUGH LIQUID); POUR INTO CLEAN POT. BRING TO A FULL BOIL OVER HIGH HEAT, STIRRING CONSTANTLY. ADD SUGAR IN A STEADY STREAM, STIRRING CONSTANTLY. RETURN TO A FULL BOIL, STIRRING CONSTANTLY TO DISSOLVE SUGAR. IMMEDIATELY STIR IN PECTIN; RETURN TO A FULL BOIL. BOIL HARD FOR I MINUTE, STIRRING CONSTANTLY. REMOVE FROM HEAT AND SKIM OFF ANY FOAM. STIR FOR 5 TO 8 MINUTES TO PREVENT FLOATING GARLIC (SOME GARLIC MAY SETTLE TO THE BOTTOM AS IT COOLS).

LADLE INTO PREPARED JARS TO WITHIN 1/4 INCH (0.5 CM) OF RIM; WIPE RIMS. APPLY PREPARED LIDS AND RINGS; TIGHTEN JUST UNTIL FINGERTIP-TIGHT. PROCESS JARS IN A BOILING WATER CANNER FOR IO MINUTES

(SEE PAGE 27). TRANSFER JARS TO A TOWEL-LINED SURFACE AND LET REST AT ROOM TEMPERATURE UNTIL SET. CHECK SEALS; REFRIGERATE ANY UNSEALED JARS FOR UP TO 3 WEEKS. MAKES ABOUT FOUR 8-OUNCE (250 ML) JARS OR EIGHT 4-OUNCE (125 ML) JARS.

TIP: A FOOD PROCESSOR MAKES FINELY MINCING THE LARGE AMOUNT OF GARLIC EASIER.

RECIPE SUGGESTION: USE THIS JELLY TO GLAZE ROAST CHICKEN.

SERVING SUGGESTION: SERVE WITH CREAM CHEESE ON CRACKERS.

USING GARLIC IN PRESERVES

"HEAD" REFERS TO THE WHOLE BULB, AND THE CLOVES ARE THE INDIVIDUAL SEGMENTS OR WEDGES. CHOOSE HEADS THAT ARE FIRM AND TIGHTLY CLOSED, WITH THE OUTER PAPER INTACT AND NO SIGNS OF SPROUTING. STORE IN AN UNGLAZED CLAY GARLIC KEEPER, A PAPER BAG OR MESH NETTING IN A DRY PLACE AT A COOL ROOM TEMPERATURE. BEFORE CHOPPING THE CLOVES, REMOVE THE PAPER-LIKE SKINS AND TRIM THE ENDS. USE THE FRESHEST GARLIC POSSIBLE. IF THERE ARE ANY GREEN SPROUTS INSIDE THE CLOVES, REMOVE THEM TO PREVENT A BITTER FLAVOR. THE FINER GARLIC IS CHOPPED, THE HOTTER IT WILL SEEM.

Conserves

Conserves are jam-like preserves but usually have added dried fruit, chopped or whole nuts, and/or liqueur or spices. They are generally a bit thinner than jam and a little chunkier, but should still mound nicely on a spoon. They do not typically use added commercial pectin.

To test a conserve for doneness, place a spoonful from the pot on a chilled plate. Place the plate in the freezer for a few minutes, until cooled to room temperature. Gently push the mixture with your finger; when done, it will wrinkle slightly and have the texture of a soft jam (spreadable but not runny). It will mound on a spoon but be soft enough to tumble from it when turned. If it becomes sticky, it is overcooked. To fix that, stir in a little apple juice or water, then reheat the mixture, stirring constantly over low heat.

CHERRY AND PLUM CONSERVE

MAKE THIS RED CONSERVE WHEN CHERRIES ARE IN SEASON. YOU CAN USE PLUMCOTS OR DARK PLUMS INSTEAD OF THE RED PLUMS, IF YOU LIKE.

4 CUPS	COARSELY CHOPPED PITTED SWEET CHERRIES, SUCH AS BING	1 L
4 CUPS	CHOPPED RED PLUMS	1 L
3/4 CUP	GRANULATED SUGAR	175 ML
1 CUP	COARSELY CHOPPED DRIED SOUR CHERRIES	250 ML
1/3 CUP	CHERRY BRANDY (OPTIONAL)	75 ML

IN A DUTCH OVEN OR A LARGE, DEEP, HEAVY-BOTTOMED POT, COMBINE CHERRIES AND PLUMS. ADD SUGAR IN A STEADY STREAM, STIRRING CONSTANTLY. BRING TO A FULL BOIL OVER HIGH HEAT, STIRRING CONSTANTLY TO DISSOLVE SUGAR. REDUCE HEAT AND BOIL GENTLY, STIRRING OFTEN, FOR 15 MINUTES. STIR IN DRIED CHERRIES; BOIL, STIRRING OFTEN AND REDUCING HEAT FURTHER AS MIXTURE THICKENS, FOR ABOUT 10 MINUTES OR UNTIL MIXTURE REACHES A SOFT, JAM-LIKE CONSISTENCY. TEST FOR DONENESS (SEE PAGE 142). STIR IN BRANDY (IF USING). REMOVE FROM HEAT AND LET REST FOR 1 MINUTE. STIR TO DISTRIBUTE DRIED CHERRIES.

LADLE INTO STERILIZED JARS TO WITHIN $\frac{1}{2}$ INCH (1 CM) OF RIM; WIPE RIMS. APPLY PREPARED LIDS AND RINGS; TIGHTEN RINGS JUST UNTIL FINGERTIP-TIGHT. PROCESS JARS IN A BOILING WATER CANNER FOR 10 MINUTES (SEE PAGE 27). TRANSFER JARS TO A TOWEL-LINED SURFACE AND LET REST AT ROOM TEMPERATURE UNTIL SET. CHECK SEALS; REFRIGERATE ANY UNSEALED JARS FOR UP TO 3 WEEKS. MAKES ABOUT SEVEN 8-OUNCE (250 ML) JARS.

TIP: IN SOME AREAS, YOU CAN PURCHASE PITTED CHERRIES IN LARGE BUCKETS. FREEZE IN PREMEASURED SMALLER AMOUNTS.

RECIPE SUGGESTION: USE CONSERVE IN SAUCE FOR PORK CHOPS, DUCK OR CHICKEN. REMOVE BROWNED MEAT FROM SKILLET, USE WINE OR FRUIT JUICE TO DEGLAZE THE PAN, THEN STIR IN CONSERVE AND A LITTLE CHOPPED FRESH ROSEMARY. ADD MEAT BACK TO PAN AND SIMMER, COVERED, FOR ABOUT 5 MINUTES.

CARROT, APPLE AND PINEAPPLE CONSERVE

THIS CONSERVE IS EXCELLENT ON A BRAN OR OATMEAL MUFFIN. IT'S SO TASTY I KEPT EATING IT OUT OF THE SAMPLE JAR!

7 CUPS	CHOPPED PEELED APPLES THAT SOFTEN (SEE BOX, PAGE 157)	1.75 L
2 CUPS	FINELY SHREDDED CARROTS	500 ML
1 CUP	ALL-NATURAL APPLE JUICE (SEE TIP, OPPOSITE) OR UNSWEETENED APPLE CIDER	250 ML
2 CUPS	GRANULATED SUGAR	500 ML
1 CUP	PACKED BROWN SUGAR	250 ML
1 TSP	GROUND CINNAMON	5 ML
1	CAN (14 OZ/398 ML) CRUSHED PINEAPPLE, WITH JUICE	1
1/2 CUP	GOLDEN RAISINS	125 ML
1/2 CUP	CHOPPED PECANS (OPTIONAL)	125 ML
2 TBSP	AMBER RUM (OPTIONAL)	30 ML

IN A DUTCH OVEN OR A LARGE, DEEP, HEAVY-BOTTOMED POT, COMBINE APPLES, CARROTS AND APPLE JUICE. BRING TO A BOIL OVER HIGH HEAT, STIRRING OFTEN. REDUCE HEAT AND SIMMER, COVERED, STIRRING OCCASIONALLY, FOR ABOUT 8 MINUTES OR UNTIL APPLES ARE SOFTENED. ADD GRANULATED SUGAR IN A STEADY STREAM, STIRRING CONSTANTLY. STIR IN BROWN SUGAR, CINNAMON AND PINEAPPLE WITH JUICE. INCREASE HEAT TO HIGH AND BRING TO A FULL BOIL, STIRRING CONSTANTLY TO DISSOLVE SUGAR. REDUCE HEAT AND BOIL GENTLY, UNCOVERED, STIRRING OFTEN AND REDUCING HEAT FURTHER AS MIXTURE THICKENS, FOR ABOUT 20 MINUTES

OR UNTIL BEGINNING TO THICKEN. STIR IN RAISINS, PECANS AND RUM (IF USING); BOIL GENTLY, STIRRING OFTEN, FOR 5 MINUTES OR UNTIL MIXTURE REACHES A SOFT, JAM-LIKE CONSISTENCY. TEST FOR DONENESS (SEE PAGE 142). REMOVE FROM HEAT AND LET REST FOR 1 MINUTE. STIR TO DISTRIBUTE RAISINS AND NUTS.

LADLE INTO STERILIZED JARS TO WITHIN $\frac{1}{2}$ INCH (1 CM) OF RIM; WIPE RIMS. APPLY PREPARED LIDS AND RINGS; TIGHTEN JUST UNTIL FINGERTIP-TIGHT. PROCESS JARS IN A BOILING WATER CANNER FOR 10 MINUTES (SEE PAGE 27). TRANSFER JARS TO A TOWEL-LINED SURFACE AND LET REST AT ROOM TEMPERATURE UNTIL COOL. CHECK SEALS; REFRIGERATE ANY UNSEALED JARS FOR UP TO 3 WEEKS. MAKES ABOUT SIX 8-OUNCE (250 ML) JARS.

TIP: SUPERMARKETS NOW CARRY ALL-NATURAL (OR PURE-PRESSED) APPLE JUICE, WHICH CONTAINS SOLIDS. SHAKE BEFORE USING.

USING NUTS IN PRESERVES

USE ONLY VERY FRESH NUTS. FOR MORE FLAVOR, NUTS CAN BE TOASTED BEFORE USE. SPREAD NUTS ON A BAKING SHEET AND BAKE IN A 375°F (190°C) OVEN, STIRRING ONCE OR TWICE, FOR 5 TO 8 MINUTES (DEPENDING ON THE SIZE OF THE NUTS) OR UNTIL NUTS ARE TOASTED AND FRAGRANT. WATCH CAREFULLY, AS THEY BURN EASILY. TRANSFER IMMEDIATELY TO A BOWL AND LET COOL.

APPLE RUM RAISIN CONSERVE

SIMPLY DELICIOUS — A PERFECT BLEND OF
COMPLEMENTARY TASTES! TOAST THE NUTS,
IF DESIRED, BEFORE ADDING THEM.

8 CUPS	CHOPPED PEELED APPLES THAT SOFTEN, (SEE BOX, PAGE 157)	2 L
4 CUPS	CHOPPED PEELED APPLES THAT KEEP THEIR SHAPE	1 L
1 CUP	ALL-NATURAL APPLE JUICE (SEE TIP, OPPOSITE) OR UNSWEETENED APPLE CIDER	250 ML
2 TBSP	LEMON JUICE	30 ML
3¾ CUPS	GRANULATED SUGAR	925 ML
1½ CUPS	PACKED BROWN SUGAR	375 ML
1 CUP	SULTANA OR GOLDEN RAISINS	250 ML
½ CUP	CHOPPED WALNUTS (OPTIONAL)	125 ML
⅓ CUP	AMBER RUM (OR 2 TSP/10 ML RUM EXTRACT)	75 ML

IN A DUTCH OVEN OR A LARGE, DEEP, HEAVY-BOTTOMED
POT, COMBINE APPLES, APPLE JUICE AND LEMON JUICE.
BRING TO A BOIL OVER HIGH HEAT. REDUCE HEAT AND
SIMMER, COVERED, FOR 5 MINUTES TO SOFTEN APPLES.
ADD GRANULATED SUGAR IN A STEADY STREAM, STIRRING
CONSTANTLY. STIR IN BROWN SUGAR AND RAISINS.
BRING TO A FULL BOIL, STIRRING CONSTANTLY. REDUCE
HEAT AND BOIL GENTLY, UNCOVERED, STIRRING OFTEN
AND REDUCING HEAT FURTHER AS MIXTURE THICKENS,
FOR 20 TO 25 MINUTES OR UNTIL MIXTURE REACHES A
SOFT, JAM-LIKE CONSISTENCY. TEST FOR DONENESS
(SEE PAGE 142). STIR IN WALNUTS (IF USING) AND RUM;

BOIL GENTLY FOR 2 MINUTES, STIRRING CONSTANTLY. REMOVE FROM HEAT AND LET REST FOR 1 MINUTE. STIR TO DISTRIBUTE RAISINS AND NUTS.

LADLE INTO STERILIZED JARS TO WITHIN $\frac{1}{2}$ INCH (1 CM) OF RIM; WIPE RIMS. APPLY PREPARED LIDS AND RINGS; TIGHTEN RINGS JUST UNTIL FINGERTIP-TIGHT. PROCESS JARS IN A BOILING WATER CANNER FOR 10 MINUTES (SEE PAGE 27). TRANSFER JARS TO A TOWEL-LINED SURFACE AND LET REST AT ROOM TEMPERATURE UNTIL SET. CHECK SEALS; REFRIGERATE ANY UNSEALED JARS FOR UP TO 3 WEEKS. MAKES ABOUT SEVEN 8-OUNCE (250 ML) JARS

TIP: FOR LONGER STORAGE, KEEP NUTS IN A GLASS JAR IN THE REFRIGERATOR. NUTS, SUCH AS WALNUTS, THAT ARE HIGH IN OMEGA-3 FATS CAN EASILY GO RANCID IF STORED AT TEMPERATURES ABOVE 40°F (4°C). DO NOT USE ANY NUTS THAT HAVE AN OFF OR FISHY SMELL.

TIP: SUPERMARKETS NOW CARRY ALL-NATURAL (OR PURE-PRESSED) APPLE JUICE, WHICH CONTAINS SOLIDS. SHAKE BEFORE USING.

VARIATIONS

SPICED APPLE RAISIN CONSERVE: OMIT THE RUM AND ADD 1 TSP (5 ML) GROUND CINNAMON AND $\frac{1}{2}$ TSP (2 ML) GROUND NUTMEG WITH THE BROWN SUGAR.

APPLE CRANBERRY ORANGE CONSERVE: REPLACE THE RAISINS WITH DRIED CRANBERRIES AND THE RUM WITH GRAND MARNIER.

CATS ARE JUST TINY WOMEN IN CHEAP FUR COATS.

CRANBERRY AND PEAR CONSERVE

THIS RECIPE IS A LITTLE QUICKER TO MAKE THAN THE LONG-BOIL METHOD USUALLY USED FOR CONSERVES, AS IT HAS ADDED PECTIN TO HELP IT SET. THE FRUIT KEEPS A BIT OF CHUNKINESS, TOO, AS A RESULT.

2 CUPS	FRESH OR FROZEN CRANBERRIES	500 ML
1/2 CUP	WATER	125 ML
4 CUPS	FINELY CHOPPED PEELED PEARS	1 L
1	PACKAGE (1.75 OZ/49 OR 57 G) POWDERED PECTIN	1
5 CUPS	GRANULATED SUGAR	1.25 L
3/4 CUP	DRIED CRANBERRIES	175 ML

IN A DUTCH OVEN OR A LARGE, DEEP, HEAVY-BOTTOMED POT, COMBINE FRESH CRANBERRIES AND WATER. BRING TO A BOIL OVER HIGH HEAT. REDUCE HEAT AND SIMMER FOR 5 MINUTES. USE A POTATO MASHER TO FURTHER BREAK DOWN CRANBERRIES. STIR IN PEARS. STIR IN PECTIN UNTIL DISSOLVED. INCREASE HEAT TO HIGH AND BRING TO A FULL BOIL, STIRRING CONSTANTLY. ADD SUGAR IN A STEADY STREAM, STIRRING CONSTANTLY. RETURN TO A FULL BOIL, STIRRING CONSTANTLY TO DISSOLVE SUGAR. STIR IN DRIED CRANBERRIES. BOIL HARD FOR 1 MINUTE. REMOVE FROM HEAT AND SKIM OFF ANY FOAM. STIR FOR 5 MINUTES TO PREVENT FLOATING FRUIT.

LADLE INTO STERILIZED JARS TO WITHIN 1/2 INCH (1 CM) OF RIM; WIPE RIMS. APPLY PREPARED LIDS AND RINGS; TIGHTEN RINGS JUST UNTIL FINGERTIP-TIGHT. PROCESS JARS IN A BOILING WATER CANNER FOR 10 MINUTES (SEE

PAGE 27). TRANSFER JARS TO A TOWEL-LINED SURFACE AND LET REST AT ROOM TEMPERATURE UNTIL SET. CHECK SEALS; REFRIGERATE ANY UNSEALED JARS FOR UP TO 3 WEEKS. MAKES ABOUT SEVEN 8-OUNCE (250 ML) JARS.

TIP: FREEZE AN EXTRA BAG OF CRANBERRIES WHEN THEY'RE AVAILABLE SO YOU'LL HAVE THEM ON HAND.

TIP: TRY FLAVORED DRIED CRANBERRIES, SUCH AS CHERRY OR ORANGE, OR SUBSTITUTE CHOPPED DRIED SOUR CHERRIES.

USING PEARS IN PRESERVES

PEARS ARE ALWAYS PICKED UNDERRIPE AND MUST BE RIPENED AT HOME BEFORE USE. TO RIPEN, PLACE IN A PAPER BAG AND STORE AT ROOM TEMPERATURE. PEARS ARE RIPE WHEN THE SHOULDERS AND NECK YIELD TO SLIGHT PRESSURE. ALWAYS PEEL AND CORE PEARS, EXCEPT FOR USE IN SOME FRUIT BUTTER RECIPES.

NECTARINE, APRICOT AND CHERRY CONSERVE

NECTARINES DO NOT NEED TO BE PEELED, WHICH SAVES TIME AND ADDS FLAVOR. DRIED APRICOTS AND DRIED CHERRIES ADD A NICE TASTE AND TEXTURE.

8 CUPS	CHOPPED NECTARINES (UNPEELED)	2 L
1 TBSP	FINELY GRATED LEMON ZEST	15 ML
$\frac{1}{4}$ CUP	LEMON JUICE	60 ML
$4\frac{1}{2}$ CUPS	GRANULATED SUGAR	1.125 L
1 CUP	SLICED DRIED APRICOTS	250 ML
1 CUP	DRIED CHERRIES	250 ML
2 TBSP	APRICOT BRANDY (OPTIONAL)	30 ML

IN A DUTCH OVEN OR A LARGE, HEAVY-BOTTOMED POT, COMBINE NECTARINES, LEMON ZEST AND LEMON JUICE. BRING TO A BOIL OVER HIGH HEAT, STIRRING CONSTANTLY. REDUCE HEAT AND SIMMER, COVERED, FOR 12 TO 15 MINUTES OR UNTIL SOFTENED. ADD SUGAR IN A STEADY STREAM, STIRRING CONSTANTLY. STIR IN APRICOTS AND CHERRIES; RETURN TO A BOIL, STIRRING CONSTANTLY TO DISSOLVE SUGAR. REDUCE HEAT AND BOIL GENTLY, UNCOVERED, STIRRING OFTEN AND REDUCING HEAT FURTHER AS MIXTURE THICKENS, FOR 25 TO 30 MINUTES OR UNTIL MIXTURE REACHES A SOFT, JAM-LIKE CONSISTENCY. TEST FOR DONENESS (SEE PAGE 142). STIR IN BRANDY (IF USING); SIMMER FOR 1 MINUTE. REMOVE FROM HEAT AND LET REST FOR 1 MINUTE. STIR TO DISTRIBUTE DRIED FRUIT.

LADLE INTO STERILIZED JARS TO WITHIN $\frac{1}{2}$ INCH (1 CM) OF RIM; WIPE RIMS. APPLY PREPARED LIDS AND RINGS;

TIGHTEN RINGS JUST UNTIL FINGERTIP-TIGHT. PROCESS JARS IN A BOILING WATER CANNER FOR 10 MINUTES (SEE PAGE 27). TRANSFER JARS TO A TOWEL-LINED SURFACE AND LET REST AT ROOM TEMPERATURE UNTIL SET. CHECK SEALS; REFRIGERATE ANY UNSEALED JARS FOR UP TO 3 WEEKS. MAKES ABOUT SIX 8-OUNCE (250 ML) JARS.

RECIPE SUGGESTION: USE TO FILL CRÊPES.

USING NECTARINES IN PRESERVES

CHOOSE NECTARINES THAT HAVE A SMOOTH SKIN WITH RED AND YELLOW COLORING. NECTARINES SHOULD GIVE SLIGHTLY TO THE TOUCH. PLACE SLIGHTLY UNDERRIPE FRUIT IN A PAPER BAG AND LEAVE AT ROOM TEMPERATURE FOR A COUPLE OF DAYS TO RIPEN. AVOID FRUIT THAT IS OVERLY HARD OR GREEN. DO NOT PEEL NECTARINES FOR PRESERVES, BUT DO REMOVE THE PIT. NECTARINES ARE INTERCHANGEABLE WITH PEACHES IN PRESERVES RECIPES.

PINEAPPLE, MANGO AND PAPAYA CONSERVE

THIS CONSERVE OFFERS EXOTIC TASTES OF THE TROPICS, WITH A TOUCH OF SWEET SPICE.

2	MEDIUM ORANGES	2
1	CAN (19 OZ/540 ML) CRUSHED PINEAPPLE, WITH JUICE	1
2 CUPS	PURÉED PAPAYA	500 ML
1½ CUPS	DICED MANGO (SEE BOX, PAGE 265)	375 ML
¼ CUP	LIME OR LEMON JUICE	60 ML
½ TSP	GROUND ALLSPICE	2 ML
½ TSP	GROUND CINNAMON	2 ML
4½ CUPS	GRANULATED SUGAR	1.125 L
⅓ CUP	AMBER OR COCONUT RUM (OPTIONAL)	75 ML
⅓ CUP	TOASTED SLIVERED ALMONDS (OPTIONAL)	75 ML

USING A FINE GRATER, REMOVE 2 TBSP (30 ML) ORANGE RIND; SET ASIDE. PEEL AND SECTION ORANGES (SEE BOX, PAGE 75), REMOVING ALL PITH, SEEDS AND MEMBRANES, AND CHOP THE FRUIT, RESERVING ANY JUICES.

IN A DUTCH OVEN OR A LARGE, HEAVY-BOTTOMED POT, COMBINE ORANGE RIND, ORANGES WITH JUICE, PINEAPPLE WITH JUICE, PAPAYA, MANGO, LIME JUICE, ALLSPICE AND CINNAMON. BRING TO A BOIL OVER HIGH HEAT, STIRRING CONSTANTLY. REDUCE HEAT AND BOIL GENTLY FOR 5 MINUTES, STIRRING OFTEN. ADD SUGAR IN A STEADY STREAM, STIRRING CONSTANTLY. INCREASE HEAT TO HIGH AND BRING TO A FULL BOIL, STIRRING CONSTANTLY TO DISSOLVE SUGAR. REDUCE HEAT AND BOIL GENTLY, STIRRING OFTEN AND REDUCING HEAT FURTHER AS

MIXTURE THICKENS, FOR 30 TO 40 MINUTES OR UNTIL MIXTURE REACHES A SOFT, JAM-LIKE CONSISTENCY. TEST FOR DONENESS (SEE PAGE 142). STIR IN RUM AND ALMONDS (IF USING); BOIL GENTLY FOR 2 MINUTES, STIRRING CONSTANTLY. REMOVE FROM HEAT AND LET REST FOR 1 MINUTE. STIR TO DISTRIBUTE NUTS.

LADLE INTO STERILIZED JARS TO WITHIN $\frac{1}{2}$ INCH (1 CM) OF RIM; WIPE RIMS. APPLY PREPARED LIDS AND RINGS; TIGHTEN RINGS JUST UNTIL FINGERTIP-TIGHT. PROCESS JARS IN A BOILING WATER CANNER FOR 10 MINUTES (SEE PAGE 27). TRANSFER JARS TO A TOWEL-LINED SURFACE AND LET REST AT ROOM TEMPERATURE UNTIL SET. CHECK SEALS; REFRIGERATE ANY UNSEALED JARS FOR UP TO 3 WEEKS. MAKES ABOUT SIX 8-OUNCE (250 ML) JARS.

TIP: TO PREPARE THE PAPAYA BEFORE PURÉEING IT, PEEL OFF THE SKIN WITH A VEGETABLE PEELER, CUT THE FLESH IN HALF LENGTHWISE AND SCOOP OUT THE SEEDS WITH A SPOON. DISCARD THE SEEDS.

TIP: IF YOU PREFER, YOU CAN REPLACE THE RUM WITH 1 TSP (5 ML) COCONUT EXTRACT OR RUM EXTRACT.

USING PAPAYAS IN PRESERVES

CHOOSE FRUIT WITH SMOOTH, WRINKLE-FREE SKIN. PAPAYAS CAN BE RIPENED AT HOME; THEY ARE RIPE WHEN THE FRUIT GIVES SLIGHTLY WHEN PRESSED. THEY WILL KEEP IN THE REFRIGERATOR FOR SEVERAL DAYS AFTER RIPENING. BEFORE USE, PEEL AND CUT IN HALF; USING A SPOON, REMOVE SEEDS FROM THE CENTER AND DISCARD.

Fruit Butters

Fruit butters are made from puréed fruit, sugar and sometimes spices, and are cooked slowly until very thick and spreadable. They do not contain any butter but may be used in place of butter on toast, English muffins, scones, etc. They're great to make when you have an abundance of fruit or fruit that is very ripe and soft. Apples that soften when cooked (see page 157) are best for fruit butters.

To test a fruit butter for doneness, place a spoonful from the pot on a plate. Let stand for a few minutes. If there is no liquid seeping from the edges, it is done. It should be thick enough to mound on a spoon once cooled.

APRICOT BUTTER

THIS BUTTER IS TANGY AND FRESH, WITH A HINT OF SPICE TO ENHANCE THE APRICOTS.

3 LBS	RIPE APRICOTS	1.5 KG
1 CUP	WATER	250 ML
3½ CUPS	GRANULATED OR PACKED BROWN SUGAR	875 ML
¼ TSP	GROUND CINNAMON	1 ML
¼ TSP	GROUND CARDAMOM OR NUTMEG	1 ML

CUT APRICOTS IN HALF ALONG CREASE; REMOVE PIT. TRIM AWAY ANY DARK OR BRUISED AREAS. CHOP COARSELY.

IN A DUTCH OVEN OR A LARGE, DEEP, HEAVY-BOTTOMED POT, COMBINE APRICOTS AND WATER. BRING TO A BOIL OVER HIGH HEAT. REDUCE HEAT TO MEDIUM-LOW AND BOIL GENTLY FOR ABOUT 20 MINUTES OR UNTIL APRICOTS ARE VERY SOFT.

LADLE FRUIT AND LIQUID INTO A LARGE MESH SIEVE AND PRESS PULP THROUGH; DISCARD SKINS (OR EXTRACT PULP USING A FOOD MILL). RETURN PULP TO CLEAN DUTCH OVEN. ADD SUGAR IN A STEADY STREAM, STIRRING CONSTANTLY. STIR IN CINNAMON AND CARDAMOM; BRING TO A BOIL OVER HIGH HEAT, STIRRING CONSTANTLY TO DISSOLVE SUGAR. REDUCE HEAT AND BOIL GENTLY, STIRRING OFTEN AND REDUCING HEAT FURTHER AS MIXTURE THICKENS, FOR 25 TO 30 MINUTES OR UNTIL THICKENED. TEST FOR DONENESS (SEE PAGE 154).

LADLE INTO STERILIZED JARS TO WITHIN $1/2$ INCH (1 CM) OF RIM; WIPE RIMS. APPLY PREPARED LIDS AND RINGS; TIGHTEN JUST UNTIL FINGERTIP-TIGHT. PROCESS JARS IN A BOILING WATER CANNER FOR 10 MINUTES (SEE PAGE 27). TRANSFER JARS TO A TOWEL-LINED SURFACE AND LET REST AT ROOM TEMPERATURE UNTIL COOL. CHECK SEALS; REFRIGERATE ANY UNSEALED JARS FOR UP TO 3 WEEKS. MAKES ABOUT FOUR 8-OUNCE (250 ML) JARS.

RECIPE SUGGESTIONS: STIR INTO PLAIN YOGURT TO SWEETEN, AND EAT WITH FRESH BERRIES. OR LAYER IN A PARFAIT GLASS, INTERSPERSED WITH GRANOLA CLUSTERS OR BRAN CEREAL.

APPLE BUTTER

WHEN YOU COOK THIS BUTTER, YOUR HOUSE WILL SMELL LIKE YOU ARE BAKING AN APPLE PIE. THIS IS A GOOD RECIPE FOR USING UP LARGE QUANTITIES OF APPLES, ESPECIALLY WHEN THEY ARE NO LONGER CRISP.

4 LBS	APPLES THAT SOFTEN (SEE BOX, OPPOSITE)	2 KG
1½ CUPS	UNSWEETENED APPLE CIDER OR ALL-NATURAL APPLE JUICE	375 ML
3½ CUPS	PACKED BROWN SUGAR	875 ML
2 TBSP	LEMON JUICE	30 ML
1 TSP	GROUND CINNAMON	5 ML
¼ TSP	GROUND NUTMEG	1 ML
¼ TSP	GROUND CLOVES	1 ML

CUT APPLES INTO QUARTERS; REMOVE STEMS AND BLOSSOM ENDS. SLICE EACH QUARTER INTO 4 OR 5 SLICES. IN A DUTCH OVEN OR A LARGE, DEEP, HEAVY-BOTTOMED POT, COMBINE APPLES AND CIDER. BRING TO A BOIL OVER HIGH HEAT. REDUCE HEAT AND BOIL GENTLY, COVERED, FOR ABOUT 15 MINUTES OR UNTIL APPLES ARE VERY SOFT.

LADLE FRUIT AND LIQUID INTO A MESH SIEVE AND PRESS PULP THROUGH; DISCARD PEEL AND SEEDS (OR EXTRACT PULP USING A FOOD MILL). RETURN PULP TO CLEAN DUTCH OVEN. ADD SUGAR IN A STEADY STREAM, STIRRING CONSTANTLY. STIR IN LEMON JUICE AND SPICES; COOK OVER LOW HEAT, STIRRING CONSTANTLY TO DISSOLVE SUGAR. INCREASE HEAT TO HIGH AND BRING TO A BOIL, STIRRING CONSTANTLY. REDUCE HEAT AND BOIL GENTLY, UNCOVERED, STIRRING OFTEN AND REDUCING

HEAT FURTHER AS MIXTURE THICKENS, FOR ABOUT
1 HOUR OR UNTIL THICKENED. TEST FOR DONENESS (SEE
PAGE 154).

LADLE INTO STERILIZED JARS TO WITHIN $\frac{1}{2}$ INCH (1 CM)
OF RIM; WIPE RIMS. APPLY PREPARED LIDS AND RINGS;
TIGHTEN JUST UNTIL FINGERTIP-TIGHT. PROCESS JARS IN
A BOILING WATER CANNER FOR 10 MINUTES (SEE PAGE 27).
TRANSFER JARS TO A TOWEL-LINED SURFACE AND LET
REST AT ROOM TEMPERATURE UNTIL COOL. CHECK SEALS;
REFRIGERATE ANY UNSEALED JARS FOR UP TO 3 WEEKS.
MAKES ABOUT FOUR 8-OUNCE (250 ML) JARS.

TIP: YOU'LL NEED ABOUT 12 MEDIUM APPLES FOR THIS
RECIPE.

TIP: SUPERMARKETS NOW CARRY ALL-NATURAL (OR PURE-
PRESSED) APPLE JUICE, WHICH CONTAINS SOLIDS. SHAKE
BEFORE USING.

APPLES THAT SOFTEN

MCINTOSH, PAULA RED, CORTLAND, EMPIRE, RUSSET, GALA,
RHODE ISLAND GREENING, PIPPIN

APPLES THAT KEEP THEIR SHAPE

GOLDEN DELICIOUS, JONAGOLD, SPARTAN, GINGER GOLD,
CRISPIN (MUTSU), IDARED, NORTHERN SPY

CRAN-APPLE BUTTER

TWO FALL FAVORITES PARTNER IN THIS
CRANBERRY RED BUTTER. SPREAD ON APPLE,
CARROT OR BRAN MUFFINS OR LOAF SLICES.

2 LBS	APPLES THAT SOFTEN (SEE BOX, PAGE 157)	1 KG
3 CUPS	FRESH OR FROZEN CRANBERRIES	750 ML
2 CUPS	UNSWEETENED APPLE CIDER	500 ML
2 TBSP	GRATED ORANGE ZEST	30 ML
3 CUPS	GRANULATED SUGAR	750 ML
1/4 TSP	GROUND NUTMEG	1 ML

CUT APPLES INTO QUARTERS; REMOVE STEMS AND
BLOSSOM ENDS. SLICE EACH QUARTER INTO 4 OR
5 SLICES. IN A DUTCH OVEN OR A LARGE, DEEP, HEAVY-
BOTTOMED POT, COMBINE APPLES, CRANBERRIES, CIDER
AND ORANGE ZEST. BRING TO A BOIL OVER HIGH HEAT.
REDUCE HEAT AND BOIL GENTLY, COVERED, FOR ABOUT
15 MINUTES OR UNTIL APPLES ARE VERY SOFT.

LADLE FRUIT AND LIQUID INTO A MESH SIEVE AND
PRESS PULP THROUGH; DISCARD PEEL AND SEEDS (OR
EXTRACT PULP USING A FOOD MILL). RETURN PULP TO
CLEAN DUTCH OVEN. ADD SUGAR IN A STEADY STREAM,
STIRRING CONSTANTLY. STIR IN NUTMEG; COOK OVER
LOW HEAT, STIRRING CONSTANTLY TO DISSOLVE
SUGAR. INCREASE HEAT TO HIGH AND BRING TO A BOIL,
STIRRING CONSTANTLY. REDUCE HEAT AND BOIL GENTLY,
UNCOVERED, STIRRING OFTEN AND REDUCING HEAT
FURTHER AS MIXTURE THICKENS, FOR 20 TO 25 MINUTES
OR UNTIL THICKENED. TEST FOR DONENESS (SEE PAGE 154).

LADLE INTO STERILIZED JARS TO WITHIN $\frac{1}{2}$ INCH (1 CM) OF RIM; WIPE RIMS. APPLY PREPARED LIDS AND RINGS; TIGHTEN JUST UNTIL FINGERTIP-TIGHT. PROCESS JARS IN A BOILING WATER CANNER FOR 10 MINUTES (SEE PAGE 27). TRANSFER JARS TO A TOWEL-LINED SURFACE AND LET REST AT ROOM TEMPERATURE UNTIL COOL. CHECK SEALS; REFRIGERATE ANY UNSEALED JARS FOR UP TO 3 WEEKS. MAKES ABOUT FIVE 8-OUNCE (250 ML) JARS.

TIP: YOU'LL NEED ABOUT 6 MEDIUM APPLES FOR THIS RECIPE.

TIP: CRANBERRIES CAN BE EASILY FROZEN. BUY THEM WHEN THEY'RE ABUNDANT DURING THE HOLIDAY SEASON, PLACE EACH BAG IN A PLASTIC FREEZER BAG TO PROTECT IT, AND PUT THEM RIGHT INTO THE FREEZER.

WHAT I DON'T LIKE ABOUT OFFICE CHRISTMAS PARTIES IS LOOKING FOR A JOB THE NEXT DAY. — PHYLLIS DILLER

PEACH BUTTER

THIS RECIPE MAY ALSO BE MADE WITH
NECTARINES (ALSO UNPEELED). YOU CAN LEAVE OUT
THE RUM, BUT IT DOES ADD NICELY TO THE FLAVOR.

3½ LBS	UNPEELED FIRM RIPE PEACHES	1.75 KG
¾ CUP	WATER	175 ML
½ CUP	AMBER RUM	125 ML
3 CUPS	GRANULATED SUGAR	750 ML
½ CUP	PACKED BROWN SUGAR	125 ML

CUT PEACHES IN HALF; TWIST TO SEPARATE HALVES. CUT
HALVES CONTAINING PIT IN HALF AGAIN; HOLD AND TWIST
PIT TO REMOVE IT. CUT PEACHES INTO LARGE WEDGES.
IN A DUTCH OVEN OR A LARGE, DEEP, HEAVY-BOTTOMED
POT, COMBINE PEACHES AND WATER. COVER AND BRING
TO A BOIL OVER HIGH HEAT. REDUCE HEAT AND SIMMER,
STIRRING OFTEN, FOR ABOUT 22 MINUTES OR UNTIL
PEACHES ARE VERY SOFT.

LADLE FRUIT AND LIQUID INTO A LARGE MESH SIEVE
AND PRESS PULP THROUGH; DISCARD SKINS (OR EXTRACT
PULP USING A FOOD MILL). RETURN PULP TO CLEAN DUTCH
OVEN. STIR IN RUM. ADD GRANULATED SUGAR IN A STEADY
STREAM, STIRRING CONSTANTLY. STIR IN BROWN SUGAR;
COOK OVER LOW HEAT, STIRRING CONSTANTLY TO
DISSOLVE SUGAR. INCREASE HEAT TO HIGH AND BRING TO
A BOIL, STIRRING CONSTANTLY. REDUCE HEAT AND BOIL
GENTLY, STIRRING OFTEN AND REDUCING HEAT FURTHER
AS MIXTURE THICKENS, FOR 50 TO 60 MINUTES OR UNTIL
THICKENED. TEST FOR DONENESS (SEE PAGE 154).

LADLE INTO STERILIZED JARS TO WITHIN $\frac{1}{2}$ INCH (1 CM) OF RIM; WIPE RIMS. APPLY PREPARED LIDS AND RINGS; TIGHTEN JUST UNTIL FINGERTIP-TIGHT. PROCESS JARS IN A BOILING WATER CANNER FOR 10 MINUTES (SEE PAGE 27). TRANSFER JARS TO A TOWEL-LINED SURFACE AND LET REST AT ROOM TEMPERATURE UNTIL COOL. CHECK SEALS; REFRIGERATE ANY UNSEALED JARS FOR UP TO 3 WEEKS. MAKES ABOUT FOUR 8-OUNCE (250 ML) JARS.

TIP: YOU'LL NEED ABOUT 10 LARGE PEACHES FOR THIS RECIPE.

VARIATIONS

PEACH AMARETTO BUTTER: REPLACE THE RUM WITH AMARETTO (ALMOND-FLAVORED LIQUEUR), OMIT THE BROWN SUGAR AND INCREASE THE GRANULATED SUGAR TO 4 CUPS (1 L).

PEACH MARSALA BUTTER: REPLACE THE RUM WITH $\frac{1}{4}$ CUP (60 ML) SWEET MARSALA WINE, OMIT THE BROWN SUGAR AND INCREASE THE GRANULATED SUGAR TO 4 CUPS (1 L).

SPICED PEACH BUTTER: OMIT THE RUM. STIR IN 1 TSP (5 ML) GROUND CINNAMON, $\frac{1}{2}$ TSP (2 ML) GROUND NUTMEG AND A PINCH OF GROUND CLOVES WITH THE SUGAR.

PEACH ORANGE BUTTER: USE ORANGE JUICE IN PLACE OF THE WATER AND REPLACE THE RUM WITH $\frac{1}{4}$ CUP (60 ML) GRAND MARNIER.

TIRED? THERE'S A NAP FOR THAT.

PEAR BUTTER

THIS CARAMEL-COLORED BUTTER HAS A LOVELY PEAR FLAVOR AND A HINT OF SPICE.

10 LBS	RIPE PEARS	5 KG
2½ CUPS	UNSWEETENED APPLE CIDER	625 ML
4½ CUPS	GRANULATED SUGAR	1.125 L
1 TSP	GROUND CINNAMON	5 ML
1 TSP	GROUND GINGER	5 ML

CUT PEARS LENGTHWISE INTO QUARTERS AND REMOVE STEMS, BLOSSOM ENDS AND CORES (DO NOT PEEL); COARSELY CHOP. IN A DUTCH OVEN OR A LARGE, DEEP, HEAVY-BOTTOMED POT, COMBINE PEARS AND CIDER. BRING TO A BOIL OVER HIGH HEAT. REDUCE HEAT AND BOIL GENTLY, COVERED, FOR ABOUT 40 MINUTES OR UNTIL PEARS ARE VERY SOFT, USING A POTATO MASHER AFTER ABOUT 30 MINUTES TO BREAK DOWN PIECES FURTHER.

LADLE FRUIT AND LIQUID INTO A LARGE MESH SIEVE AND PRESS PULP THROUGH; DISCARD PEEL (OR EXTRACT PULP USING A FOOD MILL). RETURN PULP TO CLEAN DUTCH OVEN. ADD SUGAR IN A STEADY STREAM, STIRRING CONSTANTLY. STIR IN CINNAMON AND GINGER; COOK OVER LOW HEAT, STIRRING CONSTANTLY TO DISSOLVE SUGAR. INCREASE HEAT TO HIGH AND BRING TO A BOIL, STIRRING CONSTANTLY. REDUCE HEAT AND BOIL GENTLY, UNCOVERED, STIRRING OFTEN AND REDUCING HEAT FURTHER AS MIXTURE THICKENS, FOR 35 TO 40 MINUTES OR UNTIL THICKENED. TEST FOR DONENESS (SEE PAGE 154).

LADLE INTO STERILIZED JARS TO WITHIN $\frac{1}{2}$ INCH (1 CM) OF RIM; WIPE RIMS. APPLY PREPARED LIDS AND RINGS; TIGHTEN JUST UNTIL FINGERTIP-TIGHT. PROCESS JARS IN A BOILING WATER CANNER FOR 10 MINUTES (SEE PAGE 27). TRANSFER JARS TO A TOWEL-LINED SURFACE AND LET REST AT ROOM TEMPERATURE UNTIL COOL. CHECK SEALS; REFRIGERATE ANY UNSEALED JARS FOR UP TO 3 WEEKS. MAKES ABOUT SIX 8-OUNCE (250 ML) JARS.

TIP: BARTLETT OR PACKHAM PEARS ARE GOOD CHOICES FOR FRUIT BUTTERS, AS THEY HAVE SOFT FLESH THAT BREAKS DOWN DURING COOKING.

TIP: PEARS RIPEN WELL AFTER BEING PICKED, SO THEY ARE PICKED GREEN FOR BETTER QUALITY IN TRANSPORTING. TO SPEED RIPENING, PLACE THEM IN A PAPER BAG. WHEN RIPE, A PEAR YIELDS TO LIGHT PRESSURE NEAR THE BOTTOM OF THE NECK.

VARIATION
PEAR ORANGE BUTTER: SUBSTITUTE ORANGE JUICE FOR THE APPLE CIDER AND REPLACE THE CINNAMON AND GINGER WITH $\frac{1}{2}$ TSP (2 ML) GROUND NUTMEG.

HOW OLD WOULD YOU BE IF YOU
DIDN'T KNOW HOW OLD YOU WERE?
— SATCHEL PAIGE

PLUM GOOD APPLE BUTTER

A GREAT FRUIT DUO THAT MAKES TASTY FRUIT BUTTER. STIR INTO PLAIN YOGURT OR SPREAD ON MUFFINS.

2 LBS	APPLES THAT SOFTEN (SEE BOX, PAGE 157)	1 KG
2 LBS	RED PLUMS, PITTED AND SLICED	1 KG
1½ CUPS	UNSWEETENED APPLE CIDER OR ALL-NATURAL APPLE JUICE	375 ML
3 CUPS	GRANULATED SUGAR	750 ML
1 TSP	GROUND CINNAMON	5 ML

CUT APPLES INTO QUARTERS; REMOVE STEMS AND BLOSSOM ENDS. SLICE EACH QUARTER INTO 4 OR 5 SLICES. IN A DUTCH OVEN OR A LARGE, DEEP, HEAVY-BOTTOMED POT, COMBINE APPLES, PLUMS AND CIDER. BRING TO A BOIL OVER HIGH HEAT. REDUCE HEAT AND SIMMER, COVERED, FOR ABOUT 20 MINUTES OR UNTIL FRUIT IS VERY SOFT.

LADLE FRUIT AND LIQUID INTO A MESH SIEVE AND PRESS PULP THROUGH; DISCARD PEEL AND SEEDS (OR EXTRACT PULP USING A FOOD MILL). RETURN PULP TO CLEAN DUTCH OVEN. ADD SUGAR IN A STEADY STREAM, STIRRING CONSTANTLY. STIR IN CINNAMON; COOK OVER LOW HEAT, STIRRING CONSTANTLY TO DISSOLVE SUGAR. INCREASE HEAT TO HIGH AND BRING TO A BOIL, STIRRING CONSTANTLY. REDUCE HEAT AND BOIL GENTLY, UNCOVERED, STIRRING OFTEN AND REDUCING HEAT FURTHER AS MIXTURE THICKENS, FOR 45 TO 50 MINUTES OR UNTIL THICKENED. TEST FOR DONENESS (SEE PAGE 154).

LADLE INTO STERILIZED JARS TO WITHIN $\frac{1}{2}$ INCH (1 CM) OF RIM; WIPE RIMS. APPLY PREPARED LIDS AND RINGS; TIGHTEN JUST UNTIL FINGERTIP-TIGHT. PROCESS JARS IN A BOILING WATER CANNER FOR 10 MINUTES (SEE PAGE 27). TRANSFER JARS TO A TOWEL-LINED SURFACE AND LET REST AT ROOM TEMPERATURE UNTIL COOL. CHECK SEALS; REFRIGERATE ANY UNSEALED JARS FOR UP TO 3 WEEKS. MAKES ABOUT FIVE 8-OUNCE (250 ML) JARS.

TIP: YOU'LL NEED ABOUT 6 MEDIUM APPLES AND 16 TO 18 MEDIUM PLUMS FOR THIS RECIPE.

TIP: SUPERMARKETS NOW CARRY ALL-NATURAL APPLE JUICE, WHICH CONTAINS SOLIDS. SHAKE BEFORE USING.

USING PLUMS IN PRESERVES

CHOOSE FIRM PLUMS, EITHER RIPE OR SLIGHTLY UNDERRIPE. DO NOT PEEL, BUT DO REMOVE THE PIT BEFORE COOKING, UNLESS YOU'RE USING DAMSON PLUMS. THE PITS OF DAMSON PLUMS SEPARATE NATURALLY FROM THE FLESH WHILE THE FRUIT IS BOILING AND CAN THEN BE EASILY REMOVED FROM THE POT WITH A SLOTTED SPOON.

Chutneys

Chutneys are flavorful condiments — mild or spicy — that originated in East India. They are made with fruit (like jams), but also include vinegar, spices and vegetables (like relishes, though generally sweeter). They sometimes contain dried fruit and may include nuts. The flavor improves with age, so let chutneys rest for at least a month before using. Enjoy them with cheeses and meats or vegetarian dishes.

An extra step is needed when processing chutneys and other savory relishes, pickles, salsas and sauces. After turning off the heat and removing the pot lid, jars are left in the canner for 5 minutes. This allows the pressure in the jars to stabilize and reduces the possibility of liquid leaking from the jars.

CRABAPPLE CHUTNEY

IN THIS LARGE-BATCH CHUTNEY, YOU GET TO MIX (CRAB)APPLES AND ORANGES.

12 CUPS	QUARTERED CRABAPPLES	3 L
8 CUPS	GRANULATED SUGAR	2 L
3	LARGE ORANGES, PEELED AND CHOPPED	3
I LB	RAISINS	500 G
I TBSP	GROUND CINNAMON	15 ML
I TBSP	GROUND CLOVES	15 ML
2 CUPS	CIDER VINEGAR	500 ML

IN A DUTCH OVEN OR A LARGE, HEAVY-BOTTOMED POT, COMBINE ALL INGREDIENTS AND LET STAND AT ROOM TEMPERATURE OVERNIGHT. NEXT DAY, BRING TO A BOIL, REDUCE HEAT AND BOIL GENTLY, STIRRING OFTEN, UNTIL CRABAPPLES ARE SOFT AND MIXTURE IS DARK IN COLOR, ABOUT 45 TO 60 MINUTES, UNTIL MIXTURE IS JUST THICK ENOUGH TO MOUND ON A SPOON.

LADLE INTO STERILIZED JARS TO WITHIN $\frac{1}{2}$ INCH (1 CM) OF RIM. REMOVE ANY AIR POCKETS AND ADJUST HEADSPACE, IF NECESSARY, BY ADDING HOT CHUTNEY; WIPE RIMS. APPLY PREPARED LIDS AND RINGS; TIGHTEN RINGS JUST UNTIL FINGERTIP-TIGHT. PROCESS JARS IN A BOILING WATER CANNER FOR 10 MINUTES (SEE PAGE 27). TURN OFF CANNER AND REMOVE LID. LET JARS STAND IN WATER FOR 5 MINUTES. TRANSFER JARS TO A TOWEL-LINED SURFACE AND LET REST AT ROOM TEMPERATURE UNTIL COOLED. CHECK SEALS; REFRIGERATE ANY UNSEALED JARS FOR UP TO 3 WEEKS. MAKES ABOUT TWELVE 8-OUNCE (250 ML) JARS.

TIP: TO PREVENT BOIL-OVERS AND SPATTERING, ENSURE YOU HAVE A LARGE ENOUGH POT TO COOK THE MIXTURE IN AND STIR MORE OFTEN AS MIXTURE THICKENS TO PREVENT SCORCHING.

TIP: USE A RUBBER SPATULA OR A PLASTIC BUBBLE REMOVER TO REMOVE AIR POCKETS ONCE YOU FILL JARS.

CRANBERRY PEAR CHUTNEY

THIS CHUTNEY IS PACKED WITH WONDERFUL FLAVORS
AND ACCENTS OF ORANGE AND GINGER.

2 CUPS	WATER	500 ML
I CUP	RAISINS	250 ML
2 CUPS	GRANULATED SUGAR	500 ML
2 TBSP	WHITE WINE VINEGAR	30 ML
2 TBSP	GRATED ORANGE ZEST	30 ML
I CUP	ORANGE JUICE	250 ML
2 TBSP	SLIVERED GINGERROOT	30 ML
6 CUPS	FRESH OR FROZEN CRANBERRIES	1.5 L
2	PEARS, PEELED, CORED, CHOPPED	2
I CUP	TOASTED SLIVERED ALMONDS (OPTIONAL)	250 ML

IN A DUTCH OVEN OR A LARGE, HEAVY-BOTTOMED POT,
BRING WATER TO A BOIL; ADD RAISINS. REMOVE FROM
HEAT AND LET STAND FOR 20 MINUTES. DRAIN RAISINS,
RESERVING $1/2$ CUP (125 ML) OF THE LIQUID; SET RAISINS
ASIDE IN A SMALL BOWL. RETURN RESERVED RAISIN LIQUID
TO POT. STIR IN SUGAR AND VINEGAR; COOK OVER MEDIUM
HEAT, STIRRING SLOWLY, TO DISSOLVE SUGAR. INCREASE
HEAT AND BOIL, WITHOUT STIRRING, UNTIL SYRUP TURNS
GOLDEN BROWN, FOR ABOUT 15 MINUTES. STIR IN ORANGE
ZEST AND JUICE, GINGER AND CRANBERRIES AND BOIL
GENTLY, STIRRING OFTEN, FOR ABOUT 10 MINUTES,
UNTIL MIXTURE IS JUST THICK ENOUGH TO MOUND ON A
SPOON. STIR IN RAISINS, PEARS AND ALMONDS, IF USING.
BOIL FOR I MINUTE.

LADLE INTO STERILIZED JARS TO WITHIN $1/2$ INCH
(I CM) OF RIM. REMOVE ANY AIR POCKETS AND ADJUST

HEADSPACE, IF NECESSARY, BY ADDING HOT CHUTNEY; WIPE RIMS. APPLY PREPARED LIDS AND RINGS; TIGHTEN RINGS JUST UNTIL FINGERTIP-TIGHT. PROCESS JARS IN A BOILING WATER CANNER FOR 10 MINUTES (SEE PAGE 27). TURN OFF CANNER AND REMOVE LID. LET JARS STAND IN WATER FOR 5 MINUTES. TRANSFER JARS TO A TOWEL-LINED SURFACE AND LET REST AT ROOM TEMPERATURE UNTIL COOLED. CHECK SEALS; REFRIGERATE ANY UNSEALED JARS FOR UP TO 3 WEEKS. MAKES ABOUT SIX 8-OUNCE (250 ML JARS).

TIP: IF DESIRED, GRATE THE PEELED GINGER INSTEAD OF CUTTING INTO SLIVERS.

TIP: FOR INFORMATION ON TOASTING NUTS, SEE BOX, PAGE 145.

VARIATION: CHANGE THE TYPE OF VINEGAR USED (MAKING SURE THE VINEGAR HAS AN ACIDITY EQUAL TO THE ONE CALLED FOR; SEE BOX, PAGE 199).

SERVING SUGGESTIONS: SERVE WITH POULTRY, FOWL OR PORK, OR SPREAD ON BREAD FOR A MEAT OR CHEESE SANDWICH.

RECIPE SUGGESTION: USE TO MAKE TURKEY, BRIE AND CRANBERRY PANINI (PAGE 277).

I DREAM OF A BETTER WORLD WHERE CHICKENS CAN CROSS THE ROAD WITHOUT HAVING THEIR MOTIVES QUESTIONED.

AUTUMN HARVEST CHUTNEY

*TAKE ADVANTAGE OF THE BOUNTY
OF TREE FRUITS IN EARLY AUTUMN TO
MAKE THIS BEAUTIFUL, TASTY CHUTNEY.*

4 CUPS	CHOPPED PEELED TART COOKING APPLES	1 L
3 CUPS	CHOPPED PEELED PEARS	750 ML
2 CUPS	CHOPPED PLUMS	500 ML
1 CUP	FINELY CHOPPED ONION	250 ML
1¾ CUPS	PACKED BROWN SUGAR	425 ML
1 TSP	PICKLING OR CANNING SALT	5 ML
1 TSP	GROUND CINNAMON	5 ML
1 TSP	GROUND GINGER	5 ML
½ TSP	GROUND NUTMEG	2 ML
¼ TSP	HOT PEPPER FLAKES	1 ML
1½ CUPS	CIDER VINEGAR	375 ML
2 CUPS	FRESH OR FROZEN CRANBERRIES (THAWED IF FROZEN)	500 ML

IN A DUTCH OVEN OR A LARGE, HEAVY-BOTTOMED POT,
COMBINE APPLES, PEARS, PLUMS, ONION, SUGAR, SALT,
CINNAMON, GINGER, NUTMEG, HOT PEPPER FLAKES AND
VINEGAR. BRING TO A BOIL OVER MEDIUM HEAT, STIRRING
OFTEN. REDUCE HEAT AND BOIL GENTLY, STIRRING
OCCASIONALLY, FOR ABOUT 30 MINUTES OR UNTIL ONIONS
ARE TRANSLUCENT AND MIXTURE IS SLIGHTLY THICKENED.
STIR IN CRANBERRIES, INCREASE HEAT TO MEDIUM AND
BOIL GENTLY, STIRRING OFTEN, FOR ABOUT 10 MINUTES
OR UNTIL CRANBERRIES ARE TENDER AND START TO POP.

LADLE INTO STERILIZED JARS TO WITHIN ½ INCH
(1 CM) OF RIM. REMOVE ANY AIR POCKETS AND ADJUST

HEADSPACE, IF NECESSARY, BY ADDING HOT CHUTNEY; WIPE RIMS. APPLY PREPARED LIDS AND RINGS; TIGHTEN RINGS JUST UNTIL FINGERTIP-TIGHT. PROCESS JARS IN A BOILING WATER CANNER FOR 10 MINUTES (SEE PAGE 27). TURN OFF CANNER AND REMOVE LID. LET JARS STAND IN WATER FOR 5 MINUTES. TRANSFER JARS TO A TOWEL-LINED SURFACE AND LET REST AT ROOM TEMPERATURE UNTIL COOLED. CHECK SEALS; REFRIGERATE ANY UNSEALED JARS FOR UP TO 3 WEEKS. MAKES ABOUT SEVEN 8-OUNCE (250 ML) JARS.

TIP: THIS CHUTNEY THICKENS QUITE A BIT UPON COOLING, SO STOP COOKING WHEN IT'S THINNER THAN YOU WANT THE FINAL TEXTURE TO BE.

VARIATION: REPLACE UP TO HALF OF THE BROWN SUGAR WITH GRANULATED SUGAR TO VARY THE TASTE.

SERVING SUGGESTIONS: SERVE WITH TURKEY, PORK OR CHICKEN, OR WITH SHARP CHEESE.

STORING ONIONS

TO PREVENT MOLD AND SPROUTING, STORE ONIONS IN A DRY, BREATHABLE CONTAINER, SUCH AS A PAPER BAG OR A WICKER BASKET (NOT IN A PLASTIC BAG), AND IN A COOL, DRY PLACE (NOT IN THE REFRIGERATOR). TRIM OFF THE STEM END AND PEEL OFF DRY OR DAMAGED OUTER LAYERS BEFORE CHOPPING.

MAJOR GREY MANGO CHUTNEY

PUNGENT, BITTER, SPICY, SWEET AND TANGY FLAVORS ARE THE SIGNATURE COMBINATION FOR THIS TRADITIONAL CHUTNEY.

5 CUPS	CHOPPED PEELED SWEET MANGOS	1.25 L
1½ CUPS	CHOPPED PEELED SEEDLESS ORANGES	375 ML
1 CUP	FINELY CHOPPED ONION	250 ML
½ CUP	FINELY CHOPPED LEMON (RIND AND FLESH), SEEDS REMOVED	125 ML
⅓ CUP	FINELY CHOPPED LIME (RIND AND FLESH), SEEDS REMOVED	75 ML
¼ CUP	FINELY CHOPPED GINGERROOT	60 ML
2 TBSP	MINCED GARLIC	30 ML
1 CUP	RAISINS	250 ML
¾ CUP	PACKED BROWN SUGAR	175 ML
4 TSP	MUSTARD SEEDS	20 ML
2 TSP	PICKLING OR CANNING SALT	10 ML
1 TSP	GROUND CINNAMON	5 ML
1 TSP	GROUND CORIANDER	5 ML
½ TSP	GROUND CLOVES	2 ML
¼ TSP	GROUND CARDAMOM (OPTIONAL)	1 ML
1 CUP	CIDER VINEGAR	250 ML
⅔ CUP	LIGHT (FANCY) MOLASSES	150 ML
½ CUP	WATER	125 ML

IN A DUTCH OVEN OR A LARGE, HEAVY-BOTTOMED POT, COMBINE ALL INGREDIENTS. BRING TO A BOIL OVER MEDIUM HEAT, STIRRING OFTEN. REDUCE HEAT AND BOIL GENTLY, STIRRING OCCASIONALLY, FOR ABOUT 1 HOUR OR UNTIL ONIONS, LEMON AND LIME RINDS ARE VERY SOFT AND MIXTURE IS JUST THICK ENOUGH TO MOUND ON A SPOON.

LADLE INTO STERILIZED JARS TO WITHIN $\frac{1}{2}$ INCH (1 CM) OF RIM. REMOVE ANY AIR POCKETS AND ADJUST HEADSPACE, IF NECESSARY, BY ADDING HOT CHUTNEY; WIPE RIMS. APPLY PREPARED LIDS AND RINGS; TIGHTEN RINGS JUST UNTIL FINGERTIP-TIGHT. PROCESS JARS IN A BOILING WATER CANNER FOR 10 MINUTES (SEE PAGE 27). TURN OFF CANNER AND REMOVE LID. LET JARS STAND IN WATER FOR 5 MINUTES. TRANSFER JARS TO A TOWEL-LINED SURFACE AND LET REST AT ROOM TEMPERATURE UNTIL COOLED. CHECK SEALS; REFRIGERATE ANY UNSEALED JARS FOR UP TO 3 WEEKS. MAKES ABOUT EIGHT 8-OUNCE (250 ML) JARS.

TIP: FOR INFORMATION ON PREPPING MANGOS, SEE BOX, PAGE 265.

TIP: THIS CHUTNEY THICKENS QUITE A BIT UPON COOLING, SO STOP COOKING WHEN IT'S THINNER THAN YOU WANT THE FINAL TEXTURE TO BE.

SERVING SUGGESTION: SERVE WITH MEDIUM OR SPICY CURRIES, ACCOMPANIED BY A DOLLOP OF PLAIN YOGURT.

RECIPE SUGGESTIONS: MIX EQUAL PARTS CHUTNEY AND PLAIN GREEK YOGURT FOR A QUICK AND EASY DIP FOR CRISP FLATBREAD OR CRACKERS. OR USE THIS CHUTNEY TO MAKE APPETIZER OF THE HOUR (PAGE 267) OR MAJOR GREY'S MEAT LOAF (PAGE 270).

MEN CAN READ SMALLER PRINT THAN WOMEN CAN.
WOMEN CAN HEAR BETTER.

CLASSIC PEACH CHUTNEY

CAPTURE FRAGRANT, JUICY PEACHES AT THE HEIGHT OF THEIR SEASON IN THIS CHUTNEY, WHICH IS FRUITY WITH A TOUCH OF SPICE. PURÉEING SOME OF THE PEACHES GIVES YOU A CHUNKY CHUTNEY WITH A TOUCH OF JAMMINESS.

8 CUPS	CHOPPED PEELED PEACHES, DIVIDED	2 L
1/2	JALAPEÑO PEPPER, MINCED (OPTIONAL)	1/2
2 CUPS	FINELY CHOPPED SWEET ONION	500 ML
1 3/4 CUPS	GRANULATED SUGAR	425 ML
1 TSP	PICKLING OR CANNING SALT	5 ML
1 TSP	GROUND CINNAMON	5 ML
1/8 TSP	GROUND CLOVES	0.5 ML
1 1/4 CUPS	CIDER VINEGAR	300 ML

USING AN IMMERSION BLENDER IN A TALL CUP, OR IN A FOOD PROCESSOR OR BLENDER, PURÉE 2 CUPS (500 ML) OF THE PEACHES UNTIL SMOOTH. IN A DUTCH OVEN OR A LARGE, HEAVY-BOTTOMED POT, COMBINE PURÉED AND CHOPPED PEACHES, JALAPEÑO (IF USING), ONION, SUGAR, SALT, CINNAMON, CLOVES AND VINEGAR. BRING TO A BOIL OVER MEDIUM HEAT, STIRRING OFTEN. REDUCE HEAT AND BOIL GENTLY, STIRRING OCCASIONALLY, FOR ABOUT 40 MINUTES OR UNTIL ONIONS ARE TRANSLUCENT AND MIXTURE IS JUST THICK ENOUGH TO MOUND ON A SPOON.

LADLE INTO STERILIZED JARS TO WITHIN 1/2 INCH (1 CM) OF RIM. REMOVE ANY AIR POCKETS AND ADJUST HEADSPACE, IF NECESSARY, BY ADDING HOT CHUTNEY; WIPE RIMS. APPLY PREPARED LIDS AND RINGS; TIGHTEN RINGS JUST UNTIL FINGERTIP-TIGHT. PROCESS JARS IN

A BOILING WATER CANNER FOR 10 MINUTES (SEE PAGE 27). TURN OFF CANNER AND REMOVE LID. LET JARS STAND IN WATER FOR 5 MINUTES. TRANSFER JARS TO A TOWEL-LINED SURFACE AND LET REST AT ROOM TEMPERATURE UNTIL COOLED. CHECK SEALS; REFRIGERATE ANY UNSEALED JARS FOR UP TO 3 WEEKS. *MAKES ABOUT EIGHT 8-OUNCE (250 ML) JARS.*

TIP: USE RIPE AND FRAGRANT BUT FIRM PEACHES FOR THIS CHUTNEY. YOU'LL NEED ABOUT 20 MEDIUM, OR ABOUT $4\frac{1}{2}$ LBS (2.25 KG), TO GET 8 CUPS (2 L) CHOPPED.

TIP: FOR INSTRUCTIONS ON PEELING PEACHES, SEE PAGE 87.

TIP: ADD THE JALAPEÑO IF YOU LIKE A TOUCH OF HEAT IN YOUR CHUTNEY; LEAVE IT OUT FOR A MILD, FRUITY VERSION. IF YOU LIKE MORE HEAT, ADD A WHOLE JALAPEÑO.

SERVING SUGGESTIONS: SERVE THIS CHUTNEY WITH SPICY INDIAN CURRIES TO HELP COOL THEM OFF. OR SPREAD ON ROAST CHICKEN OR HAM SANDWICHES.

RECIPE SUGGESTION: USE THIS CHUTNEY TO MAKE PEACHY CHEESE DIP (PAGE 266).

I DON'T HAVE A PROBLEM WITH CAFFEINE — I HAVE A PROBLEM WITHOUT CAFFEINE.

PEAR GINGER CHUTNEY

TANGY, WITH A WARM HINT OF SPICE, THIS CHUNKY
CHUTNEY GOES PARTICULARLY WELL WITH GRILLED
PORK CHOPS, PORK TENDERLOIN OR BAKED HAM.

6 CUPS	FINELY CHOPPED PEELED PEARS	1.5 L
1 CUP	FINELY CHOPPED PEELED APPLE	250 ML
3/4 CUP	DARK RAISINS	175 ML
1/2 CUP	FINELY CHOPPED ONION	125 ML
1/2 CUP	FINELY CHOPPED RED BELL PEPPER	125 ML
1/2 CUP	FINELY CHOPPED CANDIED GINGER	125 ML
2 CUPS	PACKED BROWN SUGAR	500 ML
1 TBSP	MUSTARD SEEDS	15 ML
1 TSP	HOT PEPPER FLAKES	5 ML
1 TSP	PICKLING OR CANNING SALT	5 ML
1/2 TSP	GROUND NUTMEG	2 ML
1/2 TSP	GROUND CLOVES	2 ML
3/4 CUP	CIDER VINEGAR	175 ML
	FINELY GRATED ZEST OF 1 LEMON	
1/4 CUP	FRESHLY SQUEEZED LEMON JUICE	60 ML

IN A DUTCH OVEN OR A LARGE, HEAVY-BOTTOMED POT,
COMBINE ALL INGREDIENTS. BRING TO A BOIL OVER
MEDIUM-HIGH HEAT, STIRRING CONSTANTLY. REDUCE HEAT
AND SIMMER, STIRRING OCCASIONALLY, FOR ABOUT 1 HOUR
OR UNTIL PEARS, APPLE AND ONION ARE VERY SOFT AND
MIXTURE IS JUST THICK ENOUGH TO MOUND ON A SPOON.

LADLE INTO STERILIZED JARS TO WITHIN 1/2 INCH
(1 CM) OF RIM. REMOVE ANY AIR POCKETS AND ADJUST
HEADSPACE, IF NECESSARY, BY ADDING HOT CHUTNEY;
WIPE RIMS. APPLY PREPARED LIDS AND RINGS; TIGHTEN

RINGS JUST UNTIL FINGERTIP-TIGHT. PROCESS JARS IN A BOILING WATER CANNER FOR 10 MINUTES (SEE PAGE 27). TURN OFF CANNER AND REMOVE LID. LET JARS STAND IN WATER FOR 5 MINUTES. TRANSFER JARS TO A TOWEL-LINED SURFACE AND LET REST AT ROOM TEMPERATURE UNTIL COOLED. CHECK SEALS; REFRIGERATE ANY UNSEALED JARS FOR UP TO 3 WEEKS. MAKES ABOUT SIX 8-OUNCE (250 ML) JARS.

TIP: YOU CAN REPLACE THE CANDIED GINGER WITH 2 TBSP (30 ML) GRATED GINGERROOT.

USING APPLES IN PRESERVES

APPLES ARE USED IN A LOT OF PRESERVES AND ARE AVAILABLE YEAR-ROUND. FOR JAMS AND FRUIT BUTTERS, CHOOSE APPLES THAT SOFTEN AND LOSE THEIR SHAPE WHEN COOKED; FOR CONSERVES AND CHUTNEYS, CHOOSE APPLES THAT KEEP THEIR SHAPE WHEN COOKED (SEE BOX, PAGE 157). SOMETIMES, A COMBINATION OF BOTH CAN BE USED. OLDER, LESS CRISP APPLES MAY BE USED TO MAKE BUTTERS. NOTE THAT RED DELICIOUS APPLES ARE GOOD FOR EATING, BUT ARE NOT RECOMMENDED FOR COOKING.

FOR FRUIT BUTTERS, THE PEELS ARE LEFT ON APPLES, AND THE STEMS, BLOSSOM ENDS AND CORES ARE REMOVED. OTHERWISE, APPLES ARE PEELED FOR PRESERVING RECIPES. DO NOT FREEZE APPLES FOR PRESERVING, AS THEY HAVE TO BE FROZEN WITH SUGAR, WHICH IS SUITABLE FOR PIES BUT NOT FOR PRESERVES. THEY ALSO BROWN EASILY WHEN FROZEN.

PINEAPPLE MINT CHUTNEY

PINEAPPLE AND MINT ARE TWO FLAVORS
THAT JUST SEEM NATURAL TOGETHER.

6 CUPS	CHOPPED FRESH PINEAPPLE	1.5 L
1½ CUPS	FINELY CHOPPED SWEET ONION	375 ML
1 CUP	FINELY CHOPPED RED BELL PEPPER	250 ML
2	CLOVES GARLIC, MINCED	2
1¾ CUPS	GRANULATED SUGAR	425 ML
1½ TSP	PICKLING OR CANNING SALT	7 ML
¼ TSP	HOT PEPPER FLAKES	1 ML
1 CUP	WHITE VINEGAR	250 ML
½ CUP	RICE VINEGAR	125 ML
2 TBSP	CHOPPED FRESH MINT	30 ML

IN A DUTCH OVEN OR A LARGE, HEAVY-BOTTOMED POT, COMBINE PINEAPPLE, ONION, RED PEPPER, GARLIC, SUGAR, SALT, HOT PEPPER FLAKES, WHITE VINEGAR AND RICE VINEGAR. BRING TO A BOIL OVER MEDIUM HEAT, STIRRING OFTEN. REDUCE HEAT AND BOIL GENTLY, STIRRING OCCASIONALLY, FOR ABOUT 25 MINUTES OR UNTIL PINEAPPLE IS TRANSLUCENT AND MIXTURE IS JUST THICK ENOUGH TO MOUND ON A SPOON. STIR IN MINT.

LADLE INTO STERILIZED JARS TO WITHIN ½ INCH (1 CM) OF RIM. REMOVE ANY AIR POCKETS AND ADJUST HEADSPACE, IF NECESSARY, BY ADDING HOT CHUTNEY; WIPE RIMS. APPLY PREPARED LIDS AND RINGS; TIGHTEN RINGS JUST UNTIL FINGERTIP-TIGHT. PROCESS JARS IN A BOILING WATER CANNER FOR 10 MINUTES (SEE PAGE 27). TURN OFF CANNER AND REMOVE LID. LET JARS STAND IN

WATER FOR 5 MINUTES. TRANSFER JARS TO A TOWEL-LINED SURFACE AND LET REST AT ROOM TEMPERATURE UNTIL COOLED. CHECK SEALS; REFRIGERATE ANY UNSEALED JARS FOR UP TO 3 WEEKS. MAKES ABOUT SIX 8-OUNCE (250 ML) JARS.

TIP: THERE ARE MANY VARIETIES OF SWEET ONIONS AVAILABLE, SUCH AS VIDALIA, OSO SWEET, MAUI, WALLA WALLA OR SPANISH.

TIP: THE RICE VINEGAR ADDS A PLEASANT SWEET TANG, BUT YOU CAN USE ALL WHITE VINEGAR IF YOU PREFER.

VARIATION: REPLACE UP TO HALF OF THE GRANULATED SUGAR WITH BROWN SUGAR TO VARY THE TASTE.

SERVING SUGGESTIONS: THIS CHUTNEY IS EQUALLY AT HOME WITH INDIAN CURRIES, THAI FOODS AND CARIBBEAN FOODS, OR WITH PLAIN GRILLED MEATS, POULTRY AND FISH.

CHOOSING AND PREPARING PINEAPPLE

CHOOSE A PINEAPPLE THAT IS SWEET AND FRAGRANT, WITH NICE GREEN LEAVES. EXTRA-SWEET VARIETIES ARE NOW AVAILABLE. TO USE, SLICE OFF THE TOP AND BOTTOM, STAND THE FRUIT ON END, PARE OFF THE SKIN IN LENGTHWISE PIECES, REMOVE THE EYES, QUARTER LENGTHWISE AND REMOVE THE CORE.

RED ONION AND RAISIN CHUTNEY

CHOPPING ALL OF THE ONIONS MIGHT SEEM DAUNTING, BUT DON'T BE TEMPTED TO USE A POWER TOOL FOR THE JOB. HAND-CHOPPING WILL GIVE A FAR SUPERIOR TEXTURE TO THIS VERSATILE CHUTNEY.

8 CUPS	CHOPPED RED ONIONS	2 L
3	CLOVES GARLIC, MINCED	3
2 CUPS	GRANULATED SUGAR	500 ML
1 1/2 TSP	PICKLING OR CANNING SALT	7 ML
1/8 TSP	HOT PEPPER FLAKES	0.5 ML
1 CUP	WATER	250 ML
2 CUPS	RAISINS	500 ML
1 CUP	RED WINE VINEGAR	250 ML
1 TBSP	CHOPPED FRESH THYME	15 ML

IN A DUTCH OVEN OR A LARGE, HEAVY-BOTTOMED POT, COMBINE ONIONS, GARLIC, SUGAR, SALT, HOT PEPPER FLAKES AND WATER. BRING TO A SIMMER OVER MEDIUM HEAT, STIRRING OFTEN. REDUCE HEAT AND BOIL GENTLY, STIRRING OCCASIONALLY, FOR ABOUT 20 MINUTES OR UNTIL ONIONS ARE VERY SOFT. STIR IN RAISINS, VINEGAR AND THYME; SIMMER FOR ABOUT 20 MINUTES OR UNTIL ONIONS ARE TRANSLUCENT, RAISINS ARE PLUMP AND MIXTURE IS JUST THICK ENOUGH TO MOUND ON A SPOON.

LADLE INTO STERILIZED JARS TO WITHIN 1/2 INCH (1 CM) OF RIM. REMOVE ANY AIR POCKETS AND ADJUST HEADSPACE, IF NECESSARY, BY ADDING HOT CHUTNEY; WIPE RIMS. APPLY PREPARED LIDS AND RINGS; TIGHTEN

CONTINUED ON PAGE 181...

Pear Butter (page 162)

Classic Peach Chutney (page 174)

Pineapple Mint Chutney (page 178)

Harvest Relish (page 208)

RINGS JUST UNTIL FINGERTIP-TIGHT. PROCESS JARS IN A BOILING WATER CANNER FOR 10 MINUTES (SEE PAGE 27). TURN OFF CANNER AND REMOVE LID. LET JARS STAND IN WATER FOR 5 MINUTES. TRANSFER JARS TO A TOWEL-LINED SURFACE AND LET REST AT ROOM TEMPERATURE UNTIL COOLED. CHECK SEALS; REFRIGERATE ANY UNSEALED JARS FOR UP TO 3 WEEKS. MAKES ABOUT SEVEN 8-OUNCE (250 ML) JARS.

TIP: YOU'LL NEED ABOUT 5 LARGE RED ONIONS, OR ABOUT 3 LBS (1.5 KG), TO GET 8 CUPS (2 L) CHOPPED.

SERVING SUGGESTIONS: SERVE WITH GRILLED OR SMOKED SALMON, OR USE AS A CONDIMENT WITH ROAST BEEF OR A GRILLED STEAK.

USING DRIED FRUIT IN PRESERVES

DRIED FRUIT, SUCH AS APRICOTS, CRANBERRIES, CURRANTS, DATES, FIGS, PRUNES AND RAISINS, SHOULD BE PLUMP AND SOFT. STORE AT ROOM TEMPERATURE (68°F/20°C OR LESS), IN AN AREA WITHOUT EXCESS HUMIDITY, IN AN AIRTIGHT PLASTIC BAG, PLASTIC CONTAINER OR GLASS CONTAINER WITH AS LITTLE AIR IN IT AS POSSIBLE TO ENSURE THAT THE FRUIT STAYS MOIST. TO PLUMP DRIED FRUIT THAT HAS GOTTEN TOO DRIED OUT, PLACE IT IN A BOWL, COVER WITH HOT WATER AND LET SOAK FOR ABOUT 10 MINUTES. DRAIN AND DRY ON PAPER TOWELS.

HOT PEPPER ORANGE CHUTNEY

ALL YOU NEED IS SOME CRACKERS AND CREAM CHEESE
AND YOU HAVE A NICE TANGY APPETIZER. GIFTABLE!

4	LARGE SEEDLESS ORANGES	4
1 1/2 CUPS	CHOPPED RED BELL PEPPER	375 ML
1/4 CUP	FINELY CHOPPED JALAPEÑO PEPPERS	60 ML
1/2 CUP	CHOPPED ONION	125 ML
1/2 CUP	RAISINS	125 ML
1/2 CUP	MIXED CANDIED PEEL	125 ML
1 CUP	PACKED BROWN SUGAR	250 ML
3/4 CUP	WHITE WINE VINEGAR	175 ML
1/2 TSP	GROUND CINNAMON	2 ML
1/4 TSP	GROUND NUTMEG	1 ML
1/8 TSP	CAYENNE PEPPER	0.5 ML

PEEL 3 ORANGES. CUT UNPEELED ORANGE IN HALF
THROUGH STEM; SLICE THINLY CROSSWISE. CUT
3 PEELED ORANGES IN 1/2-INCH (1 CM) CHUNKS. PLACE
ALL INGREDIENTS IN A DUTCH OVEN OR A LARGE, HEAVY-
BOTTOMED POT OVER MEDIUM-HIGH HEAT AND BRING TO
A BOIL. REDUCE HEAT AND SIMMER, STIRRING OFTEN, FOR
ABOUT 45 MINUTES OR UNTIL MIXTURE IS JUST THICK
ENOUGH TO MOUND ON A SPOON.

LADLE INTO STERILIZED JARS TO WITHIN 1/2 INCH
(1 CM) OF RIM. REMOVE ANY AIR POCKETS AND ADJUST
HEADSPACE, IF NECESSARY, BY ADDING HOT CHUTNEY;
WIPE RIMS. APPLY PREPARED LIDS AND RINGS; TIGHTEN
RINGS JUST UNTIL FINGERTIP-TIGHT. PROCESS JARS IN A
BOILING WATER CANNER FOR 10 MINUTES (SEE PAGE 27).
TURN OFF CANNER AND REMOVE LID. LET JARS STAND IN

WATER FOR 5 MINUTES. TRANSFER JARS TO A TOWEL-LINED SURFACE AND LET REST AT ROOM TEMPERATURE UNTIL COOLED. CHECK SEALS; REFRIGERATE ANY UNSEALED JARS FOR UP TO 3 WEEKS. MAKES ABOUT SIX 8-OUNCE (250 ML) JARS.

TIP: IF YOU HAVE A LARGE ENOUGH POT, YOU MAY DOUBLE THIS RECIPE.

TIP: USE A RUBBER SPATULA OR A PLASTIC BUBBLE REMOVER TO REMOVE AIR POCKETS ONCE YOU FILL JARS.

NOTE: YOU CAN PURCHASE CANDIED (OR GLACÉ) PEEL AT BULK FOOD STORES.

VARIATION: FOR A DIFFERENT FLAVOR, CHANGE THE TYPE OF VINEGAR USED (MAKING SURE THE VINEGAR HAS 5% ACIDITY).

I WANT MY CHILDREN TO HAVE
ALL THE THINGS I COULD NEVER AFFORD.
THEN I WANT TO MOVE IN WITH THEM.
— PHYLLIS DILLER

SWEET AND SPICY TOMATO CHUTNEY

THIS CHUTNEY IS SIMILAR IN FLAVOR TO CHILI SAUCE, BUT NOT AS SWEET, AND IT DELIVERS THE TANG AND CHUNKY TEXTURE CHARACTERISTIC OF CHUTNEY.

8 CUPS	CHOPPED SEEDED PEELED PLUM (ROMA) TOMATOES	2 L
2 CUPS	CHOPPED ONIONS	500 ML
I CUP	CHOPPED RED BELL PEPPER	250 ML
2	CLOVES GARLIC, MINCED	2
I	HOT RED OR GREEN CHILE PEPPER, SEEDED AND MINCED	I
1½ CUPS	GRANULATED SUGAR	375 ML
1½ TSP	PICKLING OR CANNING SALT	7 ML
I TSP	GROUND CINNAMON	5 ML
I TSP	GROUND GINGER	5 ML
½ TSP	GROUND ALLSPICE	2 ML
1½ CUPS	CIDER VINEGAR	375 ML

IN A DUTCH OVEN OR A LARGE, HEAVY-BOTTOMED POT, COMBINE ALL INGREDIENTS. BRING TO A BOIL OVER MEDIUM HEAT, STIRRING OFTEN. REDUCE HEAT AND BOIL GENTLY, STIRRING OCCASIONALLY, FOR ABOUT 45 MINUTES OR UNTIL ONIONS ARE TRANSLUCENT AND MIXTURE IS JUST THICK ENOUGH TO MOUND ON A SPOON.

LADLE INTO STERILIZED JARS TO WITHIN ½ INCH (1 CM) OF RIM. REMOVE ANY AIR POCKETS AND ADJUST HEADSPACE, IF NECESSARY, BY ADDING HOT CHUTNEY; WIPE RIMS. APPLY PREPARED LIDS AND RINGS; TIGHTEN RINGS JUST UNTIL FINGERTIP-TIGHT. PROCESS JARS IN A BOILING WATER CANNER FOR 10 MINUTES (SEE PAGE 27).

TURN OFF CANNER AND REMOVE LID. LET JARS STAND IN WATER FOR 5 MINUTES. TRANSFER JARS TO A TOWEL-LINED SURFACE AND LET REST AT ROOM TEMPERATURE UNTIL COOLED. CHECK SEALS; REFRIGERATE ANY UNSEALED JARS FOR UP TO 3 WEEKS. MAKES ABOUT SIX 8-OUNCE (250 ML) JARS.

TIP: FOR INSTRUCTIONS ON PEELING TOMATOES, SEE BOX, PAGE 259.

VARIATION: IF YOU LIKE A HOT CHUTNEY, INCREASE THE CHILE PEPPERS TO 2. IF YOU'RE NOT SURE, JUST USE I TO START, THEN ADD HOT PEPPER SAUCE TO TASTE AFTER IT'S COOKED, IF DESIRED.

SERVING SUGGESTIONS: SERVE THIS TO SPICE UP OMELETS OR SCRAMBLED EGGS, OR WITH FISH OR PORK.

USING TOMATOES IN PRESERVES

FOR MOST PRESERVES, PLUM (ROMA) OR OTHER PASTE-TYPE TOMATOES ARE BEST, UNLESS OTHERWISE SPECIFIED IN THE RECIPE. THEY HAVE LESS LIQUID THAT NEEDS TO BE BOILED OFF TO MAKE A THICK SAUCE AND TEND TO HAVE A MORE CONSISTENT AMOUNT OF LIQUID THAN GLOBE TOMATOES. CHOOSE TOMATOES THAT HAVE FIRM, SHINY SKIN, FEEL HEAVY FOR THEIR SIZE AND HAVE NO SIGNS OF BLEMISHES OR MOLD. RIPE TOMATOES YIELD SLIGHTLY TO PRESSURE WHEN GENTLY SQUEEZED AND HAVE A SLIGHTLY FRAGRANT AROMA. A PUNGENT AROMA IS A SIGN OF OVERRIPENESS AND POSSIBLY ROT INSIDE.

GREEN TOMATO APPLE CHUTNEY

MAKE THIS SENSATIONAL CHUTNEY IN
LATE SUMMER, WHEN THE LAST OF THE
TOMATOES ARE STRUGGLING TO RIPEN AND
THE NEW HARVEST OF APPLES IS AVAILABLE.

7 CUPS	CHOPPED GREEN OR PARTIALLY RIPE TOMATOES	1.75 L
4 CUPS	CHOPPED PEELED APPLES THAT SOFTEN (SEE BOX, PAGE 157)	1 L
1½ CUPS	CHOPPED ONIONS	375 ML
1½ CUPS	PACKED BROWN SUGAR	375 ML
1 CUP	GRANULATED SUGAR	250 ML
1 CUP	CIDER VINEGAR	250 ML
1	LARGE CLOVE GARLIC, MINCED	1
2 TBSP	MUSTARD SEEDS	30 ML
2 TBSP	FINELY GRATED GINGERROOT	30 ML
1 TSP	PICKLING OR CANNING SALT	5 ML
½ TSP	HOT PEPPER FLAKES OR CAYENNE PEPPER	2 ML
¼ TSP	GROUND CLOVES	1 ML
1 CUP	SULTANA RAISINS	250 ML

IN A DUTCH OVEN OR A LARGE, HEAVY-BOTTOMED POT,
COMBINE TOMATOES, APPLES, ONIONS, BROWN SUGAR,
GRANULATED SUGAR, VINEGAR, GARLIC, MUSTARD SEEDS,
GINGER, SALT, HOT PEPPER FLAKES AND CLOVES. BRING TO
A BOIL OVER HIGH HEAT, STIRRING OFTEN. REDUCE HEAT
AND BOIL GENTLY, STIRRING OFTEN AND REDUCING HEAT
FURTHER AS MIXTURE THICKENS, FOR 40 TO 50 MINUTES.
STIR IN RAISINS; COOK, STIRRING OFTEN, FOR ABOUT
15 MINUTES, UNTIL MIXTURE IS JUST THICK ENOUGH TO
MOUND ON A SPOON.

LADLE INTO STERILIZED JARS TO WITHIN $1/2$ INCH (1 CM) OF RIM. REMOVE ANY AIR POCKETS AND ADJUST HEADSPACE, IF NECESSARY, BY ADDING HOT CHUTNEY; WIPE RIMS. APPLY PREPARED LIDS AND RINGS; TIGHTEN RINGS JUST UNTIL FINGERTIP-TIGHT. PROCESS JARS IN A BOILING WATER CANNER FOR 10 MINUTES (SEE PAGE 27). TURN OFF CANNER AND REMOVE LID. LET JARS STAND IN WATER FOR 5 MINUTES. TRANSFER JARS TO A TOWEL-LINED SURFACE AND LET REST AT ROOM TEMPERATURE UNTIL COOLED. CHECK SEALS; REFRIGERATE ANY UNSEALED JARS FOR UP TO 3 WEEKS. MAKES ABOUT SIX 8-OUNCE (250 ML) JARS

TIP: FOR THE BEST TEXTURE, CUT THE TOMATOES AND APPLES INTO $1/2$-INCH (1 CM) CHUNKS.

TIP: VARIETIES OF APPLES THAT SOFTEN WHEN COOKED INCLUDE MCINTOSH, CORTLAND, EMPIRE AND RUSSET.

TIP: TO DETERMINE WHEN THIS CHUTNEY IS THICK ENOUGH, PLACE A SPOONFUL ON A PLATE AND DRAW A SMALL SPOON THROUGH THE CENTER. IT IS DONE WHEN NO LIQUID SEEPS INTO THE SPACE. DO NOT OVERCOOK, AS CHUTNEY THICKENS AS IT COOLS.

SERVING SUGGESTIONS: SERVE WITH SCRAMBLED EGGS, QUICHE AND OMELETS, STIR INTO HASH BROWN POTATOES OR SERVE WITH CHEESE OR COLD MEAT.

DON'T BELIEVE EVERYTHING YOU THINK.

TOMATO, PEACH AND PEAR CHUTNEY

BOOK A DATE WITH YOUR CANNER IN LATE SUMMER TO MAKE THIS SWEETLY SPICED, FRUITY CHUTNEY — WHEN YOU POP OPEN A JAR IN THE DEPTH OF WINTER, YOU'LL BE GLAD YOU DID.

15	RIPE TOMATOES, PEELED (SEE BOX, PAGE 259) AND CHOPPED	15
3	LARGE PEACHES, PEELED, (SEE BOX, PAGE 87) AND CHOPPED	3
3	LARGE PEARS, PEELED AND CHOPPED	3
2	LARGE ONIONS, CHOPPED	2
1 TBSP	PICKLING OR CANNING SALT	15 ML
1	LARGE RED BELL PEPPER	1
1	LARGE GREEN BELL PEPPER	1
2 CUPS	WHITE VINEGAR	500 ML
2 CUPS	PACKED BROWN SUGAR	500 ML
1 TBSP	WHOLE CLOVES	15 ML
1	1-INCH (2.5 CM) PIECE CINNAMON STICK	1

IN A DUTCH OVEN OR A LARGE, HEAVY-BOTTOMED POT, COMBINE ALL INGREDIENTS (EXCEPT SPICES) AND BRING TO A BOIL OVER MEDIUM-HIGH HEAT. REDUCE HEAT AND SIMMER, STIRRING OFTEN, FOR ABOUT $1\frac{1}{2}$ HOURS. TIE CLOVES AND CINNAMON IN A SQUARE OF CHEESECLOTH. ADD SPICE BAG DURING LAST 15 MINUTES; COOK UNTIL MIXTURE IS JUST THICK ENOUGH TO MOUND ON A SPOON. REMOVE SPICE PACKET.

LADLE INTO STERILIZED JARS TO WITHIN $\frac{1}{2}$ INCH (1 CM) OF RIM. REMOVE ANY AIR POCKETS AND ADJUST HEADSPACE, IF NECESSARY, BY ADDING HOT CHUTNEY;

WIPE RIMS. APPLY PREPARED LIDS AND RINGS; TIGHTEN RINGS JUST UNTIL FINGERTIP-TIGHT. PROCESS JARS IN A BOILING WATER CANNER FOR 10 MINUTES (SEE PAGE 27). TURN OFF CANNER AND REMOVE LID. LET JARS STAND IN WATER FOR 5 MINUTES. TRANSFER JARS TO A TOWEL-LINED SURFACE AND LET REST AT ROOM TEMPERATURE UNTIL COOLED. CHECK SEALS; REFRIGERATE ANY UNSEALED JARS FOR UP TO 3 WEEKS. MAKES TEN TO TWELVE 8-OUNCE (250 ML) JARS.

SERVING SUGGESTION: DELICIOUS SERVED WITH ANY MEAT. PLACE THIS ON YOUR BUFFET WHEN HAVING "MAKE YOUR OWN SANDWICHES."

STORING TOMATOES

IF YOU BUY A LARGE QUANTITY OF TOMATOES, IT IS BEST TO SPREAD THEM OUT TO PROVIDE AIR CIRCULATION AND REDUCE DETERIORATION. LINE SHALLOW BOXES WITH CLEAN NEWSPAPER AND ARRANGE TOMATOES IN A SINGLE LAYER, OR A MAXIMUM OF TWO LAYERS. STORE OUT OF THE SUN, IN A COOL PLACE SUCH AS A GARAGE OR BASEMENT (BUT NOT IN THE REFRIGERATOR), AND CHECK DAILY TO REMOVE ANY THAT START TO SPOIL.

Relishes

With their (usually) finely chopped ingredients immersed in vinegar, sugar and spices, relishes are an easy way to add interest to meats, cheeses, sandwiches and even egg dishes. If you have produce that is slightly larger than you want to use for pickles, or perhaps not quite pretty enough — but not spoiled or of poor quality — relish is a terrific way to use it up. A little chopping, soaking and simmering, and you're ready to fill jars with sweet and tangy goodness.

SWEET GREEN RELISH

YOU CAN'T GO WRONG WITH THIS PLAIN AND SIMPLE, CLASSIC GREEN RELISH. TRY IT ON SLIDERS (PAGE 268).

10 CUPS	FINELY CHOPPED PICKLING CUCUMBERS (SEE TIP, PAGE 193)	2.5 L
1/3 CUP	PICKLING OR CANNING SALT	75 ML
2 1/2 CUPS	GRANULATED SUGAR	625 ML
1/4 TSP	FRESHLY GROUND BLACK PEPPER	1 ML
2 CUPS	WHITE VINEGAR	500 ML

IN A LARGE BOWL, COMBINE CUCUMBERS AND SALT. ADD COLD WATER TO COVER BY 1 INCH (2.5 CM). PLACE A PLATE ON TOP TO WEIGH DOWN CUCUMBERS. COVER AND LET STAND AT A COOL ROOM TEMPERATURE FOR AT LEAST 8 HOURS OR FOR UP TO 18 HOURS.

IN A COLANDER LINED WITH CHEESECLOTH, WORKING IN BATCHES, DRAIN CUCUMBERS AND RINSE WELL. DRAIN

AGAIN AND SQUEEZE OUT EXCESS LIQUID. SET ASIDE IN COLANDER TO CONTINUE DRAINING.

IN A LARGE POT, COMBINE SUGAR, PEPPER AND VINEGAR. BRING TO A BOIL OVER MEDIUM HEAT, STIRRING OFTEN UNTIL SUGAR IS DISSOLVED. INCREASE HEAT TO MEDIUM-HIGH, ADD DRAINED CUCUMBERS AND RETURN TO A BOIL, STIRRING OFTEN. REDUCE HEAT AND BOIL GENTLY, STIRRING OFTEN, FOR ABOUT 15 MINUTES OR UNTIL CUCUMBERS ARE TRANSLUCENT AND MIXTURE IS SLIGHTLY THICKENED.

LADLE HOT RELISH INTO STERILIZED JARS TO WITHIN $1/2$ INCH (1 CM) OF RIM. REMOVE ANY AIR POCKETS AND ADJUST HEADSPACE, IF NECESSARY, BY ADDING HOT RELISH; WIPE RIMS. APPLY PREPARED LIDS AND RINGS; TIGHTEN RINGS JUST UNTIL FINGERTIP-TIGHT. PROCESS JARS IN A BOILING WATER CANNER FOR 10 MINUTES (SEE PAGE 27). TURN OFF CANNER AND REMOVE LID. LET JARS STAND IN WATER FOR 5 MINUTES. TRANSFER JARS TO A TOWEL-LINED SURFACE AND LET REST AT ROOM TEMPERATURE UNTIL COOLED. CHECK SEALS; REFRIGERATE ANY UNSEALED JARS FOR UP TO 3 WEEKS. MAKES ABOUT SEVEN 8-OUNCE (250 ML) JARS.

SERVING SUGGESTION: THIS CLASSIC RELISH IS A MUST FOR HAMBURGERS, HOT DOGS AND GRILLED SAUSAGES ON A BUN.

RECIPE SUGGESTION: STIR RELISH INTO TUNA, SALMON OR EGG SALAD SANDWICH FILLINGS.

DILL CUCUMBER RELISH

DILL ADDS AN HERBY FRESHNESS
TO THIS TANGY RELISH.

8 CUPS	FINELY CHOPPED PICKLING CUCUMBERS (SEE TIP, OPPOSITE)	2 L
2 CUPS	FINELY CHOPPED ONIONS	500 ML
1/3 CUP	PICKLING OR CANNING SALT	75 ML
1 1/2 CUPS	GRANULATED SUGAR	375 ML
1 TBSP	DILL SEEDS	15 ML
2 TSP	MUSTARD SEEDS	10 ML
3 1/2 CUPS	WHITE VINEGAR	875 ML
1/4 CUP	FINELY CHOPPED FRESH DILL	60 ML

IN A LARGE BOWL, COMBINE CUCUMBERS, ONIONS AND SALT. ADD COLD WATER TO COVER BY 1 INCH (2.5 CM). PLACE A PLATE ON TOP TO WEIGH DOWN VEGETABLES. COVER AND LET STAND AT A COOL ROOM TEMPERATURE FOR AT LEAST 8 HOURS OR FOR UP TO 18 HOURS.

IN A COLANDER LINED WITH CHEESECLOTH, WORKING IN BATCHES, DRAIN VEGETABLES AND RINSE WELL. DRAIN AGAIN AND SQUEEZE OUT EXCESS LIQUID. SET ASIDE IN COLANDER TO CONTINUE DRAINING.

IN A LARGE POT, COMBINE SUGAR, DILL SEEDS, MUSTARD SEEDS AND VINEGAR. BRING TO A BOIL OVER MEDIUM HEAT, STIRRING OFTEN UNTIL SUGAR IS DISSOLVED. INCREASE HEAT TO MEDIUM-HIGH, ADD DRAINED VEGETABLES AND RETURN TO A BOIL, STIRRING OFTEN. REDUCE HEAT AND BOIL GENTLY, STIRRING OFTEN, FOR ABOUT 15 MINUTES OR UNTIL VEGETABLES ARE TRANSLUCENT AND MIXTURE IS SLIGHTLY THICKENED.

STIR IN FRESH DILL AND BOIL GENTLY, STIRRING, FOR 1 MINUTE.

LADLE HOT RELISH INTO STERILIZED JARS TO WITHIN $\frac{1}{2}$ INCH (1 CM) OF RIM. REMOVE ANY AIR POCKETS AND ADJUST HEADSPACE, IF NECESSARY, BY ADDING HOT RELISH; WIPE RIMS. APPLY PREPARED LIDS AND RINGS; TIGHTEN RINGS JUST UNTIL FINGERTIP-TIGHT. PROCESS JARS IN A BOILING WATER CANNER FOR 10 MINUTES (SEE PAGE 27). TURN OFF CANNER AND REMOVE LID. LET JARS STAND IN WATER FOR 5 MINUTES. TRANSFER JARS TO A TOWEL-LINED SURFACE AND LET REST AT ROOM TEMPERATURE UNTIL COOLED. CHECK SEALS; REFRIGERATE ANY UNSEALED JARS FOR UP TO 3 WEEKS. MAKES ABOUT SEVEN 8-OUNCE (250 ML) JARS.

TIP: PICKLING CUCUMBERS HAVE A NICE FIRM TEXTURE FOR RELISH. IF THEY AREN'T AVAILABLE, PEELED AND SEEDED FIELD CUCUMBERS CAN BE USED INSTEAD, THOUGH THE COLOR OF THE RELISH WILL BE PALE.

TIP: USE THE FEATHERY FRESH DILL SPRIGS, RATHER THAN THE MORE MATURE DILL HEADS, FOR THE BEST FLAVOR AND TEXTURE IN THIS RELISH.

SERVING SUGGESTION: THIS DILLY RELISH IS PERFECT ON GRILLED BURGERS OR FISH.

RECIPE SUGGESTIONS: STIR TOGETHER EQUAL PARTS RELISH AND MAYONNAISE FOR A QUICK TARTAR SAUCE (OR SEE RECIPE, PAGE 278), OR STIR INTO POTATO SALAD, TUNA OR SALMON SALAD.

CORN RELISH

WHEN CORN IS FRESH AND PEPPERS ARE PLENTIFUL,
COOK UP A BATCH OF THIS SWEET AND TANGY RELISH
TO BRIGHTEN MEALS THROUGHOUT THE YEAR.

6 CUPS	CORN KERNELS (FROZEN OR BLANCHED FRESH)	1.5 L
3	MEDIUM ONIONS, FINELY CHOPPED	3
1	RED BELL PEPPER, FINELY CHOPPED	1
1	GREEN BELL PEPPER, FINELY CHOPPED	1
1/2 CUP	FINELY CHOPPED CELERY	125 ML
2 CUPS	CIDER VINEGAR	500 ML
1 CUP	GRANULATED SUGAR	250 ML
2 TBSP	PICKLING OR CANNING SALT	30 ML
2 TBSP	DRY MUSTARD	30 ML
1/2 TSP	CELERY SEEDS	2 ML
1/4 TSP	GROUND TURMERIC	1 ML
1/4 TSP	FRESHLY GROUND BLACK PEPPER	1 ML

IN A LARGE POT, COMBINE ALL INGREDIENTS. BRING TO A
BOIL OVER MEDIUM HEAT, STIRRING OFTEN UNTIL SUGAR
IS DISSOLVED. REDUCE HEAT AND BOIL GENTLY, STIRRING
OFTEN, FOR ABOUT 30 MINUTES OR UNTIL ONIONS
ARE TRANSLUCENT.

LADLE HOT RELISH INTO STERILIZED JARS TO WITHIN
1/2 INCH (1 CM) OF RIM. REMOVE ANY AIR POCKETS AND
ADJUST HEADSPACE, IF NECESSARY, BY ADDING HOT
RELISH; WIPE RIMS. APPLY PREPARED LIDS AND RINGS;
TIGHTEN RINGS JUST UNTIL FINGERTIP-TIGHT. PROCESS
JARS IN A BOILING WATER CANNER FOR 10 MINUTES
(SEE PAGE 27). TURN OFF CANNER AND REMOVE LID. LET

JARS STAND IN WATER FOR 5 MINUTES. TRANSFER JARS TO A TOWEL-LINED SURFACE AND LET REST AT ROOM TEMPERATURE UNTIL COOLED. CHECK SEALS; REFRIGERATE ANY UNSEALED JARS FOR UP TO 3 WEEKS. *MAKES ABOUT EIGHT 8-OUNCE (250 ML) JARS.*

TIP: YOU'LL NEED ABOUT 12 LARGE COBS OF CORN TO GET 6 CUPS (1.5 L) KERNELS.

SERVING SUGGESTION: SERVE WITH GRILLED STEAK, PORK CHOPS OR CHICKEN.

USING CORN IN PRESERVES

FRESH CORN ON THE COB IS USED IN ALL RECIPES UNLESS OTHERWISE SPECIFIED. TO PRESERVE THE FRESH TEXTURE AND FLAVOR, WAIT TO REMOVE HUSKS AND SILKS UNTIL JUST BEFORE COOKING. COOK WHOLE OR HALVED COBS IN A LARGE POT OF LIGHTLY SALTED BOILING WATER FOR ABOUT 5 MINUTES, OR UNTIL KERNELS ARE EASILY PIERCED WITH A FORK. PLUNGE COBS INTO COLD WATER TO STOP THE COOKING. HOLDING EACH COB IN A DEEP BOWL, USE A SMALL, SERRATED KNIFE TO SLICE OFF THE KERNELS.

THREE-ONION RELISH

THREE ONION COUSINS — COOKING ONIONS, LEEKS AND GREEN ONIONS — COME TOGETHER IN THIS DELIGHTFULLY DIFFERENT, SAVORY RELISH.

6 CUPS	THINLY SLICED ONIONS	1.5 L
2 CUPS	SLICED LEEKS (WHITE AND LIGHT GREEN PARTS ONLY)	500 ML
1/4 CUP	PICKLING OR CANNING SALT	60 ML
1 1/2 CUPS	GRANULATED SUGAR	375 ML
2 TSP	CORIANDER SEEDS, CRUSHED	10 ML
1 TSP	DRIED THYME	5 ML
2 1/4 CUPS	CIDER VINEGAR	550 ML
2 CUPS	THINLY SLICED GREEN ONIONS	500 ML

IN A LARGE BOWL, COMBINE ONIONS, LEEKS AND SALT. COVER AND LET STAND AT A COOL ROOM TEMPERATURE FOR 2 HOURS.

IN A COLANDER LINED WITH CHEESECLOTH, WORKING IN BATCHES, DRAIN ONION MIXTURE AND RINSE WELL. DRAIN AGAIN AND SQUEEZE OUT EXCESS LIQUID. SET ASIDE IN COLANDER TO CONTINUE DRAINING.

IN A LARGE POT, COMBINE SUGAR, CORIANDER SEEDS, THYME AND VINEGAR. BRING TO A BOIL OVER MEDIUM HEAT, STIRRING OFTEN UNTIL SUGAR IS DISSOLVED. INCREASE HEAT TO MEDIUM-HIGH, ADD DRAINED ONIONS AND RETURN TO A BOIL, STIRRING OFTEN. REDUCE HEAT AND BOIL GENTLY, STIRRING OFTEN, FOR ABOUT 15 MINUTES OR UNTIL ONIONS ARE TRANSLUCENT AND MIXTURE IS SLIGHTLY THICKENED. STIR IN GREEN ONIONS AND RETURN TO A BOIL, STIRRING OFTEN.

LADLE HOT RELISH INTO STERILIZED JARS TO WITHIN $\frac{1}{2}$ INCH (1 CM) OF RIM. REMOVE ANY AIR POCKETS AND ADJUST HEADSPACE, IF NECESSARY, BY ADDING HOT RELISH; WIPE RIMS. APPLY PREPARED LIDS AND RINGS; TIGHTEN RINGS JUST UNTIL FINGERTIP-TIGHT. PROCESS JARS IN A BOILING WATER CANNER FOR 10 MINUTES (SEE PAGE 27). TURN OFF CANNER AND REMOVE LID. LET JARS STAND IN WATER FOR 5 MINUTES. TRANSFER JARS TO A TOWEL-LINED SURFACE AND LET REST AT ROOM TEMPERATURE UNTIL COOLED. CHECK SEALS; REFRIGERATE ANY UNSEALED JARS FOR UP TO 3 WEEKS. MAKES ABOUT SIX 8-OUNCE (250 ML) JARS.

TIP: THIS RELISH LOOKS NICE IF YOU CUT THE ONIONS IN HALF LENGTHWISE, THEN CROSSWISE INTO THIN SLICES.

TIP: BE SURE TO WASH THE LEEKS WELL TO REMOVE ALL OF THE SAND AND GRIT. TRIM OFF THE ROOT END AND DARK GREEN PARTS, THEN CUT THE WHITE AND LIGHT GREEN PORTION IN HALF LENGTHWISE. RINSE WELL BETWEEN THE LAYERS AND DRAIN, THEN CUT CROSSWISE INTO THIN SLICES.

SERVING SUGGESTIONS: TOP A JUICY STEAK WITH THIS RELISH AND YOU'LL NEVER GO BACK TO A BOTTLED SAUCE. IT'S ALSO WONDERFUL AS A SANDWICH SPREAD.

REMEMBER: "STRESSED" SPELLED
BACKWARDS IS "DESSERTS."

PEPPER RELISH

THIS IS A MILD VERSION OF JALAPEÑO PEPPER JELLY (PAGE 136). IT TAKES ON THE COLOR OF THE RED PEPPERS AND MAKES AN ATTRACTIVE CHRISTMAS GIFT.

6	GREEN BELL PEPPERS, FINELY CHOPPED	6
6	RED BELL PEPPERS, FINELY CHOPPED	6
1½ CUPS	WHITE VINEGAR	375 ML
5 CUPS	GRANULATED SUGAR	1.25 L
2	POUCHES (EACH 3 OZ/85 ML) LIQUID PECTIN	2

IN A DUTCH OVEN OR A LARGE, HEAVY-BOTTOMED POT, COMBINE PEPPERS, VINEGAR AND SUGAR. MIX WELL. BRING TO ROLLING BOIL AND BOIL HARD FOR 1 MINUTE, STIRRING CONSTANTLY. REMOVE FROM HEAT AND STIR IN PECTIN. RETURN TO HIGH HEAT AND BOIL, STIRRING, FOR 5 TO 10 MINUTES OR UNTIL SLIGHTLY THICKENED.

LADLE HOT RELISH INTO STERILIZED JARS TO WITHIN ½ INCH (1 CM) OF RIM. REMOVE ANY AIR POCKETS AND ADJUST HEADSPACE, IF NECESSARY, BY ADDING HOT RELISH; WIPE RIMS. APPLY PREPARED LIDS AND RINGS; TIGHTEN RINGS JUST UNTIL FINGERTIP-TIGHT. PROCESS JARS IN A BOILING WATER CANNER FOR 10 MINUTES (SEE PAGE 27). TURN OFF CANNER AND REMOVE LID. LET JARS STAND IN WATER FOR 5 MINUTES. TRANSFER JARS TO A TOWEL-LINED SURFACE AND LET REST AT ROOM TEMPERATURE UNTIL COOLED. CHECK SEALS; REFRIGERATE ANY UNSEALED JARS FOR UP TO 3 WEEKS. MAKES ABOUT FIVE PINT (500 ML) JARS.

TIP: YOU CAN CHOP THE PEPPERS BY HAND, BY PULSING THEM IN A FOOD PROCESSOR IN BATCHES (BEING CAREFUL NOT TO PURÉE THEM) OR BY GRINDING THEM THROUGH A FOOD GRINDER.

SERVING SUGGESTIONS: SERVE WITH SHARP OR CREAMY CHEESE, OR AS A TOPPER FOR BURGERS OR SAUSAGES ON A BUN.

USING VINEGAR IN PRESERVES

THE WHITE VINEGAR, CIDER VINEGAR, WHITE WINE VINEGAR AND RED WINE VINEGAR USED IN THESE RECIPES ARE 5% ACETIC ACID. WHITE BALSAMIC AND REGULAR BALSAMIC VINEGARS ARE 6% ACETIC ACID. THE RICE VINEGAR USED IN THESE RECIPES IS NATURAL VINEGAR WITHOUT ADDED SUGAR AND SALT (DO NOT USE SEASONED RICE VINEGAR) AND IS 4.3% ACID. DO NOT SUBSTITUTE VINEGARS OF DIFFERENT ACIDITY LEVELS, AS THIS CAN ADVERSELY AFFECT THE FINAL PH OF THE PRODUCT AND THE FLAVOR BALANCE.

SWEET AND HOT PEPPER RELISH

*A COLORFUL AND FLAVORFUL BLEND OF PEPPERS
CREATES A RELISH WITH A NICE BALANCE OF
SWEETNESS, TANG AND HEAT.*

4 CUPS	DICED RED BELL PEPPERS	1 L
3 CUPS	DICED GREEN BELL PEPPERS	750 ML
2 CUPS	DICED SWEET BANANA PEPPERS	500 ML
1 1/2 CUPS	FINELY CHOPPED ONIONS	375 ML
1/2 CUP	FINELY CHOPPED SEEDED CAYENNE OR OTHER HOT RED CHILE PEPPERS	125 ML
1/3 CUP	PICKLING OR CANNING SALT	75 ML
1 1/2 CUPS	GRANULATED SUGAR	375 ML
1 TBSP	CELERY SEEDS	15 ML
1/2 TSP	FRESHLY GROUND BLACK PEPPER	2 ML
2 CUPS	CIDER VINEGAR	500 ML

IN A LARGE BOWL, COMBINE RED AND GREEN PEPPERS, BANANA PEPPERS, ONIONS, CAYENNE PEPPERS AND SALT. COVER AND LET STAND AT A COOL ROOM TEMPERATURE FOR 4 HOURS.

IN A COLANDER LINED WITH CHEESECLOTH, WORKING IN BATCHES, DRAIN VEGETABLES AND RINSE WELL. DRAIN AGAIN AND SQUEEZE OUT EXCESS LIQUID. SET ASIDE IN COLANDER TO CONTINUE DRAINING.

IN A LARGE POT, COMBINE SUGAR, CELERY SEEDS, BLACK PEPPER AND VINEGAR. BRING TO A BOIL OVER MEDIUM HEAT, STIRRING OFTEN UNTIL SUGAR IS DISSOLVED. INCREASE HEAT TO MEDIUM-HIGH, ADD DRAINED VEGETABLES AND RETURN TO A BOIL, STIRRING OFTEN. REDUCE HEAT AND SIMMER GENTLY, STIRRING

OFTEN, FOR ABOUT 15 MINUTES OR JUST UNTIL ONIONS ARE TRANSLUCENT AND VEGETABLES ARE HEATED THROUGH.

LADLE HOT RELISH INTO STERILIZED JARS TO WITHIN $1/2$ INCH (1 CM) OF RIM. REMOVE ANY AIR POCKETS AND ADJUST HEADSPACE, IF NECESSARY, BY ADDING HOT RELISH; WIPE RIMS. APPLY PREPARED LIDS AND RINGS; TIGHTEN RINGS JUST UNTIL FINGERTIP-TIGHT. PROCESS JARS IN A BOILING WATER CANNER FOR 10 MINUTES (SEE PAGE 27). TURN OFF CANNER AND REMOVE LID. LET JARS STAND IN WATER FOR 5 MINUTES. TRANSFER JARS TO A TOWEL-LINED SURFACE AND LET REST AT ROOM TEMPERATURE UNTIL COOLED. CHECK SEALS; REFRIGERATE ANY UNSEALED JARS FOR UP TO 3 WEEKS. MAKES ABOUT SIX 8-OUNCE (250 ML) JARS.

VARIATION: IF SWEET BANANA PEPPERS AREN'T AVAILABLE, SUBSTITUTE AN EQUAL AMOUNT OF OTHER MILD PEPPERS, SUCH AS CUBANELLE, ANAHEIM OR ORANGE OR YELLOW BELL PEPPERS.

VARIATION: THIS VERSION IS MODERATELY HOT. IF YOU PREFER A HOTTER RELISH, REDUCE THE BANANA PEPPERS TO $1 1/2$ CUPS (375 ML) AND INCREASE THE CAYENNE PEPPERS TO 1 CUP (250 ML).

SERVING SUGGESTION: SERVE WITH GRILLED FISH, POULTRY OR ROAST PORK.

RECIPE SUGGESTION: STIR TOGETHER EQUAL PARTS RELISH AND PLAIN GREEK YOGURT OR SOUR CREAM FOR A QUICK CHIP DIP.

GREEN TOMATO RELISH

THERE'S NO NEED TO WORRY ABOUT A GARDEN FULL OF TOMATOES WHEN THE FROST IS LOOMING. PICK THE GREEN TOMATOES AND TURN THEM INTO THIS SWEETLY SPICED RELISH.

7 1/2 LBS	GREEN TOMATOES, THINLY SLICED	3.75 KG
5	GREEN BELL PEPPERS, QUARTERED, SEEDED AND SLICED	5
4	RED BELL PEPPERS, QUARTERED, SEEDED AND SLICED	4
4	LARGE ONIONS, HALVED AND SLICED	4
I CUP	PICKLING OR CANNING SALT	250 ML
6 CUPS	GRANULATED SUGAR	1.5 L
2 TBSP	PICKLING SPICE	30 ML
I TBSP	GROUND TURMERIC	15 ML
I TSP	GROUND CINNAMON	5 ML
I TSP	GROUND CLOVES	5 ML
4 CUPS	WHITE VINEGAR	I L

IN A LARGE BOWL, COMBINE TOMATOES, GREEN PEPPERS, RED PEPPERS, ONIONS AND SALT. COVER AND LET STAND AT A COOL ROOM TEMPERATURE OVERNIGHT.

IN A COLANDER LINED WITH CHEESECLOTH, WORKING IN BATCHES, DRAIN VEGETABLES AND RINSE WELL. DRAIN AGAIN AND SQUEEZE OUT EXCESS LIQUID. SET ASIDE IN COLANDER TO CONTINUE DRAINING.

IN A LARGE POT, COMBINE DRAINED VEGETABLES, SUGAR, PICKLING SPICE, TURMERIC, CINNAMON, CLOVES AND VINEGAR. BRING TO A BOIL OVER MEDIUM HEAT, STIRRING OFTEN. REDUCE HEAT AND SIMMER GENTLY, STIRRING

OFTEN, FOR ABOUT 30 MINUTES OR UNTIL ONIONS ARE TRANSLUCENT AND RELISH IS SLIGHTLY THICKENED.

LADLE HOT RELISH INTO STERILIZED JARS TO WITHIN $1/2$ INCH (1 CM) OF RIM. REMOVE ANY AIR POCKETS AND ADJUST HEADSPACE, IF NECESSARY, BY ADDING HOT RELISH; WIPE RIMS. APPLY PREPARED LIDS AND RINGS; TIGHTEN RINGS JUST UNTIL FINGERTIP-TIGHT. PROCESS JARS IN A BOILING WATER CANNER FOR 15 MINUTES (SEE PAGE 27). TURN OFF CANNER AND REMOVE LID. LET JARS STAND IN WATER FOR 5 MINUTES. TRANSFER JARS TO A TOWEL-LINED SURFACE AND LET REST AT ROOM TEMPERATURE UNTIL COOLED. CHECK SEALS; REFRIGERATE ANY UNSEALED JARS FOR UP TO 3 WEEKS. MAKES ABOUT TEN PINT (500 ML) JARS.

TIP: THIS IS A BIG BATCH OF RELISH, AND ALL TEN JARS MAY NOT FIT IN YOUR CANNER AT ONCE. ONLY FILL AND SEAL AS MANY JARS AS FIT IN YOUR CANNER AND KEEP THE REMAINING RELISH HOT. ONCE THE FIRST BATCH IS ALMOST FINISHED PROCESSING, FILL THE REMAINING JARS WITH THE REMAINING HOT RELISH.

SERVING SUGGESTIONS: THIS RELISH MAKES A NICE ACCOMPANIMENT TO A GRILLED CHEESE SANDWICH OR A SAVORY MEAT PIE, OR A DELICIOUS SPREAD FOR A TURKEY OR CHICKEN SANDWICH.

*I JUST BURNED 600 CALORIES.
IT WAS YOUR DINNER.*

ZUCCHINI RELISH

WHEN ZUCCHINI ABOUND AND THREATEN TO TAKE OVER YOUR KITCHEN, CHOP THEM UP AND SIMMER THEM INTO THIS ZESTY RELISH.

16 CUPS	FINELY CHOPPED ZUCCHINI	4 L
4	LARGE ONIONS, FINELY CHOPPED	4
1	GREEN BELL PEPPER, FINELY CHOPPED	1
1/2 CUP	PICKLING OR CANNING SALT	125 ML
	ICE WATER	
1 1/2 CUPS	GRANULATED SUGAR	375 ML
1 1/2 CUPS	PACKED BROWN SUGAR	375 ML
2 TBSP	GROUND TURMERIC	30 ML
2 TBSP	CELERY SEEDS	30 ML
3 CUPS	WHITE VINEGAR	750 ML
1/2 CUP	WATER	125 ML

IN A LARGE BOWL, COMBINE ZUCCHINI, ONIONS, GREEN PEPPERS AND SALT; ADD ICE WATER TO COVER. COVER AND LET STAND AT A COOL ROOM TEMPERATURE OVERNIGHT.

IN A COLANDER LINED WITH CHEESECLOTH, WORKING IN BATCHES, DRAIN VEGETABLES AND RINSE WELL. DRAIN AGAIN AND SQUEEZE OUT EXCESS LIQUID. SET ASIDE IN COLANDER TO CONTINUE DRAINING.

IN A LARGE POT, COMBINE GRANULATED SUGAR, BROWN SUGAR, TURMERIC, CELERY SEEDS, VINEGAR AND WATER. BRING TO A BOIL OVER MEDIUM HEAT, STIRRING OFTEN UNTIL SUGAR IS DISSOLVED. INCREASE HEAT TO MEDIUM-HIGH, ADD DRAINED VEGETABLES AND RETURN TO A BOIL, STIRRING OFTEN. REDUCE HEAT AND BOIL

GENTLY, STIRRING OFTEN, FOR ABOUT 15 MINUTES OR UNTIL ONIONS ARE TRANSLUCENT AND MIXTURE IS SLIGHTLY THICKENED.

LADLE HOT RELISH INTO STERILIZED JARS TO WITHIN $1/2$ INCH (1 CM) OF RIM. REMOVE ANY AIR POCKETS AND ADJUST HEADSPACE, IF NECESSARY, BY ADDING HOT RELISH; WIPE RIMS. APPLY PREPARED LIDS AND RINGS; TIGHTEN RINGS JUST UNTIL FINGERTIP-TIGHT. PROCESS JARS IN A BOILING WATER CANNER FOR 15 MINUTES (SEE PAGE 27). TURN OFF CANNER AND REMOVE LID. LET JARS STAND IN WATER FOR 5 MINUTES. TRANSFER JARS TO A TOWEL-LINED SURFACE AND LET REST AT ROOM TEMPERATURE UNTIL COOLED. CHECK SEALS; REFRIGERATE ANY UNSEALED JARS FOR UP TO 3 WEEKS. MAKES ABOUT TEN PINT (500 ML) JARS.

TIP: THIS IS A BIG BATCH OF RELISH, AND ALL TEN JARS MAY NOT FIT IN YOUR CANNER AT ONCE. ONLY FILL AND SEAL AS MANY JARS AS FIT IN YOUR CANNER AND KEEP THE REMAINING RELISH HOT. ONCE THE FIRST BATCH IS ALMOST FINISHED PROCESSING, FILL THE REMAINING JARS WITH THE REMAINING HOT RELISH.

SERVING SUGGESTIONS: SERVE AS A CONDIMENT FOR ROAST BEEF, OR AS A TOPPING FOR CRACKERS FOR QUICK HORS D'OEUVRES.

A WISE MAN ONCE SAID:
"I SHOULD ASK MY WIFE."

PICCALILLI

A CLASSIC RECIPE FOR A CLASSIC RELISH — AND A
PERFECT WAY TO USE UP GREEN TOMATOES.

12	GREEN TOMATOES	12
6	GREEN BELL PEPPERS	6
6	RED BELL PEPPERS	6
4	ONIONS	4
6 CUPS	WHITE VINEGAR, DIVIDED	1.5 L
3½ CUPS	GRANULATED SUGAR	875 ML
¼ CUP	PICKLING OR CANNING SALT	60 ML
¼ CUP	MUSTARD SEEDS	60 ML
1 TBSP	CELERY SEEDS	15 ML
2 TSP	GROUND ALLSPICE	10 ML
1 TSP	GROUND CINNAMON	5 ML

FINELY CHOP TOMATOES, GREEN PEPPERS, RED PEPPERS
AND ONIONS. PLACE IN A LARGE DUTCH OVEN OR LARGE
POT. ADD 4 CUPS (1 L) VINEGAR AND BRING TO A FULL
BOIL OVER HIGH HEAT. REDUCE HEAT AND SIMMER FOR
30 MINUTES, STIRRING OCCASIONALLY. DRAIN AND
RETURN TO POT. STIR IN REMAINING VINEGAR, SUGAR,
SALT, MUSTARD SEEDS, CELERY SEEDS, ALLSPICE AND
CINNAMON. BRING TO A BOIL OVER HIGH HEAT, STIRRING
OFTEN. REDUCE HEAT AND SIMMER FOR 3 MINUTES.

LADLE HOT RELISH INTO STERILIZED JARS TO WITHIN
½ INCH (1 CM) OF RIM. REMOVE ANY AIR POCKETS AND
ADJUST HEADSPACE, IF NECESSARY, BY ADDING HOT
RELISH; WIPE RIMS. APPLY PREPARED LIDS AND RINGS;
TIGHTEN RINGS JUST UNTIL FINGERTIP-TIGHT. PROCESS
JARS IN A BOILING WATER CANNER FOR 15 MINUTES (SEE

PAGE 27). TURN OFF CANNER AND REMOVE LID. LET JARS STAND IN WATER FOR 5 MINUTES. TRANSFER JARS TO A TOWEL-LINED SURFACE AND LET REST AT ROOM TEMPERATURE UNTIL COOLED. CHECK SEALS; REFRIGERATE ANY UNSEALED JARS FOR UP TO 3 WEEKS. MAKES ABOUT 6 PINT (500 ML) JARS.

TIP: YOU CAN CHOP THE VEGETABLES BY HAND, BY PULSING THEM IN A FOOD PROCESSOR IN BATCHES (BEING CAREFUL NOT TO PURÉE THEM) OR BY GRINDING THEM THROUGH A FOOD GRINDER.

SERVING SUGGESTIONS: SERVE ON A CHEESE AND CHARCUTERIE PLATTER, OR ON TOP OF CRACKERS SPREAD WITH PÂTÉ.

USING SALT IN PRESERVES

SALT IS AN INTEGRAL INGREDIENT IN PRESERVING. IT DRAWS JUICES OUT OF VEGETABLES AND FRUITS, ALLOWING THE PICKLING LIQUID OR BRINE TO ENTER THE CELLS AND PRESERVE THE FOOD. IT ALSO CONTRIBUTES GREATLY TO THE TEXTURE OF PICKLES, AND IS ESSENTIAL FOR THE FORMATION OF LACTIC ACID IN FERMENTED FOODS SUCH AS SAUERKRAUT. PURE SALT WITHOUT ANY ADDITIVES IS NECESSARY FOR GOOD-QUALITY PICKLES AND OTHER PRESERVES; IT IS LABELED "PICKLING SALT" OR "CANNING SALT." TABLE SALT AND OTHER IODIZED SALTS CAUSE CLOUDINESS IN BRINES. REMEMBER, YOU CAN'T GET SAFE RESULTS IF YOU DON'T USE THE CORRECT AMOUNT OF SALT.

HARVEST RELISH

THIS DARK AND INTENSELY FLAVORED COMBINATION OF VEGETABLES AND FRUIT REMINDS US OF THE POPULAR BRITISH PRODUCT CALLED BRANSTON PICKLE.

15	SMALL CORNICHON OR GHERKIN PICKLES, FINELY CHOPPED	15
5	CLOVES GARLIC, FINELY CHOPPED	5
2	CARROTS, FINELY CHOPPED	2
2	ZUCCHINI (UNPEELED), FINELY CHOPPED	2
2	APPLES, PEELED AND FINELY CHOPPED	2
2	ONIONS, FINELY CHOPPED	2
3 CUPS	FINELY CHOPPED PEELED RUTABAGA	750 ML
2 CUPS	FINELY CHOPPED CAULIFLOWER FLORETS	500 ML
1 CUP	FINELY CHOPPED DRIED DATES	250 ML
2 CUPS	PACKED DARK BROWN SUGAR	500 ML
2 TSP	MUSTARD SEEDS	10 ML
2 TSP	GROUND ALLSPICE	10 ML
1 TSP	CAYENNE PEPPER	5 ML
1 TSP	PICKLING OR CANNING SALT	5 ML
1 1/2 CUPS	MALT VINEGAR (SEE TIP, OPPOSITE)	375 ML
1/4 CUP	FRESHLY SQUEEZED LEMON JUICE	60 ML

IN A LARGE, DEEP POT, COMBINE ALL INGREDIENTS. BRING TO A BOIL OVER MEDIUM-HIGH HEAT, STIRRING CONSTANTLY. REDUCE HEAT AND SIMMER, STIRRING OCCASIONALLY, FOR ABOUT 1 1/2 HOURS OR UNTIL RUTABAGA AND CARROTS ARE COOKED BUT STILL FIRM TO THE BITE AND MIXTURE IS THICK ENOUGH TO MOUND ON A SPOON.

LADLE HOT RELISH INTO STERILIZED JARS TO WITHIN $\frac{1}{2}$ INCH (1 CM) OF RIM. REMOVE ANY AIR POCKETS AND ADJUST HEADSPACE, IF NECESSARY, BY ADDING HOT RELISH; WIPE RIMS. APPLY PREPARED LIDS AND RINGS; TIGHTEN RINGS JUST UNTIL FINGERTIP-TIGHT. PROCESS JARS IN A BOILING WATER CANNER FOR 20 MINUTES (SEE PAGE 27). TURN OFF CANNER AND REMOVE LID. LET JARS STAND IN WATER FOR 5 MINUTES. TRANSFER JARS TO A TOWEL-LINED SURFACE AND LET REST AT ROOM TEMPERATURE UNTIL COOLED. CHECK SEALS; REFRIGERATE ANY UNSEALED JARS FOR UP TO 3 WEEKS. MAKES ABOUT EIGHT 8-OUNCE (250 ML) JARS.

TIP: MALT VINEGAR, WHICH IS AMBER-COLORED AND MILD-TASTING, IS TRADITIONALLY USED IN BRITAIN AS A CONDIMENT ON FISH AND CHIPS. IT IS USUALLY SHELVED ALONGSIDE OTHER VINEGARS. IN A PINCH, YOU CAN SUBSTITUTE CIDER VINEGAR, BUT IT WILL SLIGHTLY ALTER THE FLAVOR OF THE RELISH.

TIP: ALLOW THE RELISH TO AGE FOR AT LEAST A MONTH BEFORE USING, AS THIS WILL IMPROVE AND MELLOW THE FLAVOR.

SERVING SUGGESTIONS: SERVE WITH COLD ROAST PORK, HAM OR CHICKEN, WITH GOOD-QUALITY AGED CHEDDAR CHEESE, OR AS AN ACCOMPANIMENT FOR INDIAN CURRIES.

FRUSTRATION IS TRYING TO FIND YOUR GLASSES WITHOUT YOUR GLASSES.

BLUEBERRY RELISH

THIS FABULOUS FRUITY RELISH ADDS FLASH TO CHICKEN, PORK, HAM, LAMB AND GAME MEAT.

4 CUPS	BLUEBERRIES	1 L
1 CUP	SWEETENED DRIED CRANBERRIES	250 ML
2½ CUPS	PACKED BROWN SUGAR	625 ML
1 TBSP	GRATED GINGERROOT	15 ML
⅛ TSP	GROUND NUTMEG	0.5 ML
PINCH	HOT PEPPER FLAKES	PINCH
	FINELY GRATED ZEST OF 2 LEMONS	
½ CUP	FRESHLY SQUEEZED LEMON JUICE	125 ML
	FINELY GRATED ZEST OF 1 ORANGE	
½ CUP	FRESHLY SQUEEZED ORANGE JUICE	125 ML
½ CUP	RED WINE VINEGAR OR CIDER VINEGAR	125 ML

IN A POT, COMBINE ALL INGREDIENTS. BRING TO A BOIL OVER MEDIUM-HIGH HEAT, STIRRING CONSTANTLY. REDUCE HEAT AND SIMMER, STIRRING FREQUENTLY, FOR 45 TO 60 MINUTES OR UNTIL THICK ENOUGH TO MOUND ON A SPOON.

LADLE HOT RELISH INTO STERILIZED JARS TO WITHIN ½ INCH (1 CM) OF RIM. REMOVE ANY AIR POCKETS AND ADJUST HEADSPACE, IF NECESSARY, BY ADDING HOT RELISH; WIPE RIMS. APPLY PREPARED LIDS AND RINGS; TIGHTEN RINGS JUST UNTIL FINGERTIP-TIGHT. PROCESS JARS IN A BOILING WATER CANNER FOR 10 MINUTES (SEE PAGE 27). TURN OFF CANNER AND REMOVE LID. LET JARS STAND IN WATER FOR 5 MINUTES. TRANSFER JARS TO A TOWEL-LINED SURFACE AND LET REST AT ROOM TEMPERATURE UNTIL COOLED. CHECK SEALS; REFRIGERATE

ANY UNSEALED JARS FOR UP TO 3 WEEKS. MAKES ABOUT THREE 8-OUNCE (250 ML) JARS.

TIP: THIS RELISH THICKENS NATURALLY — WITHOUT ADDED PECTIN — AS A RESULT OF THE LONG SIMMER. TO PREVENT IT FROM STICKING AND BURNING AS IT THICKENS, BE SURE TO STIR FREQUENTLY AND REDUCE HEAT AS NECESSARY TO KEEP IT AT A SIMMER AS IT GETS THICKER. USE A HEAVY-BOTTOMED, GOOD-QUALITY SAUCEPAN TO FURTHER PREVENT SCORCHING.

TIP: ONCE JARS OF RELISH ARE OPENED, STORE THEM IN THE REFRIGERATOR AND USE UP WITHIN 1 MONTH.

SERVING SUGGESTIONS: SERVE THIS RELISH ALONGSIDE YOUR NEXT TURKEY DINNER IN PLACE OF CRANBERRY SAUCE, OR PAIR IT WITH A CREAMY CHEESE, SUCH AS BRIE OR GOAT CHEESE, ON CRACKERS FOR AN EASY APPETIZER.

STORING FRESH GINGER

STORE UNPEELED GINGERROOT (FRESH GINGER) IN THE REFRIGERATOR, WRAPPED IN PAPER TOWELS AND SEALED IN A ZIP-LOCK BAG. OR GRATE AND FREEZE IN SMALL PACKAGES. PEEL OFF THE BROWN SKIN BEFORE GRATING OR CHOPPING.

BLUSHING PEACH AND PEPPER RELISH

TOP CRACKERS WITH GOAT CHEESE AND A DOLLOP OF THIS STUNNING ORANGE-RED RELISH. CONGRATULATIONS, YOU'VE GOT YOURSELF AN AWESOME APPETIZER. IT'S SIMILAR IN TASTE TO THAI DIPPING SAUCE, SO IT IS ALSO A PERFECT MATCH FOR CRISPY SPRING ROLLS.

6 LBS	RED BELL PEPPERS (ABOUT 12 LARGE), QUARTERED AND SEEDED	3 KG
5	HOT RED CHILE PEPPERS (SUCH AS SERRANO CHILES), STEMS REMOVED (SEEDS INCLUDED, IF DESIRED)	5
12	RIPE PEACHES, PEELED (SEE BOX, PAGE 87) AND COARSELY CHOPPED	12
2	LEMONS, HALVED AND SEEDED	2
1 TSP	PICKLING OR CANNING SALT	5 ML
1 CUP	WHITE WINE VINEGAR OR CIDER VINEGAR	250 ML
5 CUPS	GRANULATED SUGAR	1.25 L

IN A FOOD PROCESSOR, IN BATCHES AS NECESSARY, PULSE RED PEPPERS AND CHILE PEPPERS UNTIL COARSELY CHOPPED. TRANSFER TO A LARGE, DEEP STAINLESS STEEL SAUCEPAN OR DUTCH OVEN. ADD PEACHES, LEMONS, SALT AND VINEGAR. BRING TO A BOIL OVER MEDIUM-HIGH HEAT, STIRRING CONSTANTLY. REDUCE HEAT AND SIMMER, STIRRING FREQUENTLY, FOR 30 MINUTES. DISCARD LEMONS. ADD SUGAR, INCREASE HEAT TO HIGH AND BRING TO A BOIL, STIRRING CONSTANTLY. REDUCE HEAT AND SIMMER, STIRRING FREQUENTLY, FOR ABOUT 45 MINUTES OR UNTIL THICK ENOUGH TO MOUND ON A SPOON.

LADLE HOT RELISH INTO STERILIZED JARS TO WITHIN $1/2$ INCH (1 CM) OF RIM. REMOVE ANY AIR POCKETS AND ADJUST HEADSPACE, IF NECESSARY, BY ADDING HOT RELISH; WIPE RIMS. APPLY PREPARED LIDS AND RINGS; TIGHTEN RINGS JUST UNTIL FINGERTIP-TIGHT. PROCESS JARS IN A BOILING WATER CANNER FOR 10 MINUTES (SEE PAGE 27). TURN OFF CANNER AND REMOVE LID. LET JARS STAND IN WATER FOR 5 MINUTES. TRANSFER JARS TO A TOWEL-LINED SURFACE AND LET REST AT ROOM TEMPERATURE UNTIL COOLED. CHECK SEALS; REFRIGERATE ANY UNSEALED JARS FOR UP TO 3 WEEKS. MAKES ABOUT EIGHT 8-OUNCE (250 ML) JARS.

TIP: THE HEAT OF CHILES IS MOSTLY FOUND IN THE SEEDS AND MEMBRANE. IF YOU LIKE YOUR FOOD FIERY, LEAVE THEM IN. FOR A MILDER CHILE TASTE, REMOVE SOME OR ALL OF THE SEEDS AND THE MEMBRANE. AVOID TOUCHING YOUR LIPS, EYES OR OTHER SENSITIVE AREAS WHILE HANDLING CHILES. WASH YOUR HANDS AND UNDER YOUR NAILS THOROUGHLY AFTERWARDS.

USING PEACHES IN PRESERVES

CHOOSE FIRM FRUIT THAT IS EITHER RIPE OR SLIGHTLY UNDERRIPE (BUT WITHOUT GREEN AREAS). PEEL AND PIT BEFORE USING (SEE PAGE 87).

THE MAYOR'S WIFE'S BLUE PLUM RELISH

*A CONSTANT FAVORITE THAT GOES
WITH PRACTICALLY EVERYTHING.*

2½ LBS	BLUE PRUNE PLUMS, FINELY CHOPPED	1.25 KG
2	ONIONS, GRATED	2
2 LBS	COOKING APPLES, PEELED AND GRATED	I KG
2 CUPS	WHITE VINEGAR	500 ML
4 CUPS	GRANULATED SUGAR	I L
4 OZ	PRESERVED OR CANDIED GINGER, FINELY CHOPPED	125 G
I TBSP	CORNSTARCH	15 ML
2 TBSP	WATER	30 ML
2 TSP	PICKLING OR CANNING SALT	10 ML
I½ TSP	GROUND ALLSPICE	7 ML
I½ TSP	GROUND CLOVES	7 ML
½ TSP	FRESHLY GROUND BLACK PEPPER	2 ML

IN LARGE POT, COMBINE PLUMS, ONIONS, APPLES AND VINEGAR. BRING TO A BOIL OVER HIGH HEAT. REDUCE HEAT AND BOIL FOR 30 MINUTES. ADD SUGAR AND BRING TO A BOIL AGAIN, STIRRING TO DISSOLVE SUGAR. REDUCE HEAT AND SIMMER, STIRRING OFTEN, FOR 15 MINUTES. ADD GINGER AND CONTINUE TO SIMMER, STIRRING OFTEN, FOR ABOUT 15 MINUTES OR UNTIL ALMOST THICK ENOUGH TO MOUND ON A SPOON.

JUST BEFORE RELISH IS COOKED, IN A SMALL BOWL, DISSOLVE CORNSTARCH IN WATER. STIR SALT, ALLSPICE, CLOVES, PEPPER AND DISSOLVED CORNSTARCH MIXTURE INTO RELISH UNTIL WELL BLENDED. BOIL FOR I MINUTE.

LADLE HOT RELISH INTO STERILIZED JARS TO WITHIN 1/2 INCH (1 CM) OF RIM. REMOVE ANY AIR POCKETS AND ADJUST HEADSPACE, IF NECESSARY, BY ADDING HOT RELISH; WIPE RIMS. APPLY PREPARED LIDS AND RINGS; TIGHTEN RINGS JUST UNTIL FINGERTIP-TIGHT. PROCESS JARS IN A BOILING WATER CANNER FOR 10 MINUTES (SEE PAGE 27). TURN OFF CANNER AND REMOVE LID. LET JARS STAND IN WATER FOR 5 MINUTES. TRANSFER JARS TO A TOWEL-LINED SURFACE AND LET REST AT ROOM TEMPERATURE UNTIL COOLED. CHECK SEALS; REFRIGERATE ANY UNSEALED JARS FOR UP TO 3 WEEKS. MAKES ABOUT SIX PINT (500 ML) JARS.

TIP: THIS RELISH IS BEST IF AGED A FEW WEEKS, OR EVEN MONTHS, BEFORE SERVING.

SERVING SUGGESTIONS: SERVE WITH ROAST PORK AND POULTRY, OR AS A CONDIMENT FOR OMELETS OR SCRAMBLED EGGS.

HOW TO REMOVE THE PIT FROM A PLUM

CUT IN HALF THROUGH THE STEM AND TWIST TO SEPARATE THE HALVES. REPEAT, CUTTING THE HALF THAT STILL HAS THE PIT IN HALF, THEN TWISTING THE STONE FROM THE CENTER. (THIS TECHNIQUE HELPS A LOT WHEN THE PITS ARE TIGHTLY IMBEDDED IN SLIGHTLY UNDERRIPE FRUIT.)

RHUBARB RELISH

IF YOU'RE LUCKY ENOUGH TO HAVE A
RHUBARB PATCH, OR NEIGHBORS WHO DO, THIS
SAVORY RELISH IS A TERRIFIC WAY TO USE UP
A BUNDLE AND DRESS UP MEALS LONG AFTER
THE GARDEN IS ASLEEP FOR THE WINTER.

4 CUPS	FINELY CHOPPED ONIONS	I L
4 CUPS	FINELY CHOPPED RHUBARB	I L
3 CUPS	PACKED BROWN SUGAR	750 ML
2 TBSP	FINELY GRATED GINGERROOT	30 ML
I TSP	GROUND CLOVES	5 ML
I TSP	GROUND CINNAMON	5 ML
I TSP	GROUND ALLSPICE	5 ML
I TSP	PICKLING OR CANNING SALT	5 ML
PINCH	CAYENNE PEPPER (OR TO TASTE)	PINCH
2 CUPS	CIDER VINEGAR	500 ML

IN A LARGE, DEEP POT, COMBINE ALL INGREDIENTS.
BRING TO A BOIL OVER MEDIUM-HIGH HEAT, STIRRING
CONSTANTLY. REDUCE HEAT AND SIMMER, STIRRING
OCCASIONALLY, FOR ABOUT I HOUR OR UNTIL RHUBARB AND
ONIONS ARE VERY SOFT AND MIXTURE IS THICK ENOUGH
TO MOUND ON A SPOON.

LADLE HOT RELISH INTO STERILIZED JARS TO WITHIN
$1/2$ INCH (I CM) OF RIM. REMOVE ANY AIR POCKETS AND
ADJUST HEADSPACE, IF NECESSARY, BY ADDING HOT
RELISH; WIPE RIMS. APPLY PREPARED LIDS AND RINGS;
TIGHTEN RINGS JUST UNTIL FINGERTIP-TIGHT. PROCESS
JARS IN A BOILING WATER CANNER FOR 15 MINUTES

CONTINUED ON PAGE 217...

Bread and Butter Pickles (page 218)

Sweet and Tangy Green Beans (page 230)

Classic Pickled Beet Slices (page 232)

Dill Pickled Carrot Sticks (page 234) and Sweet and Tangy Zucchini Pickles (page 242)

(SEE PAGE 27). TURN OFF CANNER AND REMOVE LID. LET JARS STAND IN WATER FOR 5 MINUTES. TRANSFER JARS TO A TOWEL-LINED SURFACE AND LET REST AT ROOM TEMPERATURE UNTIL COOLED. CHECK SEALS; REFRIGERATE ANY UNSEALED JARS FOR UP TO 3 WEEKS. MAKES ABOUT FOUR 8-OUNCE (250 ML) JARS.

TIP: THIS RELISH THICKENS NATURALLY — WITHOUT ADDED PECTIN — AS A RESULT OF THE LONG SIMMER. TO PREVENT IT FROM STICKING AND BURNING AS IT THICKENS, BE SURE TO STIR FREQUENTLY AND REDUCE HEAT AS NECESSARY TO KEEP IT AT A SIMMER AS IT GETS THICKER. USE A HEAVY-BOTTOMED, GOOD-QUALITY SAUCEPAN TO FURTHER PREVENT SCORCHING.

TIP: USE A RUBBER SPATULA OR A PLASTIC BUBBLE REMOVER TO REMOVE AIR POCKETS ONCE YOU FILL JARS.

SERVING SUGGESTION: SERVE WITH MEAT PIE, MEATLOAF, QUICHE OR INDIAN CURRIES.

THE BEST WAY TO FORGET YOUR TROUBLES
IS TO WEAR TIGHT SHOES.

Pickles

Pickles are easy to make and most require just a few ingredients: vegetables, vinegar, salt and seasonings. They're a great intro for those new to canning, and experts can garner fame and admiration with their prize-worthy pickles. Plan ahead so you have time to pickle your vegetables as soon as possible after they're picked. Remember, you want to preserve the freshness, not old, tired vegetables on the verge of spoiling! Make sure to read through the recipe before getting started — some recipes require an overnight soak.

BREAD AND BUTTER PICKLES

HOMEMADE ARE THE BEST!! TRY THESE ON SLIDERS (PAGE 268).

10 CUPS	THINLY SLICED PICKLING CUCUMBERS	2.5 L
2	GREEN BELL PEPPERS, DICED	2
2	CLOVES GARLIC, MINCED	2
3	LARGE ONIONS, THINLY SLICED	3
1/3 CUP	PICKLING OR CANNING SALT	75 ML
12 CUPS	ICE CUBES	3 L
3 CUPS	WHITE VINEGAR	750 ML
4 CUPS	GRANULATED SUGAR	1 L
1 1/2 TSP	GROUND TURMERIC	7 ML
1 1/2 TSP	CELERY SEEDS	7 ML
1 1/2 TSP	MUSTARD SEEDS	7 ML

IN A LARGE POT OR BOWL, COMBINE CUCUMBERS, PEPPERS, GARLIC AND ONIONS. MIX IN SALT AND ICE CUBES. COVER AND LET STAND IN A COOL PLACE FOR AT LEAST 4 HOURS OR FOR UP TO 12 HOURS. DRAIN AND DISCARD ANY LEFTOVER ICE. SET VEGETABLES ASIDE. IN A LARGE POT, COMBINE VINEGAR, SUGAR, TURMERIC, CELERY SEEDS AND MUSTARD SEEDS. BRING TO A BOIL OVER MEDIUM HEAT; BOIL FOR 3 TO 5 MINUTES. MIX IN VEGETABLES AND RETURN TO A BOIL OVER HIGH HEAT, STIRRING OFTEN. REMOVE FROM HEAT.

USING A SLOTTED SPOON, PACK VEGETABLES INTO STERILIZED JARS TO WITHIN 1 INCH (2.5 CM) OF RIM. POUR IN HOT PICKLING LIQUID TO WITHIN $\frac{1}{2}$ INCH (1 CM) OF RIM. REMOVE ANY AIR POCKETS AND ADJUST HEADSPACE, IF NECESSARY, BY ADDING LIQUID; WIPE RIMS. APPLY PREPARED LIDS AND RINGS; TIGHTEN RINGS JUST UNTIL FINGERTIP-TIGHT. PROCESS JARS IN A BOILING WATER CANNER FOR 10 MINUTES (SEE PAGE 27). TURN OFF CANNER AND REMOVE LID. LET JARS STAND IN WATER FOR 5 MINUTES. TRANSFER JARS TO A TOWEL-LINED SURFACE AND LET REST AT ROOM TEMPERATURE UNTIL COOLED. CHECK SEALS; REFRIGERATE ANY UNSEALED JARS FOR UP TO 3 WEEKS. MAKES TEN 8-OUNCE (250 ML) JARS OR FIVE PINT (500 ML) JARS.

DILL PICKLES

PUCKER UP!

1/4 CUP	PICKLING OR CANNING SALT	60 ML
3 CUPS	WATER	750 ML
1 CUP	WHITE VINEGAR	250 ML
5 1/2 LBS	PICKLING CUCUMBERS, TRIMMED	2.75 KG
	FRESH DILL SPRIGS	
1	BULB GARLIC, CLOVES SEPARATED AND PEELED	1
	BLACK PEPPERCORNS	

IN A POT, COMBINE SALT, WATER AND VINEGAR; BRING TO A BOIL OVER MEDIUM HEAT, STIRRING UNTIL SALT IS DISSOLVED. REDUCE HEAT TO LOW AND KEEP HOT.

PACK CUCUMBERS INTO STERILIZED JARS. TO EACH JAR ADD 1 TO 2 SPRIGS OF FRESH DILL, 1 TO 2 PEELED GARLIC CLOVES AND A FEW PEPPERCORNS. POUR IN HOT PICKLING LIQUID TO WITHIN 1/2 INCH (1 CM) OF RIM. REMOVE ANY AIR POCKETS AND ADJUST HEADSPACE, IF NECESSARY, BY ADDING LIQUID; WIPE RIMS. APPLY PREPARED LIDS AND RINGS; TIGHTEN RINGS JUST UNTIL FINGERTIP-TIGHT. PROCESS JARS IN A BOILING WATER CANNER FOR 20 MINUTES (SEE PAGE 27). TURN OFF CANNER AND REMOVE LID. LET JARS STAND IN WATER FOR 5 MINUTES. TRANSFER JARS TO A TOWEL-LINED SURFACE AND LET REST AT ROOM TEMPERATURE UNTIL COOLED. CHECK SEALS; REFRIGERATE ANY UNSEALED JARS FOR UP TO 3 WEEKS. MAKES FOUR TO FIVE QUART (1 L) JARS.

TIP: THIS IS A QUICK METHOD OF MAKING DILL PICKLES AND THESE TEND NOT TO KEEP AS LONG, SO BE SURE TO USE WITHIN 6 MONTHS.

TIP: IF YOU LIKE A LOT OF PICKLES (AND PLAN TO EAT THEM QUICKLY), MAKE MORE SINGLE BATCHES RATHER THAN DOUBLING THE RECIPE. YOU WANT ALL OF THE JARS TO FIT IN THE CANNER IN ONE BATCH SO THEY DON'T COOL DOWN BEFORE PROCESSING.

SERVING SUGGESTIONS: SERVE WITH DELI-STYLE SANDWICHES, BURGERS AND HOT DOGS, CHOP INTO TUNA OR POTATO SALADS, OR MUNCH AS A SNACK WITH A PIECE OF CHEESE.

RECIPE SUGGESTION: USE TO MAKE THE TARTAR SAUCE FOR CRISPY SOLE FINGERS (PAGE 278).

USING PICKLING CUCUMBERS IN PRESERVES

THESE SMALL VARIETIES OF CUCUMBERS ARE GROWN SPECIFICALLY FOR PICKLING. USE CUCUMBERS UP TO ABOUT 6 INCHES (15 CM) IN LENGTH. USE ONLY FIRM CUCUMBERS WITH NO BLEMISHES, SPLITS OR SOFT SPOTS. THE THINNER SKIN ON THESE CUCUMBERS MAKES THEM DETERIORATE FASTER, SO THEY ARE BEST USED WITHIN A DAY OR TWO OF HARVEST. ALWAYS TRIM OFF ABOUT $1/8$ INCH (3 MM) FROM THE BLOSSOM END BEFORE USING, AS THERE IS AN ENZYME IN THE BLOSSOM THAT CAN CAUSE CUCUMBERS TO SOFTEN WHEN PICKLED.

EASY SWEET PICKLES

THESE CLASSIC PICKLES ARE QUICKER TO MAKE THAN MOST SWEET PICKLES AND HAVE A LIGHTLY SPICED SWEET FLAVOR WITH A TOUCH OF TANGINESS.

4 LBS	PICKLING CUCUMBERS	2 KG
4 CUPS	ICE CUBES	1 L
3 TBSP	PICKLING OR CANNING SALT	45 ML
3 1/2 CUPS	PACKED BROWN SUGAR	875 ML
1 TBSP	MUSTARD SEEDS	15 ML
1 TSP	WHOLE ALLSPICE	5 ML
1 TSP	CELERY SEEDS	5 ML
1/4 TSP	WHOLE CLOVES	1 ML
3 CUPS	CIDER VINEGAR	750 ML

SCRUB CUCUMBERS GENTLY UNDER RUNNING WATER. CUT CROSSWISE INTO 3/4-INCH (2 CM) SLICES, TRIMMING OFF 1/8 INCH (3 MM) FROM EACH END. YOU SHOULD HAVE ABOUT 12 CUPS (3 L). IN A LARGE BOWL, COMBINE CUCUMBERS, ICE CUBES AND SALT. ADD COLD WATER TO COVER BY ABOUT 1 INCH (2.5 CM). PLACE A PLATE ON TOP TO WEIGH DOWN CUCUMBERS. COVER AND LET STAND AT A COOL ROOM TEMPERATURE FOR AT LEAST 8 HOURS OR FOR UP TO 18 HOURS.

DRAIN CUCUMBERS AND RINSE WELL. DRAIN AGAIN AND SET ASIDE. IN A LARGE POT, COMBINE BROWN SUGAR, MUSTARD SEEDS, ALLSPICE, CELERY SEEDS, CLOVES AND VINEGAR. BRING TO A BOIL OVER MEDIUM HEAT, STIRRING OFTEN UNTIL SUGAR IS DISSOLVED. BOIL FOR 1 MINUTE. ADD CUCUMBERS AND RETURN TO A BOIL, PRESSING

OCCASIONALLY TO IMMERSE CUCUMBERS IN LIQUID. REMOVE FROM HEAT.

USING A SLOTTED SPOON, PACK CUCUMBERS INTO STERILIZED JARS TO WITHIN 1 INCH (2.5 CM) OF RIM. POUR IN HOT PICKLING LIQUID TO WITHIN $\frac{1}{2}$ INCH (1 CM) OF RIM. REMOVE ANY AIR POCKETS AND ADJUST HEADSPACE, IF NECESSARY, BY ADDING LIQUID; WIPE RIMS. APPLY PREPARED LIDS AND RINGS; TIGHTEN RINGS JUST UNTIL FINGERTIP-TIGHT. PROCESS JARS IN A BOILING WATER CANNER FOR 10 MINUTES (SEE PAGE 27). TURN OFF CANNER AND REMOVE LID. LET JARS STAND IN WATER FOR 5 MINUTES. TRANSFER JARS TO A TOWEL-LINED SURFACE AND LET REST AT ROOM TEMPERATURE UNTIL COOLED. CHECK SEALS; REFRIGERATE ANY UNSEALED JARS FOR UP TO 3 WEEKS. MAKES FOUR TO FIVE PINT (500 ML) JARS.

TIP: FOR AN INTERESTING TEXTURE, USE A CRINKLE CUTTER TO SLICE THE CUCUMBERS.

TIP: USE CUCUMBERS THAT ARE EVENLY SIZED AND LESS THAN 1 INCH (2.5 CM) IN DIAMETER FOR THE BEST TEXTURE.

TIP: DEPENDING ON HOW THESE PICKLES GET PACKED, YOU MAY GET EITHER FOUR OR FIVE PINT (500 ML) JARS. IT'S BEST TO PREPARE AN 8-OUNCE (250 ML) JAR AS WELL, IN CASE YOU DON'T HAVE QUITE ENOUGH FOR THE FIFTH PINT.

LIFE IS TOO SHORT TO EAT RICE CAKES.

B.L.'S BEST MUSTARD PICKLES

A ZESTY, SWEET AND TANGY MIXED PICKLE
TO PRESERVE YOUR GARDEN BOUNTY.

8	LARGE STALKS CELERY	8
2	CUCUMBERS, PEELED AND SEEDED	2
3	LARGE ONIONS	3
1	SMALL CAULIFLOWER	1
6	GREEN TOMATOES	6
1	RED BELL PEPPER	1
1/4 CUP	PICKLING OR CANNING SALT	60 ML
4 CUPS	GRANULATED SUGAR	1 L
1/3 CUP	DRY MUSTARD	75 ML
1 1/2 TSP	GROUND TURMERIC	7 ML
1 TBSP	CELERY SALT	15 ML
1 TBSP	CURRY POWDER	15 ML
1/2 CUP	ALL-PURPOSE FLOUR	125 ML
2 CUPS	WHITE VINEGAR	500 ML
1 CUP	MALT VINEGAR	250 ML

CHOP ALL VEGETABLES INTO SIMILAR-SIZE CHUNKS.
IN A LARGE POT, ROASTING PAN OR BOWL, COMBINE
VEGETABLES AND SALT. COVER AND LET STAND AT ROOM
TEMPERATURE FOR 1 HOUR. DRAIN OFF 2 CUPS (500 ML) OF
THE LIQUID AND DISCARD.

IN A LARGE POT, COMBINE SUGAR, MUSTARD,
TURMERIC, CELERY SALT, CURRY POWDER AND FLOUR.
STIR IN WHITE AND MALT VINEGARS GRADUALLY TO
AVOID LUMPS. BRING TO A BOIL OVER MEDIUM-HIGH HEAT,
STIRRING. REDUCE HEAT AND BOIL GENTLY, STIRRING,

FOR ABOUT 10 MINUTES OR UNTIL THICKENED. ADD VEGETABLES AND REMAINING LIQUID. BOIL FOR 10 MINUTES.

USING A SLOTTED SPOON, PACK VEGETABLES INTO STERILIZED JARS TO WITHIN 1 INCH (2.5 CM) OF RIM. POUR IN HOT PICKLING LIQUID TO WITHIN $\frac{1}{2}$ INCH (1 CM) OF RIM. REMOVE ANY AIR POCKETS AND ADJUST HEADSPACE, IF NECESSARY, BY ADDING LIQUID; WIPE RIMS. APPLY PREPARED LIDS AND RINGS; TIGHTEN RINGS JUST UNTIL FINGERTIP-TIGHT. PROCESS JARS IN A BOILING WATER CANNER FOR 15 MINUTES (SEE PAGE 27). TURN OFF CANNER AND REMOVE LID. LET JARS STAND IN WATER FOR 5 MINUTES. TRANSFER JARS TO A TOWEL-LINED SURFACE AND LET REST AT ROOM TEMPERATURE UNTIL COOLED. CHECK SEALS; REFRIGERATE ANY UNSEALED JARS FOR UP TO 3 WEEKS. MAKES FIVE TO SIX PINT (500 ML) JARS.

SERVING SUGGESTIONS: SERVE WITH CURED MEATS, CHEESES AND CRUSTY BREAD FOR A TRADITIONAL PUB LUNCH, OR AS A SALAD WITH BURGERS OR HOT DOGS.

USING FIELD CUCUMBERS IN PRESERVES

LOOK FOR FIELD CUCUMBERS THAT HAVEN'T BEEN WAXED. CHOOSE SMALL OR MEDIUM CUCUMBERS THAT FEEL HEAVY FOR THEIR SIZE. IF YOU USE WAXED CUCUMBERS, PEEL THEM BEFORE CHOPPING. CUT FIELD CUCUMBERS IN HALF LENGTHWISE AND SCOOP OUT THE TOUGH SEEDS BEFORE CHOPPING.

CLASSIC ICICLE PICKLES

THESE PICKLES ARE A CLASSIC TO BE ENJOYED.

3 LBS	3½- TO 4-INCH (8.5 TO 10 CM) PICKLING CUCUMBERS	1.5 KG
4 CUPS	ICE CUBES	1 L
1½ CUPS	GRANULATED SUGAR	375 ML
¼ CUP	PICKLING OR CANNING SALT	60 ML
6 CUPS	WHITE VINEGAR	1.5 L
1½ CUPS	WATER	375 ML
½ CUP	FINELY CHOPPED ONION	125 ML
	MUSTARD SEEDS	
	CELERY SEEDS	
14	CELERY STICKS (EACH 3 BY ½ INCH/ 7.5 BY 1 CM)	14

SCRUB CUCUMBERS GENTLY UNDER RUNNING WATER. TRIM OFF ⅛ INCH (3 MM) FROM EACH END AND CUT CUCUMBERS LENGTHWISE INTO QUARTERS. IN A LARGE BOWL, LAYER CUCUMBERS AND ICE CUBES, USING ABOUT ONE-QUARTER OF EACH PER LAYER. ADD COLD WATER TO COVER BY ABOUT 1 INCH (2.5 CM). PLACE A PLATE ON TOP TO WEIGH DOWN CUCUMBERS. COVER AND LET STAND AT A COOL ROOM TEMPERATURE FOR 3 HOURS.

DRAIN CUCUMBERS. SET ASIDE. IN A POT, COMBINE SUGAR, SALT, VINEGAR AND 1½ CUPS (375 ML) WATER. BRING TO A BOIL OVER MEDIUM HEAT, STIRRING OFTEN UNTIL SUGAR AND SALT ARE DISSOLVED. BOIL FOR 5 MINUTES. REDUCE HEAT TO LOW AND KEEP LIQUID HOT.

PLACE A HEAPING TABLESPOON (15 ML) OF ONION, ½ TSP (2 ML) MUSTARD SEEDS AND ¼ TSP (1 ML) CELERY

SEEDS IN EACH STERILIZED JAR. PACK CUCUMBERS AND 2 CELERY STICKS INTO JAR, LEAVING 1 INCH (2.5 CM) HEADSPACE. POUR IN HOT PICKLING LIQUID TO WITHIN $1/2$ INCH (1 CM) OF RIM. REMOVE ANY AIR POCKETS AND ADJUST HEADSPACE, IF NECESSARY, BY ADDING LIQUID; WIPE RIMS. APPLY PREPARED LIDS AND RINGS; TIGHTEN RINGS JUST UNTIL FINGERTIP-TIGHT. PROCESS JARS IN A BOILING WATER CANNER FOR 10 MINUTES (SEE PAGE 27). TURN OFF CANNER AND REMOVE LID. LET JARS STAND IN WATER FOR 5 MINUTES. TRANSFER JARS TO A TOWEL-LINED SURFACE AND LET REST AT ROOM TEMPERATURE UNTIL COOLED. CHECK SEALS; REFRIGERATE ANY UNSEALED JARS FOR UP TO 3 WEEKS. MAKES ABOUT SEVEN PINT (500 ML) JARS.

TIP: TO KEEP CUCUMBER SPEARS UPRIGHT WHEN PACKING THEM INTO JARS, HOLD THE JAR WITH ONE HAND IN A SILICONE OVEN MITT, OR WITH A DRY TOWEL, AND TILT THE JAR TOWARD YOU AT ABOUT A 45-DEGREE ANGLE. USE THE OTHER HAND OR SILICONE-COATED TONGS TO PLACE THE SPEARS UPRIGHT IN THE JAR, LEANING AGAINST THE BOTTOM INSIDE WALL. GENTLY SHAKE THE JAR ON THE ANGLE ONCE IT'S FULL TO HELP THE PIECES SETTLE, ADDING MORE IF NECESSARY.

SERVING SUGGESTION: SERVE ALONGSIDE DELI SANDWICHES, BURGERS OR HOT DOGS.

RECIPE SUGGESTION: CHOP THESE PICKLES INTO COLESLAW TO ADD TANG.

CLASSIC PICKLED ASPARAGUS

THE CRISPNESS AND TANG MAKE THESE
PICKLED SPEARS WONDERFUL TO ADD TO
A SALAD OR TO EAT ON THEIR OWN.

4 LBS	ASPARAGUS	2 KG
1/4 CUP	GRANULATED SUGAR	60 ML
2 TBSP	PICKLING OR CANNING SALT	30 ML
3 1/2 CUPS	WHITE VINEGAR	875 ML
2 1/2 CUPS	WATER	625 ML
4	CLOVES GARLIC, HALVED	4
	MUSTARD SEEDS	

CUT TIP ENDS OF ASPARAGUS INTO LENGTHS ABOUT
3/4 INCH (2 CM) SHORTER THAN THE HEIGHT OF JARS.
RESERVE BOTTOM ENDS FOR ANOTHER USE. IN A
LARGE POT OF BOILING SALTED WATER, IN BATCHES AS
NECESSARY, BLANCH ASPARAGUS SPEARS FOR ABOUT
30 SECONDS OR UNTIL BRIGHT GREEN. IMMEDIATELY
PLUNGE INTO A LARGE BOWL OR SINK OF ICE WATER AND
LET STAND UNTIL WELL CHILLED, REFRESHING WATER AS
NECESSARY TO KEEP COLD, FOR AT LEAST 30 MINUTES
OR FOR UP TO 1 HOUR.

REMOVE ASPARAGUS FROM WATER AND SPREAD OUT
ON BAKING SHEETS OR TRAYS LINED WITH LINT-FREE
TOWELS TO DRAIN. IN A LARGE POT, COMBINE SUGAR,
SALT, VINEGAR AND WATER. BRING TO A BOIL OVER
MEDIUM-HIGH HEAT, STIRRING OFTEN UNTIL SUGAR AND
SALT ARE DISSOLVED. BOIL FOR 1 MINUTE. ADD ASPARAGUS
AND SIMMER UNTIL HEATED THROUGH. REMOVE
FROM HEAT.

PLACE 2 GARLIC HALVES AND $\frac{1}{2}$ TSP (2 ML) MUSTARD SEEDS IN EACH STERILIZED JAR. CAREFULLY PACK ASPARAGUS, TIPS DOWN, INTO JARS, LEAVING ROOM FOR LIQUID. POUR IN HOT PICKLING LIQUID TO WITHIN $\frac{1}{2}$ INCH (1 CM) OF RIM. REMOVE ANY AIR POCKETS AND ADJUST HEADSPACE, IF NECESSARY, BY ADDING LIQUID; WIPE RIMS. APPLY PREPARED LIDS AND RINGS; TIGHTEN RINGS JUST UNTIL FINGERTIP-TIGHT. PROCESS JARS IN A BOILING WATER CANNER FOR 10 MINUTES (SEE PAGE 27). TURN OFF CANNER AND REMOVE LID. LET JARS STAND IN WATER FOR 5 MINUTES. TRANSFER JARS TO A TOWEL-LINED SURFACE AND LET REST AT ROOM TEMPERATURE UNTIL COOLED. CHECK SEALS; REFRIGERATE ANY UNSEALED JARS FOR UP TO 3 WEEKS. MAKES ABOUT FOUR PINT (500 ML) JARS.

TIP: FOR THE BEST TEXTURE WHEN PICKLING, CHOOSE MEDIUM-SIZE SPEARS OF ASPARAGUS, ABOUT $\frac{1}{2}$ INCH (1 CM) THICK.

TIP: SILICONE-COATED TONGS WORK WELL TO HANDLE THE HOT ASPARAGUS WHEN PACKING THE JARS. BE GENTLE WITH THE SPEARS SO THE TIPS DON'T GET CRUSHED.

SERVING SUGGESTIONS: SERVE ON A NIÇOISE-STYLE OR COBB SALAD, OR AS A COLD SIDE DISH FOR GRILLED FISH.

WHEN IT COMES TO DIETING,
REMEMBER ONE SIMPLE RULE:
IF YOU CAN'T LOSE IT, DECORATE IT.

SWEET AND TANGY GREEN BEANS

CAPTURE THAT BUMPER CROP OF GREEN BEANS
IN THIS SWEET, LIGHTLY SPICED PICKLE TO ENJOY
WELL AFTER THE SUMMER HARVEST.

3	STICKS CINNAMON (EACH 3 INCHES/ 7.5 CM LONG), BROKEN IN HALF	3
2½ CUPS	GRANULATED SUGAR	625 ML
2 TBSP	PICKLING OR CANNING SALT	30 ML
2 TBSP	MUSTARD SEEDS	30 ML
1 TBSP	CELERY SEEDS	15 ML
1 TSP	WHOLE ALLSPICE	5 ML
5 CUPS	CIDER VINEGAR	1.25 L
1½ CUPS	WATER	375 ML
3 LBS	GREEN BEANS, STEMS TRIMMED	1.5 KG

IN A LARGE POT, COMBINE CINNAMON STICKS, SUGAR, SALT, MUSTARD SEEDS, CELERY SEEDS, ALLSPICE, VINEGAR AND WATER. BRING TO A BOIL OVER MEDIUM HEAT, STIRRING OFTEN UNTIL SUGAR AND SALT ARE DISSOLVED. INCREASE HEAT TO MEDIUM-HIGH. ADD BEANS AND RETURN TO A BOIL, PRESSING OCCASIONALLY TO IMMERSE BEANS IN LIQUID. REMOVE FROM HEAT.

PLACE HALF A CINNAMON STICK IN EACH STERILIZED JAR. ADD BEANS, PACKING LIGHTLY BUT LEAVING ROOM FOR LIQUID AND LEAVING 1 INCH (2.5 CM) HEADSPACE. POUR IN HOT PICKLING LIQUID TO WITHIN ½ INCH (1 CM) OF RIM. REMOVE ANY AIR POCKETS AND ADJUST HEADSPACE, IF NECESSARY, BY ADDING LIQUID; WIPE RIMS. APPLY PREPARED LIDS AND RINGS; TIGHTEN RINGS JUST UNTIL FINGERTIP-TIGHT. PROCESS JARS IN A BOILING WATER CANNER

FOR 10 MINUTES (SEE PAGE 27). TURN OFF CANNER AND REMOVE LID. LET JARS STAND IN WATER FOR 5 MINUTES. TRANSFER JARS TO A TOWEL-LINED SURFACE AND LET REST AT ROOM TEMPERATURE UNTIL COOLED. CHECK SEALS; REFRIGERATE ANY UNSEALED JARS FOR UP TO 3 WEEKS. MAKES ABOUT SIX PINT (500 ML) JARS.

TIP: SILICONE-COATED TONGS WORK WELL TO HANDLE THE HOT BEANS WHEN PACKING THE JARS.

TIP: SIX QUARTS (6 L) OF GREEN BEANS WILL GIVE YOU ABOUT 3 LBS (1.5 KG).

SERVING SUGGESTIONS: SERVE ALONGSIDE GRILLED CHEESE SANDWICHES, OR AS A STIR-STICK GARNISH IN A COCKTAIL.

RECIPE SUGGESTION: MIX PICKLED BEANS AND LIQUID WITH CANNED KIDNEY AND WHITE BEANS FOR A SUPER-EASY THREE-BEAN SALAD.

USING GREEN BEANS IN PRESERVES

USE THE FRESHEST BEANS POSSIBLE, AS THEY TEND TO WILT QUICKLY AFTER HARVEST. LOOK FOR MATURE BEANS THAT ARE CRISPY BUT NOT WOODY OR STRINGY. TRIM OFF THE STEM END JUST BEFORE USING.

CLASSIC PICKLED BEET SLICES

BEETS ARE CERTAINLY THE STARS HERE — THEIR NATURAL SWEETNESS AND RICH FLAVOR COME THROUGH IN THIS SIMPLE PICKLE.

6 LBS	BEETS (SEE TIP, OPPOSITE)	3 KG
1 1/3 CUPS	GRANULATED SUGAR	325 ML
2 TSP	PICKLING OR CANNING SALT	10 ML
4 CUPS	WHITE VINEGAR	1 L
2 CUPS	WATER	500 ML

TRIM BEETS AND PLACE IN A LARGE POT (SEE TIP, OPPOSITE). COVER WITH COLD WATER AND BRING TO A BOIL OVER HIGH HEAT. REDUCE HEAT AND BOIL GENTLY FOR ABOUT 40 MINUTES OR UNTIL FORK-TENDER. IMMEDIATELY PLUNGE INTO A LARGE BOWL OR SINK OF COLD WATER AND LET STAND UNTIL WELL CHILLED, REFRESHING WATER AS NECESSARY TO KEEP COLD, FOR AT LEAST 30 MINUTES OR FOR UP TO 1 HOUR. PEEL OFF SKINS AND CUT BEETS CROSSWISE INTO 1/4-INCH (0.5 CM) SLICES. SET ASIDE.

IN A CLEAN LARGE POT, COMBINE SUGAR, SALT, VINEGAR AND WATER. BRING TO A BOIL OVER MEDIUM HEAT, STIRRING OFTEN UNTIL SUGAR AND SALT ARE DISSOLVED. BOIL FOR 1 MINUTE. INCREASE HEAT TO MEDIUM-HIGH, ADD BEETS AND RETURN TO A BOIL. REMOVE FROM HEAT.

USING A SLOTTED SPOON, PACK BEETS INTO STERILIZED JARS, LEAVING ABOUT 1 INCH (2.5 CM) HEADSPACE. POUR IN HOT PICKLING LIQUID TO WITHIN 1/2 INCH (1 CM) OF RIM. REMOVE ANY AIR POCKETS AND

ADJUST HEADSPACE, IF NECESSARY, BY ADDING LIQUID; WIPE RIMS. APPLY PREPARED LIDS AND RINGS; TIGHTEN RINGS JUST UNTIL FINGERTIP-TIGHT. PROCESS JARS IN A BOILING WATER CANNER FOR 30 MINUTES (SEE PAGE 27). TURN OFF CANNER AND REMOVE LID. LET JARS STAND IN WATER FOR 5 MINUTES. TRANSFER JARS TO A TOWEL-LINED SURFACE AND LET REST AT ROOM TEMPERATURE UNTIL COOLED. CHECK SEALS; REFRIGERATE ANY UNSEALED JARS FOR UP TO 3 WEEKS. MAKES ABOUT SEVEN PINT (500 ML) JARS.

TIP: MEDIUM BEETS, 2 TO $2\frac{1}{2}$ INCHES (5 TO 6 CM) IN DIAMETER, WORK BEST BECAUSE THEY ARE LESS TEDIOUS TO PEEL AND SLICE THAN SMALL BEETS AND THE SLICES FIT NICELY IN THE MOUTH OF THE CANNING JARS. IF YOU HAVE LARGER BEETS, CUT THE SLICES INTO HALF-MOONS, CUT LENGTHWISE IN WEDGES SO THEY FIT BETTER OR USE WIDE-MOUTH CANNING JARS.

TIP: IF YOU HAVE TWO LARGE POTS, COOK THE BEETS IN TWO BATCHES FOR BETTER CONTROL AND EVEN COOKING.

VARIATION
PICKLED BEETS WITH ONIONS: REDUCE BEETS TO $5\frac{1}{2}$ LBS (2.75 KG) AND ADD 1 LB (500 G) ONIONS (ABOUT 4), HALVED AND THINLY SLICED, WITH THE SUGAR.

SERVING SUGGESTIONS: SERVE WITH TRADITIONAL TOURTIÈRE OR ANOTHER MEAT PIE, ALONGSIDE HAMBURGERS OR ON TOP OF A GREEN SALAD WITH SOME BLUE CHEESE.

DILL PICKLED CARROT STICKS

THESE ARE AMONG THE EASIEST PICKLES
TO MAKE, AND YOU'LL BE DELIGHTED WITH
WHAT THE DILLY TASTE AND TANGY CRUNCH
DO TO A HUMBLE CARROT STICK.

3½ LBS	CARROTS (15 TO 20)	1.75 KG
⅓ CUP	GRANULATED SUGAR	75 ML
2 TBSP	PICKLING OR CANNING SALT	30 ML
6 CUPS	WHITE VINEGAR	1.5 L
2¾ CUPS	WATER	675 ML
6	DILL HEADS	6
6	DILL SPRIGS	6
	DILL SEEDS	

CUT CARROTS INTO 4- BY ½- BY ½-INCH (10 BY 1 BY
1 CM) STICKS, OR THE LENGTH THAT WILL FIT IN JARS
ALLOWING FOR 1 INCH (2.5 CM) HEADSPACE. SET ASIDE.
IN A POT, COMBINE SUGAR, SALT, VINEGAR AND WATER.
BRING TO A BOIL OVER MEDIUM-HIGH HEAT, STIRRING
OFTEN UNTIL SUGAR AND SALT ARE DISSOLVED. BOIL FOR
1 MINUTE. REDUCE HEAT TO LOW AND KEEP LIQUID HOT.

PLACE 1 DILL HEAD, 1 DILL SPRIG AND ¼ TSP (1 ML)
DILL SEEDS IN EACH STERILIZED JAR. PACK CARROT
STICKS INTO JAR, LEAVING ROOM FOR LIQUID. POUR IN
HOT PICKLING LIQUID TO WITHIN ½ INCH (1 CM) OF RIM.
REMOVE ANY AIR POCKETS AND ADJUST HEADSPACE,
IF NECESSARY, BY ADDING LIQUID; WIPE RIMS. APPLY
PREPARED LIDS AND RINGS; TIGHTEN RINGS JUST UNTIL
FINGERTIP-TIGHT. PROCESS JARS IN A BOILING WATER
CANNER FOR 10 MINUTES (SEE PAGE 27). TURN OFF

CANNER AND REMOVE LID. LET JARS STAND IN WATER FOR 5 MINUTES. TRANSFER JARS TO A TOWEL-LINED SURFACE AND LET REST AT ROOM TEMPERATURE UNTIL COOLED. CHECK SEALS; REFRIGERATE ANY UNSEALED JARS FOR UP TO 3 WEEKS. MAKES ABOUT SIX PINT (500 ML) JARS.

TIP: WHEN CUTTING THE CARROTS, IT IS EASIEST TO CUT THEM CROSSWISE INTO 4-INCH (10 CM) LENGTHS AND THEN INTO STICKS. YOU MAY JUST NEED TO CUT THE NARROW END OF THE CARROT IN HALF LENGTHWISE; IT'S OKAY NOT TO HAVE SQUARED-OFF STICKS.

TIP: AVOID VERY LARGE CARROTS, WHICH OFTEN HAVE A WOODY CORE AND MAKE UNPLEASANT PICKLES.

TIP: THE COMBINATION OF DILL SPRIGS, DILL HEADS AND DILL SEEDS GIVES THESE PICKLES A GOOD DILLY FLAVOR. IF YOU DON'T HAVE DILL HEADS, USE 2 LARGE DILL SPRIGS PER JAR.

SERVING SUGGESTION: SERVE ON A CRUDITÉ PLATTER OR ALONGSIDE DELI-STYLE SANDWICHES.

RECIPE SUGGESTION: CHOP INTO COLESLAW OR OTHER HEARTY GREEN SALADS.

USING CARROTS IN PRESERVES

PEEL AND TRIM THE ENDS BEFORE CHOPPING OR SHREDDING. SMALL OR MEDIUM-SIZE CARROTS ARE BEST, AS VERY LARGE CARROTS CAN HAVE WOODY CORES AND A SPONGY TEXTURE THAT MAKES FOR SOFT PICKLES.

CLASSIC PICKLED GARLIC

THE CLASSIC FRENCH SEASONING MAKES THE GARLIC AS DELICIOUS ON ITS OWN AS IT IS IN RECIPES.

7 CUPS	GARLIC CLOVES (ABOUT 21 HEADS), BLANCHED AND PEELED	1.75 L
5	EACH BAY LEAVES AND SPRIGS THYME	5
5	1-INCH (2.5 CM) PIECES ROSEMARY SPRIGS	5
1 TBSP	BLACK PEPPERCORNS	15 ML
2 TBSP	GRANULATED SUGAR	30 ML
1 TSP	PICKLING OR CANNING SALT	5 ML
3 CUPS	WHITE WINE VINEGAR	750 ML
1 CUP	DRY WHITE WINE	250 ML

PLACE BAY LEAVES, THYME, ROSEMARY AND PEPPERCORNS IN THE CENTER OF A SQUARE OF TRIPLE-LAYERED CHEESECLOTH AND TIE INTO A SPICE BAG. IN A LARGE POT, COMBINE SPICE BAG, SUGAR, SALT, VINEGAR AND WINE. BRING TO A BOIL OVER MEDIUM-HIGH HEAT, STIRRING OFTEN UNTIL SUGAR AND SALT ARE DISSOLVED. ADD GARLIC AND RETURN TO A BOIL. BOIL FOR 1 MINUTE. REMOVE FROM HEAT AND LET COOL. COVER AND LET STAND AT A COOL ROOM TEMPERATURE FOR AT LEAST 12 HOURS OR FOR UP TO 24 HOURS.

REMOVE SPICE BAG FROM GARLIC MIXTURE, SQUEEZING OUT EXCESS LIQUID. UNTIE BAG AND RESERVE HERBS AND SPICES. RETURN GARLIC MIXTURE TO MEDIUM HEAT AND BRING TO A BOIL. BOIL FOR 1 MINUTE. REMOVE FROM HEAT.

DIVIDE RESERVED HERBS AND SPICES EVENLY AMONG STERILIZED JARS, BREAKING SMALL PIECES OFF TO ADD TO SIXTH JAR IF NECESSARY. USING A SLOTTED

SPOON, PACK GARLIC INTO JARS, LEAVING ROOM FOR LIQUID AND LEAVING 1 INCH (2.5 CM) HEADSPACE. POUR IN HOT PICKLING LIQUID TO WITHIN $\frac{1}{2}$ INCH (1 CM) OF RIM. REMOVE ANY AIR POCKETS AND ADJUST HEADSPACE, IF NECESSARY, BY ADDING LIQUID; WIPE RIMS. APPLY PREPARED LIDS AND RINGS; TIGHTEN RINGS JUST UNTIL FINGERTIP-TIGHT. PROCESS JARS IN A BOILING WATER CANNER FOR 10 MINUTES (SEE PAGE 27). TURN OFF CANNER AND REMOVE LID. LET JARS STAND IN WATER FOR 5 MINUTES. TRANSFER JARS TO A TOWEL-LINED SURFACE AND LET REST AT ROOM TEMPERATURE UNTIL COOLED. CHECK SEALS; REFRIGERATE ANY UNSEALED JARS FOR UP TO 3 WEEKS. MAKES FIVE TO SIX 8-OUNCE (250 ML) JARS.

TIP: YOU CAN OFTEN FIND PEELED GARLIC CLOVES IN CONTAINERS OR BAGS IN THE PRODUCE SECTION AT SUPERMARKETS AND WAREHOUSE STORES. THESE CERTAINLY SAVE A LOT OF TIME AND EFFORT, BUT BE SURE THEY ARE VERY FRESH. RINSE AND DRAIN THEM WELL AND TRIM OFF THE TOUGH ROOT END BEFORE ADDING.

TIP: THE GARLIC MAY TURN BLUE IN THE PICKLING LIQUID. IT'S PERFECTLY SAFE TO EAT; THE COLOR CHANGE IS JUST A REACTION BETWEEN THE MINERALS IN THE GARLIC AND THE ACID FROM THE VINEGAR.

SERVING SUGGESTION: SERVE WITH MEATS OR CHEESES ON AN APPETIZER PLATTER.

RECIPE SUGGESTION: USE IN PLACE OF FRESH GARLIC IN A PASTA SAUCE OR SOUP, ADDING SOME OF THE PICKLING LIQUID IN PLACE OF ANY WINE OR VINEGAR IN THE RECIPE.

PICKLED HOT PEPPER RINGS

*FIERY PEPPERS ARE THE STARS IN
THESE SIMPLE PICKLES. THEY'LL SPICE UP ANY
SUMMER BARBECUE OR WINTER SANDWICH.*

2 LBS	HOT BANANA PEPPERS (ABOUT 12)	1 KG
1½ LBS	CAYENNE PEPPERS (ABOUT 18)	750 G
4 TSP	PICKLING OR CANNING SALT	20 ML
6½ CUPS	WHITE VINEGAR	1.625 L
2 CUPS	WATER	500 ML

TRIM OFF STEMS AND CUT OUT SEEDS FROM BANANA
AND CAYENNE PEPPERS, KEEPING PEPPERS INTACT. CUT
CROSSWISE INTO ¼-INCH (0.5 CM) SLICES. YOU SHOULD
HAVE ABOUT 14 CUPS (3.5 L) TOTAL. SET ASIDE. IN A POT,
COMBINE SALT, VINEGAR AND WATER. BRING TO A BOIL
OVER MEDIUM-HIGH HEAT, STIRRING OFTEN UNTIL SALT IS
DISSOLVED. BOIL FOR 1 MINUTE. REDUCE HEAT TO LOW AND
KEEP LIQUID HOT.

PACK PEPPERS INTO STERILIZED JARS, LEAVING ROOM
FOR LIQUID AND LEAVING 1 INCH (2.5 CM) HEADSPACE. POUR
IN HOT PICKLING LIQUID TO WITHIN ½ INCH (1 CM) OF RIM.
REMOVE ANY AIR POCKETS AND ADJUST HEADSPACE,
IF NECESSARY, BY ADDING LIQUID; WIPE RIMS. APPLY
PREPARED LIDS AND RINGS; TIGHTEN RINGS JUST UNTIL
FINGERTIP-TIGHT. PROCESS JARS IN A BOILING WATER
CANNER FOR 10 MINUTES (SEE PAGE 27). TURN OFF
CANNER AND REMOVE LID. LET JARS STAND IN WATER FOR
5 MINUTES. TRANSFER JARS TO A TOWEL-LINED SURFACE
AND LET REST AT ROOM TEMPERATURE UNTIL COOLED.

CHECK SEALS; REFRIGERATE ANY UNSEALED JARS FOR UP TO 3 WEEKS. MAKES ABOUT SIX PINT (500 ML) JARS.

TIP: CHOOSE FIRM, SHINY PEPPERS THAT FEEL LIGHT FOR THEIR SIZE. HEAVY ONES TEND TO BE FULL OF SEEDS AND HAVE THICK MEMBRANES THAT NEED TO BE CUT OUT.

TIP: CAYENNE PEPPERS ARE RED, LONG, OFTEN CURVED OR CURLED, AND ABOUT I INCH (2.5 CM) IN DIAMETER AT THE STEM.

SERVING SUGGESTIONS: SERVE ON TOP OF GRILLED SAUSAGES, HOT DOGS OR BURGERS, OR TO SPICE UP SUBMARINE SANDWICHES.

USING FRESH CHILE PEPPERS IN PRESERVES

FRESH CHILE PEPPERS, SUCH AS JALAPEÑOS, HABANEROS, SCOTCH BONNETS, THAI AND SO ON, CAN ALL BE USED TO ADD HOTNESS TO CHUTNEYS AND JELLIES. HANDLE CAREFULLY, WEARING GLOVES, AND REMOVE INNER SEEDS AND MEMBRANES BEFORE CHOPPING. FOR PRESERVES, IT IS BEST TO REMOVE THE SEEDS FROM CHILE PEPPERS BEFORE CHOPPING, AS THEY TEND TO ADD A BITTER FLAVOR WHEN COOKED FOR A LONG TIME. CHIPOTLE PEPPERS (SMOKED JALAPEÑOS) ARE ALSO AVAILABLE, USUALLY CANNED IN ADOBO SAUCE.

SWEET AND HOT PICKLED RAINBOW PEPPERS

IF YOU'VE PICKED A PECK OF PEPPERS, THIS IS THE RECIPE TO MAKE! WELL, IT DOESN'T USE A WHOLE PECK, BUT YOU CAN MAKE A SECOND OR THIRD BATCH.

I LB	YELLOW WAX (HOT BANANA) PEPPERS (ABOUT 6)	500 G
I LB	SWEET RED SHEPHERD AND/ OR BANANA PEPPERS (ABOUT 5)	500 G
I LB	CUBANELLE PEPPERS (ABOUT 4)	500 G
8 OZ	CAYENNE PEPPERS (ABOUT 6)	250 G
1/3 CUP	GRANULATED SUGAR	75 ML
I TBSP	PICKLING OR CANNING SALT	15 ML
5 CUPS	WHITE VINEGAR	1.25 L
3 1/3 CUPS	WATER	825 ML

TRIM OFF STEMS AND CUT OUT SEEDS FROM HOT BANANA, SWEET BANANA, CUBANELLE AND CAYENNE PEPPERS, KEEPING PEPPERS INTACT. CUT CROSSWISE INTO 1/4-INCH (0.5 CM) SLICES. YOU SHOULD HAVE ABOUT 14 CUPS (3.5 L) TOTAL. SET ASIDE. IN A POT, COMBINE SUGAR, SALT, VINEGAR AND WATER. BRING TO A BOIL OVER MEDIUM-HIGH HEAT, STIRRING OFTEN UNTIL SUGAR AND SALT ARE DISSOLVED. BOIL FOR I MINUTE. REDUCE HEAT TO LOW AND KEEP LIQUID HOT.

PACK PEPPERS INTO STERILIZED JARS, LEAVING ROOM FOR LIQUID AND LEAVING I INCH (2.5 CM) HEADSPACE. POUR IN HOT PICKLING LIQUID TO WITHIN 1/2 INCH (I CM) OF RIM. REMOVE ANY AIR POCKETS AND ADJUST HEADSPACE, IF NECESSARY, BY ADDING LIQUID; WIPE RIMS. APPLY

PREPARED LIDS AND RINGS; TIGHTEN RINGS JUST UNTIL FINGERTIP-TIGHT. PROCESS JARS IN A BOILING WATER CANNER FOR 10 MINUTES (SEE PAGE 27). TURN OFF CANNER AND REMOVE LID. LET JARS STAND IN WATER FOR 5 MINUTES. TRANSFER JARS TO A TOWEL-LINED SURFACE AND LET REST AT ROOM TEMPERATURE UNTIL COOLED. CHECK SEALS; REFRIGERATE ANY UNSEALED JARS FOR UP TO 3 WEEKS. MAKES ABOUT SIX PINT (500 ML) JARS.

TIP: SHEPHERD PEPPERS ARE SWEET LIKE BELL PEPPERS BUT ARE LONGER AND NARROWER AND HAVE A THINNER SKIN AND FLESH THAT ARE NICE IN THESE PICKLES.

TIP: YELLOW WAX PEPPERS ARE OFTEN LABELED AS HOT BANANA PEPPERS. THEY LOOK VERY SIMILAR TO SWEET BANANA PEPPERS, SO IT'S BEST TO TASTE A SMALL PIECE TO MAKE SURE YOU HAVE HOT PEPPERS.

TIP: TO AVOID BURNS, WEAR DISPOSABLE RUBBER GLOVES WHEN HANDLING HOT PEPPERS AND BE SURE TO WASH ALL UTENSILS AND THE CUTTING BOARD WELL AFTER PREPARING THE PEPPERS.

SERVING SUGGESTION: SPICE UP YOUR SANDWICHES, BURGERS AND HOT DOGS WITH THESE PEPPERS.

RECIPE SUGGESTION: ADD THESE PEPPERS TO A POTATO SALAD OR BEAN SALAD FOR SOME ZIP.

I ALWAYS HAVE LOTS TO SAY.
I JUST DON'T ALWAYS HAVE TO SAY IT.

SWEET AND TANGY ZUCCHINI PICKLES

THIS IS A TERRIFIC WAY TO USE UP THIS VIGOROUS VEGETABLE WHEN YOU TIRE OF ZUCCHINI LOAF!

5 LBS	ZUCCHINI (1 TO 1½ INCHES/ 2.5 TO 4 CM IN DIAMETER)	2.5 KG
¼ CUP	PICKLING OR CANNING SALT	60 ML
2½ CUPS	GRANULATED SUGAR	625 ML
1 TBSP	PICKLING SPICE	15 ML
1 TBSP	MUSTARD SEEDS	15 ML
1 TSP	CELERY SEEDS	5 ML
5 CUPS	CIDER VINEGAR	1.25 L

TRIM ENDS FROM ZUCCHINI AND CUT CROSSWISE INTO ¼-INCH (0.5 CM) SLICES. YOU SHOULD HAVE ABOUT 15 CUPS (3.75 L). IN A LARGE BOWL, LAYER ZUCCHINI AND SALT, USING ABOUT ONE-QUARTER OF EACH PER LAYER. PLACE A PLATE ON TOP TO WEIGH DOWN ZUCCHINI. COVER AND LET STAND AT A COOL ROOM TEMPERATURE FOR 3 HOURS OR UNTIL ZUCCHINI IS WILTED AND LIQUID IS RELEASED.

DRAIN ZUCCHINI AND RINSE WELL. DRAIN AGAIN. SPREAD OUT ON BAKING SHEETS OR TRAYS LINED WITH LINT-FREE TOWELS TO DRAIN FOR AT LEAST 30 MINUTES OR FOR UP TO 1 HOUR.

IN A LARGE POT, COMBINE SUGAR, PICKLING SPICE, MUSTARD SEEDS, CELERY SEEDS AND VINEGAR. BRING TO A BOIL OVER MEDIUM HEAT, STIRRING OFTEN UNTIL SUGAR IS DISSOLVED. COVER, REDUCE HEAT TO LOW AND SIMMER FOR 5 MINUTES OR UNTIL LIQUID IS FLAVORFUL.

INCREASE HEAT TO MEDIUM-HIGH. ADD ZUCCHINI AND RETURN TO A SIMMER. REDUCE HEAT AND SIMMER FOR ABOUT 10 MINUTES OR UNTIL ZUCCHINI IS TRANSLUCENT. REMOVE FROM HEAT.

USING A SLOTTED SPOON, PACK ZUCCHINI INTO STERILIZED JARS, LEAVING 1 INCH (2.5 CM) HEADSPACE. POUR IN HOT PICKLING LIQUID TO WITHIN $\frac{1}{2}$ INCH (1 CM) OF RIM. REMOVE ANY AIR POCKETS AND ADJUST HEADSPACE, IF NECESSARY, BY ADDING LIQUID; WIPE RIMS. APPLY PREPARED LIDS AND RINGS; TIGHTEN RINGS JUST UNTIL FINGERTIP-TIGHT. PROCESS JARS IN A BOILING WATER CANNER FOR 10 MINUTES (SEE PAGE 27). TURN OFF CANNER AND REMOVE LID. LET JARS STAND IN WATER FOR 5 MINUTES. TRANSFER JARS TO A TOWEL-LINED SURFACE AND LET REST AT ROOM TEMPERATURE UNTIL COOLED. CHECK SEALS; REFRIGERATE ANY UNSEALED JARS FOR UP TO 3 WEEKS. MAKES ABOUT FIVE PINT (500 ML) JARS.

TIP: ABOUT 14 MEDIUM ZUCCHINI WILL GIVE YOU 5 LBS (2.5 KG).

RECIPE SUGGESTION: ADD ZUCCHINI TO A PASTA SALAD OR A HOT PASTA, USING SOME OF THE LIQUID FOR THE DRESSING OR SAUCE.

I VOW NEVER TO WEAR A FLANNEL NIGHTGOWN IF YOU PROMISE NEVER TO DO A COMB-OVER.

243

Sauces and Salsas

Sauces are, in general, among the easiest preserves to make. If you can chop, measure and boil, you can make a sauce. They may take a little more time than other preserves, but much of that is spent boiling the ingredients on the stove, and the only effort required during that time is stirring. That stage has the benefit of the soothing bubbling sound and the glorious aroma that fills the house, so an hour or two really doesn't seem all that bad.

HOT AND SWEET MUSTARD

A MARVELOUS GIFT FOR YOUR CHRISTMAS EXCHANGE.

1 CUP	DRY MUSTARD	250 ML
3/4 CUP	GRANULATED SUGAR	175 ML
1/2 CUP	MUSTARD SEEDS	125 ML
1 TSP	SALT	5 ML
1/4 TSP	GROUND WHITE PEPPER	1 ML
1/4 TSP	CAYENNE PEPPER	1 ML
1 1/2 CUPS	DRY WHITE WINE	375 ML
1/2 CUP	WHITE WINE VINEGAR OR WHITE VINEGAR	125 ML

IN A MEDIUM SAUCEPAN, COMBINE DRY MUSTARD, SUGAR, MUSTARD SEEDS, SALT, PEPPER AND CAYENNE. GRADUALLY POUR IN WINE AND VINEGAR, WHISKING TO COMBINE. BRING TO A BOIL OVER MEDIUM HEAT, STIRRING CONSTANTLY.

REDUCE HEAT AND BOIL FOR 1 MINUTE, STIRRING
CONSTANTLY, UNTIL SLIGHTLY THICKENED.

LADLE INTO STERILIZED JARS TO WITHIN $\frac{1}{2}$ INCH
(1 CM) OF RIM. REMOVE ANY AIR POCKETS AND ADJUST
HEADSPACE, IF NECESSARY, BY ADDING HOT MUSTARD;
WIPE RIMS. APPLY PREPARED LIDS AND RINGS; TIGHTEN
RINGS JUST UNTIL FINGERTIP-TIGHT. PROCESS JARS IN A
BOILING WATER CANNER FOR 15 MINUTES (SEE PAGE 27).
TURN OFF HEAT AND REMOVE CANNER LID. LET JARS
STAND IN WATER FOR 5 MINUTES. TRANSFER JARS
TO A TOWEL-LINED SURFACE AND LET REST AT ROOM
TEMPERATURE UNTIL COOLED. CHECK SEALS; REFRIGERATE
ANY UNSEALED JARS FOR UP TO 3 WEEKS. MAKES SIX
4-OUNCE (125 ML) JARS.

TIP: IT'S BEST TO WAIT TO ENJOY THIS MUSTARD UNTIL
AT LEAST A WEEK AFTER PROCESSING, TO ALLOW THE
FLAVORS TO BLEND.

TIP: USE A RUBBER SPATULA OR A PLASTIC BUBBLE
REMOVER TO REMOVE AIR POCKETS ONCE YOU FILL JARS.

TIP: THE BEST, SAFEST WAY TO LIFT JARS OUT OF THE
CANNER IS WITH A JAR LIFTER, SPECIALIZED TONGS
COATED WITH SILICONE AND DESIGNED TO FIT AROUND
THE NECKS OF JARS.

HOMEMADE KETCHUP

MAKING YOUR OWN HOMEMADE KETCHUP WITH TOMATOES YOU GREW YOURSELF OR BOUGHT FROM A LOCAL FARM MEANS YOU KNOW EXACTLY WHAT'S IN IT, SO YOU CAN FEEL GOOD WHEN YOUR FAMILY WANTS TO SQUIRT IT ON ABSOLUTELY EVERYTHING!

2	BAY LEAVES	2
2 TBSP	CELERY SEEDS	30 ML
2 TSP	WHOLE ALLSPICE	10 ML
1 TSP	WHOLE CLOVES	5 ML
1 TSP	BLACK PEPPERCORNS	5 ML
10 LBS	PLUM (ROMA) TOMATOES, CUT INTO CHUNKS, DIVIDED	5 KG
2 CUPS	CHOPPED ONIONS	500 ML
2 CUPS	GRANULATED SUGAR	500 ML
2 TBSP	PICKLING OR CANNING SALT	30 ML
2 CUPS	CIDER VINEGAR	500 ML

PLACE BAY LEAVES, CELERY SEEDS, ALLSPICE, CLOVES AND PEPPERCORNS IN THE CENTER OF A SQUARE OF TRIPLE-LAYERED CHEESECLOTH AND TIE INTO A SPICE BAG. IN A DUTCH OVEN OR A LARGE, HEAVY-BOTTOMED POT, COMBINE SPICE BAG AND HALF THE TOMATOES; HEAT OVER MEDIUM HEAT, STIRRING OFTEN, UNTIL WILTED. ADD THE REMAINING TOMATOES AND THE ONIONS; BRING TO A BOIL, STIRRING OFTEN. REDUCE HEAT AND BOIL GENTLY, STIRRING OCCASIONALLY, FOR ABOUT 1½ HOURS OR UNTIL VEGETABLES ARE VERY SOFT. DISCARD SPICE BAG.

WORKING IN BATCHES, PRESS SAUCE THROUGH A FOOD MILL FITTED WITH THE FINE PLATE OR A VICTORIO STRAINER (SEE TIP, OPPOSITE) INTO ANOTHER LARGE POT

OR BOWL, DISCARDING SKINS AND SEEDS. RETURN TO POT, IF NECESSARY, AND STIR IN SUGAR, SALT AND VINEGAR. RETURN POT TO MEDIUM-HIGH HEAT AND BRING SAUCE TO A BOIL. REDUCE HEAT AND BOIL GENTLY, STIRRING OFTEN, FOR ABOUT 2 HOURS OR UNTIL THICK ENOUGH TO COAT A WOODEN SPOON.

LADLE INTO STERILIZED JARS TO WITHIN $\frac{1}{2}$ INCH (1 CM) OF RIM. REMOVE ANY AIR POCKETS AND ADJUST HEADSPACE, IF NECESSARY, BY ADDING HOT SAUCE; WIPE RIMS. APPLY PREPARED LIDS AND RINGS; TIGHTEN RINGS JUST UNTIL FINGERTIP-TIGHT. PROCESS JARS IN A BOILING WATER CANNER FOR 35 MINUTES (SEE PAGE 27). TURN OFF HEAT AND REMOVE CANNER LID. LET JARS STAND IN WATER FOR 5 MINUTES. TRANSFER JARS TO A TOWEL-LINED SURFACE AND LET REST AT ROOM TEMPERATURE UNTIL COOLED. CHECK SEALS; REFRIGERATE ANY UNSEALED JARS FOR UP TO 3 WEEKS. MAKES FIVE TO SIX PINT (500 ML) JARS.

TIP: IF YOU DON'T HAVE A FOOD MILL OR VICTORIO STRAINER, PEEL, SEED AND CHOP THE TOMATOES BEFORE ADDING THEM TO THE POT. AFTER DISCARDING THE SPICES, USE AN IMMERSION BLENDER TO PURÉE THE SAUCE IN THE POT UNTIL FAIRLY SMOOTH. STIR IN THE REMAINING INGREDIENTS AND PROCEED AS DIRECTED.

TIP: THIS WILL BE THINNER THAN COMMERCIAL KETCHUP BECAUSE THERE IS NO THICKENING AGENT, SUCH AS STARCH.

247

SPICY KETCHUP

IF YOUR GRILLED CHEESE SANDWICHES OR BURGERS NEED A LITTLE KICK, THIS KETCHUP WILL DO THE TRICK. TRY IT ON SLIDERS (PAGE 268).

2	BAY LEAVES	2
2 TBSP	CELERY SEEDS	30 ML
I TBSP	HOT PEPPER FLAKES	15 ML
2 TSP	WHOLE CLOVES	10 ML
10 LBS	PLUM (ROMA) TOMATOES, CUT INTO CHUNKS, DIVIDED	5 KG
2 CUPS	CHOPPED ONIONS	500 ML
1/4 CUP	CHOPPED SEEDED JALAPEÑO PEPPERS	60 ML
2 CUPS	PACKED BROWN SUGAR	500 ML
2 TBSP	PICKLING OR CANNING SALT	30 ML
2 CUPS	CIDER VINEGAR	500 ML

PLACE BAY LEAVES, CELERY SEEDS, HOT PEPPER FLAKES AND CLOVES IN THE CENTER OF A SQUARE OF TRIPLE-LAYERED CHEESECLOTH AND TIE INTO A SPICE BAG. IN A DUTCH OVEN OR A LARGE, HEAVY-BOTTOMED POT, COMBINE SPICE BAG AND HALF THE TOMATOES; HEAT OVER MEDIUM HEAT, STIRRING OFTEN, UNTIL WILTED. ADD THE REMAINING TOMATOES, ONIONS AND JALAPEÑOS; BRING TO A BOIL, STIRRING OFTEN. REDUCE HEAT AND BOIL GENTLY, STIRRING OCCASIONALLY, FOR ABOUT 1 1/2 HOURS OR UNTIL VEGETABLES ARE VERY SOFT. DISCARD SPICE BAG.

WORKING IN BATCHES, PRESS SAUCE THROUGH A FOOD MILL FITTED WITH THE FINE PLATE OR A VICTORIO STRAINER (SEE TIP, PAGE 247) INTO ANOTHER LARGE POT

OR BOWL, DISCARDING SKINS AND SEEDS. RETURN TO POT, IF NECESSARY, AND STIR IN BROWN SUGAR, SALT AND VINEGAR. RETURN POT TO MEDIUM-HIGH HEAT AND BRING SAUCE TO A BOIL. REDUCE HEAT AND BOIL GENTLY, STIRRING OFTEN, FOR ABOUT 2 HOURS OR UNTIL THICK ENOUGH TO COAT A WOODEN SPOON.

LADLE INTO STERILIZED JARS TO WITHIN $1/2$ INCH (1 CM) OF RIM. REMOVE ANY AIR POCKETS AND ADJUST HEADSPACE, IF NECESSARY, BY ADDING HOT SAUCE; WIPE RIMS. APPLY PREPARED LIDS AND RINGS; TIGHTEN RINGS JUST UNTIL FINGERTIP-TIGHT. PROCESS JARS IN A BOILING WATER CANNER FOR 35 MINUTES (SEE PAGE 27). TURN OFF HEAT AND REMOVE CANNER LID. LET JARS STAND IN WATER FOR 5 MINUTES. TRANSFER JARS TO A TOWEL-LINED SURFACE AND LET REST AT ROOM TEMPERATURE UNTIL COOLED. CHECK SEALS; REFRIGERATE ANY UNSEALED JARS FOR UP TO 3 WEEKS. MAKES FIVE TO SIX PINT (500 ML) JARS.

TIP: THIS WILL BE THINNER THAN COMMERCIAL KETCHUP BECAUSE THERE IS NO THICKENING AGENT, SUCH AS STARCH.

TIP: AFTER OPENING THE JAR OF KETCHUP, TRANSFER IT TO A PLASTIC SQUEEZE BOTTLE FOR THE FULL TRADITIONAL KETCHUP EFFECT.

HOUSEWORK WON'T KILL YOU, BUT WHY TAKE THE CHANCE. — PHYLLIS DILLER

CLASSIC BARBECUE SAUCE

WHEN FRESH TOMATOES ARE AT THEIR PEAK, MAKE THIS BARBECUE SAUCE; AFTER ONE TASTE, YOU'LL NEVER GO BACK TO THE BOTTLED KIND AGAIN! IT'S SWEET, TANGY AND SAVORY, ALL IN ONE. TRY IT ON STICKY BAKED CHICKEN (PAGE 276)

10 LBS	PLUM (ROMA) TOMATOES, CUT INTO CHUNKS, DIVIDED	5 KG
3 CUPS	CHOPPED ONIONS	750 ML
2 CUPS	CHOPPED CELERY	500 ML
4	CLOVES GARLIC, CHOPPED	4
2	BAY LEAVES	2
2 TBSP	PICKLING OR CANNING SALT	30 ML
2 TBSP	DRY MUSTARD	30 ML
2 TBSP	CHILI POWDER	30 ML
1 TSP	FRESHLY GROUND BLACK PEPPER	5 ML
1 1/2 CUPS	GRANULATED SUGAR	375 ML
2 CUPS	WHITE VINEGAR	500 ML
1/2 CUP	FANCY (LIGHT) MOLASSES	125 ML

IN A DUTCH OVEN OR A LARGE, HEAVY-BOTTOMED POT, HEAT HALF THE TOMATOES OVER MEDIUM HEAT, STIRRING OFTEN, UNTIL WILTED. ADD THE REMAINING TOMATOES AND BRING TO A BOIL, STIRRING OFTEN. ADD ONIONS, CELERY, GARLIC, BAY LEAVES, SALT, MUSTARD, CHILI POWDER AND PEPPER; RETURN TO A BOIL, STIRRING OFTEN. REDUCE HEAT AND BOIL GENTLY, STIRRING OCCASIONALLY, FOR ABOUT 1 1/2 HOURS OR UNTIL VEGETABLES ARE VERY SOFT. DISCARD BAY LEAVES.

WORKING IN BATCHES, PRESS THROUGH A FOOD MILL FITTED WITH THE FINE PLATE OR A VICTORIO STRAINER

(SEE TIP, PAGE 247) INTO ANOTHER LARGE POT OR BOWL, DISCARDING SKINS AND SEEDS. RETURN TO POT, IF NECESSARY, AND STIR IN SUGAR, VINEGAR AND MOLASSES. RETURN POT TO MEDIUM-HIGH HEAT AND BRING SAUCE TO A BOIL. REDUCE HEAT AND BOIL GENTLY, STIRRING OFTEN, FOR ABOUT 2 HOURS OR UNTIL THICK ENOUGH TO COAT A WOODEN SPOON.

LADLE INTO STERILIZED JARS TO WITHIN $\frac{1}{2}$ INCH (1 CM) OF RIM. REMOVE ANY AIR POCKETS AND ADJUST HEADSPACE, IF NECESSARY, BY ADDING HOT SAUCE; WIPE RIMS. APPLY PREPARED LIDS AND RINGS; TIGHTEN RINGS JUST UNTIL FINGERTIP-TIGHT. PROCESS JARS IN A BOILING WATER CANNER FOR 35 MINUTES (SEE PAGE 27). TURN OFF HEAT AND REMOVE CANNER LID. LET JARS STAND IN WATER FOR 5 MINUTES. TRANSFER JARS TO A TOWEL-LINED SURFACE AND LET REST AT ROOM TEMPERATURE UNTIL COOLED. CHECK SEALS; REFRIGERATE ANY UNSEALED JARS FOR UP TO 3 WEEKS. MAKES ABOUT SIX PINT (500 ML) JARS.

TIP: AS THE SAUCE GETS THICKER, YOU'LL NEED TO STIR MORE OFTEN AND REDUCE THE HEAT TO PREVENT IT FROM SCORCHING AND SPLATTERING TOO MUCH.

EVERY MORNING IS THE DAWN OF A NEW ERROR.

SMOKY PEPPER CHILI SAUCE

THIS THICK AND RICH CHILI SAUCE, SPIKED WITH HEAT AND SMOKINESS FROM CHIPOTLE PEPPERS, WILL CERTAINLY PERK UP SCRAMBLED EGGS, BURGERS OR MEAT PIES. TRY IT ON SLIDERS (PAGE 268).

12 CUPS	CHOPPED PEELED PLUM (ROMA) TOMATOES (SEE BOX, PAGE 259)	3 L
4 CUPS	CHOPPED ONIONS	1 L
3 CUPS	CHOPPED RED BELL PEPPERS	750 ML
2 CUPS	FINELY CHOPPED CELERY	500 ML
2 TBSP	MINCED GARLIC	30 ML
3 CUPS	PACKED BROWN SUGAR	750 ML
2 TBSP	PICKLING OR CANNING SALT	30 ML
1 TSP	GROUND ALLSPICE	5 ML
1 TSP	GROUND CINNAMON	5 ML
1 TSP	GROUND CUMIN	5 ML
1½ CUPS	CIDER VINEGAR	375 ML
2	DRIED ANCHO OR MILD NEW MEXICO CHILE PEPPERS	2
1 CUP	BOILING WATER	250 ML
2	DRAINED CHIPOTLE PEPPERS IN ADOBO SAUCE, MINCED	2
2 TBSP	ADOBO SAUCE	30 ML

IN A DUTCH OVEN OR A LARGE, HEAVY-BOTTOMED POT, COMBINE TOMATOES, ONIONS, RED PEPPERS, CELERY, GARLIC, BROWN SUGAR, SALT, ALLSPICE, CINNAMON, CUMIN AND VINEGAR. BRING TO A BOIL OVER MEDIUM-HIGH HEAT, STIRRING OFTEN. REDUCE HEAT AND BOIL GENTLY, STIRRING OFTEN, FOR 2 TO 2½ HOURS OR UNTIL CHILI SAUCE IS REDUCED BY ABOUT HALF AND IS THICK ENOUGH TO MOUND ON A SPOON.

CONTINUED ON PAGE 253...

Black Bean Tomato Salsa (page 262)

Hot and Sweet Mustard (page 244), Spicy Ketchup (page 248)
and Dill Cucumber Relish (page 192)

Appetizer of the Hour (page 267)

Black Currant Linzer Slices (page 286)

IN A HEATPROOF BOWL, COMBINE DRIED CHILE PEPPERS AND BOILING WATER. LET STAND FOR ABOUT 30 MINUTES OR UNTIL PEPPERS ARE SOFTENED. REMOVE PEPPERS FROM LIQUID AND DISCARD LIQUID. DISCARD STEM AND SEEDS AND FINELY CHOP PEPPERS. STIR INTO CHILI SAUCE WITH CHIPOTLES AND ADOBO SAUCE AND BOIL GENTLY, STIRRING OFTEN, FOR 10 MINUTES TO BLEND THE FLAVORS.

LADLE INTO STERILIZED JARS TO WITHIN $\frac{1}{2}$ INCH (1 CM) OF RIM. REMOVE ANY AIR POCKETS AND ADJUST HEADSPACE, IF NECESSARY, BY ADDING HOT SAUCE; WIPE RIMS. APPLY PREPARED LIDS AND RINGS; TIGHTEN RINGS JUST UNTIL FINGERTIP-TIGHT. PROCESS JARS IN A BOILING WATER CANNER FOR 20 MINUTES (SEE PAGE 27). TURN OFF HEAT AND REMOVE CANNER LID. LET JARS STAND IN WATER FOR 5 MINUTES. TRANSFER JARS TO A TOWEL-LINED SURFACE AND LET REST AT ROOM TEMPERATURE UNTIL COOLED. CHECK SEALS; REFRIGERATE ANY UNSEALED JARS FOR UP TO 3 WEEKS. MAKES SIX TO SEVEN PINT (500 ML) JARS.

TIP: ANCHO CHILE PEPPERS ARE DRIED POBLANO PEPPERS. THEY ADD A TOUCH OF TOASTED FLAVOR WITHOUT MUCH HEAT. LOOK FOR THEM IN THE PRODUCE SECTION OF SUPERMARKETS AND AT SPECIALTY FOOD STORES.

TIP: CHIPOTLE PEPPERS ARE SMOKED JALAPEÑO PEPPERS. THEY PACK QUITE A PUNCH OF HEAT AND SMOKY FLAVOR. CHIPOTLES ARE OFTEN SOLD IN CANS IN A THICK SAUCE, CALLED ADOBO SAUCE, AND ARE AVAILABLE IN WELL-STOCKED SUPERMARKETS.

TENDER FRUIT CHILI SAUCE

*TOMATOES ARE BOTANICALLY FRUIT,
SO THIS COMBINATION IS A NATURAL, CAPTURING
THE FRUITS OF THE LATE SUMMER HARVEST
IN A SWEETLY SPICED SAUCE.*

6 CUPS	CHOPPED PEELED PLUM (ROMA) TOMATOES (SEE BOX, PAGE 259)	1.5 L
4 CUPS	CHOPPED PEELED PEACHES (SEE BOX, PAGE 87)	1 L
3 CUPS	CHOPPED PEELED PEARS	750 ML
2 CUPS	CHOPPED PURPLE, BLUE OR RED PLUMS	500 ML
2 CUPS	CHOPPED ONIONS	500 ML
1 CUP	CHOPPED GREEN BELL PEPPER	250 ML
2 CUPS	GRANULATED SUGAR	500 ML
1 TBSP	PICKLING OR CANNING SALT	15 ML
1 TBSP	PICKLING SPICE, TIED IN A SPICE BAG (SEE TIP, OPPOSITE)	15 ML
1 TSP	GROUND CINNAMON	5 ML
1/2 TSP	GROUND MACE OR NUTMEG	2 ML
1/4 TSP	GROUND CLOVES	1 ML
2 CUPS	WHITE VINEGAR	500 ML

IN A DUTCH OVEN OR A LARGE, HEAVY-BOTTOMED POT, COMBINE TOMATOES, PEACHES, PEARS, PLUMS, ONIONS, GREEN PEPPER, SUGAR, SALT, PICKLING SPICE, CINNAMON, MACE, CLOVES AND VINEGAR. BRING TO A BOIL OVER MEDIUM-HIGH HEAT, STIRRING OFTEN. REDUCE HEAT AND BOIL GENTLY, STIRRING OFTEN, FOR 2 TO 2 1/2 HOURS OR UNTIL CHILI SAUCE IS REDUCED BY ABOUT HALF AND IS THICK ENOUGH TO MOUND ON A SPOON. DISCARD SPICE BAG.

LADLE INTO STERILIZED JARS TO WITHIN $\frac{1}{2}$ INCH (1 CM) OF RIM. REMOVE ANY AIR POCKETS AND ADJUST HEADSPACE, IF NECESSARY, BY ADDING HOT SAUCE; WIPE RIMS. APPLY PREPARED LIDS AND RINGS; TIGHTEN RINGS JUST UNTIL FINGERTIP-TIGHT. PROCESS JARS IN A BOILING WATER CANNER FOR 20 MINUTES (SEE PAGE 27). TURN OFF HEAT AND REMOVE CANNER LID. LET JARS STAND IN WATER FOR 5 MINUTES. TRANSFER JARS TO A TOWEL-LINED SURFACE AND LET REST AT ROOM TEMPERATURE UNTIL COOLED. CHECK SEALS; REFRIGERATE ANY UNSEALED JARS FOR UP TO 3 WEEKS. MAKES FOUR TO FIVE PINT (500 ML) JARS.

TIP: SOME PEAR VARIETIES LOSE THEIR FLAVOR WHEN HEATED, SO CHOOSE A VARIETY SUITED TO COOKING, SUCH AS BARTLETT, BOSC OR PACKHAM.

TIP: TO MAKE A SPICE BAG, CUT A 4-INCH (10 CM) SQUARE PIECE OF TRIPLE-LAYERED CHEESECLOTH. PLACE THE PICKLING SPICE IN THE CENTER OF THE SQUARE AND BRING THE EDGES TOGETHER INTO A BUNDLE. TIE TIGHTLY WITH KITCHEN STRING. ALTERNATIVELY, USE A LARGE MESH TEA BALL.

SERVING SUGGESTIONS: SERVE SPOONED ON TOP OF CRACKERS SPREAD WITH CREAM CHEESE FOR A CHANGE FROM RED PEPPER JELLY. OR SPREAD ON A SANDWICH STACKED WITH HAM AND OLD (SHARP) CHEDDAR CHEESE.

HE WHO LAUGHS LAST THINKS SLOWEST.

CLASSIC TOMATO SAUCE

*JUST AS THE TITLE SAYS, THIS SAUCE IS
LIGHTLY SEASONED WITH CLASSIC FLAVORS THAT
REALLY HIGHLIGHT THE VINE-RIPENED BEAUTY
OF FRESHLY HARVESTED TOMATOES.*

10 LBS	PLUM (ROMA) TOMATOES, CUT INTO CHUNKS, DIVIDED	5 KG
3 CUPS	CHOPPED ONIONS	750 ML
3 CUPS	CHOPPED RED BELL PEPPERS	750 ML
2 CUPS	CHOPPED CELERY	500 ML
4	CLOVES GARLIC, CHOPPED	4
2	BAY LEAVES	2
1/2 CUP	GRANULATED SUGAR	125 ML
1 TBSP	PICKLING OR CANNING SALT	15 ML
1 TBSP	DRIED OREGANO	15 ML
1 TBSP	DRIED BASIL	15 ML
1 TSP	FRESHLY GROUND BLACK PEPPER	5 ML
	RED WINE VINEGAR (SEE TIP, OPPOSITE)	

IN A DUTCH OVEN OR A LARGE, HEAVY-BOTTOMED
POT, HEAT HALF THE TOMATOES OVER MEDIUM HEAT,
STIRRING OFTEN, UNTIL WILTED. ADD THE REMAINING
TOMATOES AND BRING TO A BOIL, STIRRING OFTEN. ADD
ONIONS, RED PEPPERS, CELERY, GARLIC, BAY LEAVES,
SUGAR, SALT, OREGANO, BASIL AND PEPPER; RETURN TO A
BOIL, STIRRING OFTEN. REDUCE HEAT AND BOIL GENTLY,
STIRRING OCCASIONALLY, FOR ABOUT 1 1/2 HOURS OR UNTIL
VEGETABLES ARE VERY SOFT. DISCARD BAY LEAVES.

WORKING IN BATCHES, PRESS SAUCE THROUGH A
FOOD MILL FITTED WITH THE FINE PLATE OR A VICTORIO
STRAINER (SEE TIP, PAGE 247) INTO ANOTHER LARGE POT

OR BOWL, DISCARDING SKINS AND SEEDS. RETURN TO POT, IF NECESSARY. RETURN POT TO MEDIUM-HIGH HEAT AND BRING SAUCE TO A BOIL. REDUCE HEAT AND BOIL GENTLY, STIRRING OFTEN, FOR ABOUT 30 MINUTES OR UNTIL THICK ENOUGH TO THINLY COAT A WOODEN SPOON (IT WILL BE THINNER THAN COMMERCIAL PASTA SAUCE).

PLACE 2 TBSP (30 ML) VINEGAR IN THE BOTTOM OF EACH HOT JAR. LADLE INTO STERILIZED JARS TO WITHIN $\frac{1}{2}$ INCH (1 CM) OF RIM. REMOVE ANY AIR POCKETS AND ADJUST HEADSPACE, IF NECESSARY, BY ADDING HOT SAUCE; WIPE RIMS. APPLY PREPARED LIDS AND RINGS; TIGHTEN RINGS JUST UNTIL FINGERTIP-TIGHT. PROCESS JARS IN A BOILING WATER CANNER FOR 35 MINUTES (SEE PAGE 27). TURN OFF HEAT AND REMOVE CANNER LID. LET JARS STAND IN WATER FOR 5 MINUTES. TRANSFER JARS TO A TOWEL-LINED SURFACE AND LET REST AT ROOM TEMPERATURE UNTIL COOLED. CHECK SEALS; REFRIGERATE ANY UNSEALED JARS FOR UP TO 3 WEEKS. MAKES ABOUT SIX PINT (500 ML) JARS.

TIP: MANY TOMATO SAUCE RECIPES USE BOTTLED LEMON JUICE INSTEAD OF VINEGAR. WE PREFER THE FLAVOR OF VINEGAR AND OFFSET THE ACIDIC TASTE WITH A BIT OF SUGAR. TO SWEETEN TO TASTE, STIR 2 CUPS (500 ML) SAUCE WITH 2 TBSP (30 ML) VINEGAR, TASTE AND ADD MORE SUGAR, IF DESIRED. THEN ADD THAT MUCH SUGAR WITH THE VINEGAR TO EACH JAR. IF YOU PREFER TO USE BOTTLED LEMON JUICE, USE 1 TBSP (15 ML) PER JAR. DO NOT USE FRESHLY SQUEEZED LEMON JUICE.

MILD TOMATO SALSA

IF YOU LIKE TO INCORPORATE SALSA INTO YOUR COOKING AND EAT IT ON ITS OWN, THIS IS THE RECIPE TO MAKE. IT'S PLEASANTLY SEASONED, AND ITS SIMPLE FLAVORS MAKE IT VERSATILE FOR USE IN DISHES THAT CALL FOR A SALSA TOUCH.

14 CUPS	CHOPPED PEELED PLUM (ROMA) TOMATOES (SEE BOX, OPPOSITE)	3.5 L
3 CUPS	CHOPPED ONIONS	750 ML
2 CUPS	CHOPPED RED BELL PEPPERS	500 ML
I CUP	CHOPPED GREEN BELL PEPPER	250 ML
2 TBSP	FINELY CHOPPED SEEDED JALAPEÑO PEPPER	30 ML
I TBSP	MINCED GARLIC	15 ML
2 TBSP	GRANULATED SUGAR	30 ML
2 TSP	PICKLING OR CANNING SALT	10 ML
1½ TSP	GROUND CUMIN	7 ML
¼ TSP	FRESHLY GROUND BLACK PEPPER	I ML
1¾ CUPS	CIDER VINEGAR	425 ML
¼ CUP	CHOPPED FRESH CILANTRO OR OREGANO (OPTIONAL)	60 ML

IN A DUTCH OVEN OR A LARGE, HEAVY-BOTTOMED POT, COMBINE TOMATOES, ONIONS, RED AND GREEN PEPPERS, JALAPEÑO, GARLIC, SUGAR, SALT, CUMIN, BLACK PEPPER AND VINEGAR. BRING TO A BOIL OVER MEDIUM-HIGH HEAT, STIRRING OFTEN. REDUCE HEAT AND BOIL GENTLY, STIRRING OFTEN, FOR ABOUT I HOUR OR UNTIL SALSA IS REDUCED BY ABOUT HALF AND IS THICK ENOUGH TO MOUND ON A SPOON. STIR IN CILANTRO (IF USING).

LADLE INTO STERILIZED JARS (SEE TIP, PAGE 263) TO WITHIN $\frac{1}{2}$ INCH (1 CM) OF RIM. REMOVE ANY AIR POCKETS AND ADJUST HEADSPACE, IF NECESSARY, BY ADDING HOT SALSA; WIPE RIMS. APPLY PREPARED LIDS AND RINGS; TIGHTEN RINGS JUST UNTIL FINGERTIP-TIGHT. PROCESS JARS IN A BOILING WATER CANNER FOR 20 MINUTES (SEE PAGE 27). TURN OFF HEAT AND REMOVE CANNER LID. LET JARS STAND IN WATER FOR 5 MINUTES. TRANSFER JARS TO A TOWEL-LINED SURFACE AND LET REST AT ROOM TEMPERATURE UNTIL COOLED. CHECK SEALS; REFRIGERATE ANY UNSEALED JARS FOR UP TO 3 WEEKS. MAKES ABOUT TEN 8-OUNCE (250 ML) OR FIVE PINT (500 ML) JARS.

HOW TO PEEL A TOMATO

DROP 6 TO 10 TOMATOES AT A TIME INTO A LARGE POT OF BOILING WATER FOR 30 SECONDS (AFTER RETURNING TO BOIL). USING A SLOTTED SPOON, TRANSFER TOMATOES TO A LARGE BOWL OR SINK OF ICE-COLD WATER AND LET COOL COMPLETELY, REFRESHING WATER AS NECESSARY TO KEEP COOL. DRAIN WELL. USING A SHARP PARING KNIFE, CUT OUT THE CORE AND LIFT OFF THE SKINS FROM THE OPENING; THE REST SHOULD SLIP OFF EASILY. IF THE SKINS SEEM DIFFICULT TO REMOVE, INCREASE THE BLANCHING TIME TO 1 MINUTE.

HOT, HOT, HOT TOMATO SALSA

AS THE NAME SAYS, THIS SALSA HAS LOTS OF HEAT: SLOW, DEEP HEAT FROM THE DRIED CHILE PEPPERS AND FRESH, ZINGY HEAT FROM TWO VARIETIES OF FRESH HOT PEPPERS. BE SURE TO LABEL THIS WITH FLAMES WHEN STORING AND SERVING IT SO YOU DON'T GET IT CONFUSED — IT'S NOT FOR THE MEEK.

14 CUPS	CHOPPED PEELED PLUM (ROMA) TOMATOES (SEE BOX, PAGE 259)	3.5 L
3 CUPS	CHOPPED ONIONS	750 ML
2 CUPS	CHOPPED RED BELL PEPPERS	500 ML
3/4 CUP	FINELY CHOPPED SEEDED YELLOW WAX (HOT BANANA) PEPPERS	175 ML
1/2 CUP	FINELY CHOPPED SEEDED JALAPEÑO PEPPERS	125 ML
2 TBSP	MINCED GARLIC	30 ML
2 TBSP	GRANULATED SUGAR	30 ML
2 TSP	PICKLING OR CANNING SALT	10 ML
1 TSP	GROUND CUMIN	5 ML
1 3/4 CUPS	CIDER VINEGAR	425 ML
2	DRIED HOT NEW MEXICO CHILE PEPPERS	2
1 CUP	BOILING WATER	250 ML
2 TBSP	CHOPPED FRESH OREGANO OR CILANTRO (OPTIONAL)	30 ML

IN A DUTCH OVEN OR A LARGE, HEAVY-BOTTOMED POT, COMBINE TOMATOES, ONIONS, RED PEPPERS, YELLOW WAX PEPPERS, JALAPEÑOS, GARLIC, SUGAR, SALT, CUMIN AND VINEGAR. BRING TO A BOIL OVER MEDIUM-HIGH HEAT, STIRRING OFTEN. REDUCE HEAT AND BOIL GENTLY, STIRRING OFTEN, FOR ABOUT 1 HOUR OR UNTIL SALSA

IS REDUCED BY ABOUT HALF AND IS THICK ENOUGH TO MOUND ON A SPOON.

IN A HEATPROOF BOWL, COMBINE DRIED CHILE PEPPERS AND BOILING WATER. LET STAND FOR ABOUT 30 MINUTES OR UNTIL PEPPERS ARE SOFTENED. REMOVE PEPPERS FROM LIQUID AND DISCARD LIQUID. DISCARD STEM AND SEEDS AND FINELY CHOP PEPPERS. STIR INTO SALSA WITH OREGANO (IF USING) AND BOIL GENTLY, STIRRING OFTEN, FOR 5 MINUTES TO BLEND THE FLAVORS.

LADLE INTO STERILIZED JARS (SEE TIP, PAGE 263) TO WITHIN $1/2$ INCH (1 CM) OF RIM. REMOVE ANY AIR POCKETS AND ADJUST HEADSPACE, IF NECESSARY, BY ADDING HOT SALSA; WIPE RIMS. APPLY PREPARED LIDS AND RINGS; TIGHTEN RINGS JUST UNTIL FINGERTIP-TIGHT. PROCESS JARS IN A BOILING WATER CANNER FOR 20 MINUTES (SEE PAGE 27). TURN OFF HEAT AND REMOVE CANNER LID. LET JARS STAND IN WATER FOR 5 MINUTES. TRANSFER JARS TO A TOWEL-LINED SURFACE AND LET REST AT ROOM TEMPERATURE UNTIL COOLED. CHECK SEALS; REFRIGERATE ANY UNSEALED JARS FOR UP TO 3 WEEKS. MAKES ABOUT TEN 8-OUNCE (250 ML) OR FIVE PINT (500 ML) JARS.

TIP: TO AVOID BURNS, WEAR DISPOSABLE RUBBER GLOVES WHEN HANDLING HOT PEPPERS AND BE SURE TO WASH ALL UTENSILS AND THE CUTTING BOARD WELL AFTER PREPARING THE PEPPERS.

KNITTING KEEPS ME FROM UNRAVELING.

BLACK BEAN TOMATO SALSA

WHEN YOU'RE READY TO VENTURE BEYOND CLASSIC TOMATO SALSA, THIS IS GREAT COMBINATION TO TRY — IT'S SURE TO BECOME A FAVORITE.

2 TSP	CUMIN SEEDS	10 ML
12 CUPS	CHOPPED PEELED PLUM (ROMA) TOMATOES (SEE BOX, PAGE 259)	3 L
1 1/2 CUPS	CHOPPED ONIONS	375 ML
1 CUP	CHOPPED RED BELL PEPPER	250 ML
1 CUP	CHOPPED GREEN BELL PEPPER	250 ML
1/4 CUP	FINELY CHOPPED SEEDED JALAPEÑO PEPPERS	60 ML
2 TBSP	MINCED GARLIC	30 ML
1/4 CUP	GRANULATED SUGAR	60 ML
2 TSP	PICKLING OR CANNING SALT	10 ML
2 CUPS	CIDER VINEGAR	500 ML
2 CUPS	DRAINED RINSED CANNED OR COOKED BLACK BEANS	500 ML
1/4 CUP	CHOPPED FRESH CILANTRO OR OREGANO	60 ML

IN A SMALL DRY SKILLET, OVER MEDIUM HEAT, TOAST CUMIN, STIRRING CONSTANTLY, FOR ABOUT 1 MINUTE OR UNTIL FRAGRANT AND SLIGHTLY DARKER BUT NOT YET POPPING. IMMEDIATELY TRANSFER TO A DUTCH OVEN OR A LARGE, HEAVY-BOTTOMED POT. ADD TOMATOES, ONIONS, RED AND GREEN PEPPERS, JALAPEÑOS, GARLIC, SUGAR, SALT AND VINEGAR TO THE POT. BRING TO A BOIL OVER MEDIUM-HIGH HEAT, STIRRING OFTEN. REDUCE HEAT AND BOIL GENTLY, STIRRING OFTEN, FOR ABOUT 1 HOUR OR UNTIL SALSA IS REDUCED BY ABOUT HALF AND IS THICK ENOUGH TO MOUND ON A SPOON. STIR BEANS

INTO SALSA AND BOIL GENTLY, STIRRING OFTEN, FOR ABOUT 10 MINUTES OR UNTIL BEANS ARE VERY HOT. STIR IN CILANTRO.

LADLE INTO STERILIZED JARS TO WITHIN $\frac{1}{2}$ INCH (1 CM) OF RIM. REMOVE ANY AIR POCKETS AND ADJUST HEADSPACE, IF NECESSARY, BY ADDING HOT SALSA; WIPE RIMS. APPLY PREPARED LIDS AND RINGS; TIGHTEN RINGS JUST UNTIL FINGERTIP-TIGHT. PROCESS JARS IN A BOILING WATER CANNER FOR 20 MINUTES (SEE PAGE 27). TURN OFF HEAT AND REMOVE CANNER LID. LET JARS STAND IN WATER FOR 5 MINUTES. TRANSFER JARS TO A TOWEL-LINED SURFACE AND LET REST AT ROOM TEMPERATURE UNTIL COOLED. CHECK SEALS; REFRIGERATE ANY UNSEALED JARS FOR UP TO 3 WEEKS. MAKES ABOUT TEN 8-OUNCE (250 ML) OR FIVE PINT (500 ML) JARS.

TIP: IF USING CANNED BLACK BEANS, YOU'LL NEED ONE 19-OZ (540 ML) CAN. IF YOU HAVE SMALLER CANS, YOU'LL NEED TWO. DON'T BE TEMPTED TO ADD THE EXTRA BEANS TO THE SALSA — IT WILL ALTER THE ACID BALANCE. ADD THEM TO A SALAD, MASH THEM WITH SOME SALSA TO MAKE BURRITOS OR FREEZE THEM FOR LATER USE.

TIP: IF YOU USE 8-OUNCE (250 ML) JARS, THEY MAY NOT ALL FIT IN YOUR CANNER AT ONCE. LET EXTRA JARS COOL, THEN REFRIGERATE THEM AND USE THEM UP FIRST. TO AVOID THIS PROBLEM, PACK SOME IN PINT (500 ML) JARS AND SOME IN 8-OUNCE (250 ML) JARS. THAT WAY, YOU ALSO HAVE DIFFERENT SIZES AND CAN OPEN THE SIZE YOU'LL USE UP WITHIN A FEW WEEKS.

MANGO CILANTRO SALSA

WHEN CASES OF MANGOS ARE ON SPECIAL, IT'S TIME TO SALSA!

8 CUPS	FINELY CHOPPED SWEET MANGOS	2 L
1/2 CUP	GRANULATED SUGAR, DIVIDED	125 ML
1 1/2 CUPS	FINELY CHOPPED RED ONION	375 ML
1 CUP	FINELY CHOPPED ORANGE OR RED BELL PEPPER	250 ML
1/4 CUP	FINELY CHOPPED SEEDED YELLOW WAX (HOT BANANA) PEPPER OR JALAPEÑO PEPPERS	60 ML
1 TSP	PICKLING OR CANNING SALT	5 ML
1/2 TSP	GROUND CUMIN	2 ML
3/4 CUP	WHITE VINEGAR	175 ML
1/4 CUP	FRESHLY SQUEEZED LIME JUICE	60 ML
1/4 CUP	CHOPPED FRESH CILANTRO	60 ML

IN A BOWL, GENTLY COMBINE MANGOS AND HALF THE SUGAR. SET ASIDE. IN A DUTCH OVEN OR A LARGE, HEAVY-BOTTOMED POT, COMBINE THE REMAINING SUGAR, ONION, ORANGE PEPPER, YELLOW WAX PEPPER, SALT, CUMIN AND VINEGAR. BRING TO A BOIL OVER MEDIUM-HIGH HEAT, STIRRING OFTEN. REDUCE HEAT AND BOIL GENTLY, STIRRING OFTEN, FOR ABOUT 5 MINUTES OR UNTIL ONIONS ARE ALMOST TRANSLUCENT. STIR IN MANGO MIXTURE AND BOIL GENTLY, STIRRING OFTEN, FOR ABOUT 10 MINUTES OR UNTIL MANGO JUST STARTS TO BREAK DOWN. STIR IN LIME JUICE AND CILANTRO.

LADLE INTO STERILIZED JARS TO WITHIN 1/2 INCH (1 CM) OF RIM. REMOVE ANY AIR POCKETS AND ADJUST HEADSPACE, IF NECESSARY, BY ADDING HOT SALSA; WIPE

RIMS. APPLY PREPARED LIDS AND RINGS; TIGHTEN RINGS JUST UNTIL FINGERTIP-TIGHT. PROCESS JARS IN A BOILING WATER CANNER FOR 20 MINUTES (SEE PAGE 27). TURN OFF HEAT AND REMOVE CANNER LID. LET JARS STAND IN WATER FOR 5 MINUTES. TRANSFER JARS TO A TOWEL-LINED SURFACE AND LET REST AT ROOM TEMPERATURE UNTIL COOLED. CHECK SEALS; REFRIGERATE ANY UNSEALED JARS FOR UP TO 3 WEEKS. MAKES ABOUT EIGHT 8-OUNCE (250 ML) OR FOUR PINT (500 ML) JARS.

TIP: MIXING THE MANGOS WITH SOME OF THE SUGAR HELPS TO SOFTEN THEM AND REDUCES THE AMOUNT OF COOKING REQUIRED, KEEPING THE FLAVOR FRESHER.

TIP: USE RIPE BUT FIRM MANGOS FOR THE BEST TEXTURE AND FLAVOR. YOU'LL NEED ABOUT 6 LARGE MANGOS TO GET 8 CUPS (2 L) FINELY CHOPPED.

SERVING SUGGESTION: SERVE ON TOP OF GRILLED FISH OR BARBECUED PORK.

HOW TO PREPARE A MANGO

THE NEATEST AND MOST EFFICIENT WAY TO PREPARE A FIRM, RIPE MANGO IS TO PEEL IT WITH A SHARP VEGETABLE PEELER. AFTER PEELING OFF THE SKIN, HOLD THE MANGO UPRIGHT, WITH THE STEM DOWN, ON A CUTTING BOARD. USING A SHARP KNIFE, CUT CLOSE TO THE FLAT SIDE OF THE SEED ON BOTH SIDES, CREATING TWO "CHEEKS." CAREFULLY CUT ALL REMAINING FLESH FROM AROUND THE SEED. CHOP THE FLESH INTO PIECES OF THE DESIRED SIZE.

Recipes Using Preserves

Preserves are wonderful ingredients to add to other recipes. This section shows you how to incorporate them into a variety of appetizers, main courses and desserts.

PEACHY CHEESE DIP

SERVE THIS YUMMY DIP GARNISHED WITH CHIVES AND CLASSIC PEACH CHUTNEY (PAGE 174), AND SET OUT WITH CRACKERS.

8 OZ	CREAM CHEESE, SOFTENED	250 G
8 OZ	PACKAGE IMPERIAL CHEESE (OR COLD-PACK SHARP CHEDDAR), SOFTENED	250 G
2 TBSP	SHERRY	30 ML
1 TSP	CURRY POWDER	5 ML
3/4 CUP	SPICED PEACH JAM (PAGE 53) OR CLASSIC PEACH CHUTNEY (PAGE 174)	175 ML

USING A FOOD PROCESSOR OR ELECTRIC MIXER, PROCESS CREAM CHEESE AND IMPERIAL CHEESE UNTIL BLENDED. ADD SHERRY, CURRY POWDER AND JAM, PROCESSING UNTIL SMOOTH. COVER AND REFRIGERATE UNTIL READY TO USE.

MAKES ABOUT 2 CUPS (500 ML).

APPETIZER OF THE HOUR

LAST-MINUTE COMPANY? WHIP THIS UP WHEN THEY WALK THROUGH THE DOOR AND SERVE IT WITH COCKTAIL CRACKERS.

8 OZ	CREAM CHEESE, SOFTENED	250 G
1/2 TSP	MADRAS CURRY POWDER	2 ML
1/4 CUP	JALAPEÑO PEPPER JELLY (PAGE 136)	60 ML
1/4 CUP	MAJOR GREY MANGO CHUTNEY (PAGE 172) OR MANGO CILANTRO SALSA (PAGE 265)	60 ML
1/4 CUP	TOASTED PINE NUTS (SEE TIP, BELOW)	60 ML
1/4 CUP	DRIED CRANBERRIES OR RAISINS	60 ML
1/4 CUP	FINELY CHOPPED GREEN ONIONS	60 ML

IN A MEDIUM BOWL, BEAT CREAM CHEESE UNTIL SOFT. ADD CURRY POWDER AND MIX WELL. SPREAD INTO A SHALLOW GLASS SERVING DISH. TOP WITH JALAPEÑO JELLY AND CHUTNEY. SPRINKLE WITH PINE NUTS, CRANBERRIES AND GREEN ONIONS. MAKES ABOUT 1 CUP (250 ML).

TIP: TOASTING NUTS HELPS BRING OUT THEIR FLAVOR. THE QUICKEST METHOD IS ON THE STOVETOP. SPREAD NUTS OUT IN AN UNGREASED NONSTICK SKILLET AND PLACE OVER MEDIUM HEAT. SHAKE OR STIR FREQUENTLY, TO PREVENT BURNING, FOR 4 TO 5 MINUTES OR UNTIL FRAGRANT AND STARTING TO BROWN. TIP ONTO A COLD PLATE TO STOP THE COOKING PROCESS AND LET COOL COMPLETELY.

SLIDERS

TWO-BITE BURGERS IN COCKTAIL BUNS WITH ALL THE FIXINS — EVERYONE LOVES THESE.

ALL-THE-FIXINS MAYONNAISE

I CUP	MAYONNAISE	250 ML
1/4 CUP	HOMEMADE KETCHUP (PAGE 246) OR SPICY KETCHUP (PAGE 248)	60 ML
2 TBSP	PREPARED YELLOW MUSTARD	30 ML
2 TBSP	SWEET GREEN RELISH (PAGE 190)	30 ML

BURGERS

2	SLICES BREAD, TORN INTO SMALL PIECES	2
I	EGG, LIGHTLY BEATEN	I
1/4 CUP	MILK	60 ML
2 TBSP	SMOKY PEPPER CHILI SAUCE (PAGE 252) OR KETCHUP	30 ML
I TSP	WORCESTERSHIRE SAUCE	5 ML
I LB	LEAN GROUND BEEF	500 G
I	ONION, GRATED	I
	SALT AND BLACK PEPPER	

TO SERVE

12	COCKTAIL ROLLS (SEE TIP, OPPOSITE) OR SLIDER BUNS, TOASTED	12
	SHREDDED LETTUCE	
	SLICED TOMATO	
	BREAD AND BUTTER PICKLES (PAGE 218)	

ALL-THE-FIXINS MAYONNAISE: IN A BOWL, COMBINE MAYONNAISE, KETCHUP, MUSTARD AND RELISH. SET ASIDE.

BURGERS: IN ANOTHER BOWL, COMBINE BREAD PIECES, EGG, MILK, CHILI SAUCE AND WORCESTERSHIRE SAUCE. LET STAND UNTIL BREAD HAS ABSORBED LIQUID. IN A LARGE BOWL, COMBINE BEEF AND ONION. ADD BREAD MIXTURE AND SALT AND PEPPER TO TASTE; MIX THOROUGHLY. FORM INTO 12 MINI PATTIES, ABOUT 2 INCHES (5 CM) WIDE AND $\frac{1}{2}$ INCH (1 CM) THICK. GRILL OR PAN-FRY PATTIES OVER MEDIUM-HIGH HEAT, TURNING ONCE, FOR 5 TO 7 MINUTES OR UNTIL NO LONGER PINK INSIDE.

TO SERVE: SPREAD MAYONNAISE ON TOASTED ROLLS. LAYER LETTUCE, TOMATO AND PICKLES ON BOTTOM HALVES OF ROLLS, TOP EACH WITH A BURGER AND COVER WITH THE TOP HALVES OF ROLLS. IF SERVING ADULTS, SECURE WITH COCKTAIL SKEWERS. MAKES 12 MINI BURGERS.

MAKE AHEAD: PLACE UNCOOKED PATTIES BETWEEN LAYERS OF WAXED PAPER IN AN AIRTIGHT CONTAINER AND REFRIGERATE FOR UP TO 4 HOURS OR FREEZE FOR UP TO 2 WEEKS. COOK FROM FROZEN, INCREASING THE COOKING TIME TO 12 TO 15 MINUTES.

TIP: COCKTAIL ROLLS ARE LIKE SMALL DINNER ROLLS AND ARE USUALLY AVAILABLE IN THE BAKERY SECTION OF THE SUPERMARKET.

VARIATION: BRUSH THE PATTIES WITH YOUR FAVORITE BARBECUE SAUCE HALFWAY THROUGH THE COOKING TIME.

NOTHING EASY IS EVER WORTH DOING.
— TEDDY ROOSEVELT

MAJOR GREY'S MEAT LOAF

JOLLY GOOD!

2 LBS	GROUND BEEF	I KG
	SALT AND BLACK PEPPER	
I to 2 TSP	CURRY POWDER	5 to 10 ML
2	LARGE EGGS, BEATEN	2
1/4 CUP	FINELY CHOPPED ONION	60 ML
2	LARGE APPLES, PEELED AND CHOPPED	2
1/2 CUP	ORANGE JUICE	125 ML
1/3 CUP	MAJOR GREY MANGO CHUTNEY (PAGE 172)	75 ML

MIX GROUND BEEF WITH ALL INGREDIENTS EXCEPT CHUTNEY. PLACE IN A 9- BY 5-INCH (23 BY 12.5 CM) LOAF PAN AND BAKE AT 350°F (180°C) FOR I HOUR. DRAIN. SPREAD CHUTNEY ON LOAF AND BAKE ANOTHER 20 MINUTES OR UNTIL A MEAT THERMOMETER INSERTED IN THE CENTER REGISTERS 160°F (71°C). GOOD HOT OR COLD. MAKES 6 TO 8 SERVINGS.

FREE PUPPIES. MOTHER: KENNEL CLUB-REGISTERED GERMAN SHEPHERD. FATHER: SUPER DOG ABLE TO LEAP TALL FENCES IN A SINGLE BOUND.

LEG OF LAMB WITH RED CURRANT SAUCE

1	LEG OF LAMB (4 TO 5 LBS/2 TO 2.5 KG)	1
1 TBSP	GIN	15 ML
2 TSP	SALT	10 ML
1/2 TSP	DRY MUSTARD	2 ML
1/4 TSP	BLACK PEPPER	1 ML

RED CURRANT SAUCE

1/2 CUP	RED CURRANT JELLY (PAGE 118)	125 ML
1 CUP	WATER	250 ML
1/4 TSP	SALT	1 ML
1/4 CUP	GIN	60 ML
3 TBSP	ALL-PURPOSE FLOUR	45 ML
1/4 CUP	WATER	60 ML

PLACE LAMB ON A RACK IN ROASTING PAN, FAT SIDE UP. COMBINE GIN, SALT, MUSTARD AND PEPPER TO MAKE A PASTE; SPREAD OVER LAMB. ROAST AT 350°F (180°C) FOR 2 1/2 HOURS OR UNTIL A MEAT THERMOMETER INSERTED IN THE THICKEST PART REGISTERS 180°F (90°C). SET ON A PLATTER AND COVER WITH FOIL.

SAUCE: REMOVE EXCESS FAT FROM ROASTING PAN. BLEND JELLY INTO PAN JUICES. ADD WATER AND HEAT OVER MEDIUM-LOW HEAT UNTIL JELLY MELTS. STIR IN SALT AND GIN. BLEND FLOUR IN WATER AND STIR INTO SAUCE. STIR UNTIL SAUCE BOILS AND THICKENS. POUR INTO GRAVY BOAT AND SERVE WITH LAMB. MAKES 8 TO 12 SERVINGS.

GLAZED ROAST PORK LOIN

THE PERFECT SUNDAY NIGHT SUPPER.

GLAZE

1/4 CUP	PORT	60 ML
6 TBSP	BLACK CURRANT JELLY (PAGE 116)	90 ML
2	CLOVES GARLIC, MINCED	2
3 LB	BONELESS PORK CENTER-CUT LOIN ROAST	1.5 KG
	SALT AND BLACK PEPPER	
1 TBSP	VEGETABLE OIL	15 ML
1 CUP	CHICKEN BROTH	250 ML
1 TSP	CORNSTARCH	5 ML

GLAZE: IN A SMALL SAUCEPAN, COMBINE PORT, BLACK CURRANT JELLY AND GARLIC; BRING TO A BOIL. REDUCE HEAT AND SIMMER FOR 10 MINUTES OR UNTIL SLIGHTLY THICKENED. REMOVE FROM HEAT AND KEEP WARM.

PREHEAT OVEN TO 325°F (160°C). SPRINKLE PORK WITH SALT AND PEPPER. IN A LARGE SKILLET, HEAT OIL OVER MEDIUM-HIGH HEAT. BROWN PORK ON ALL SIDES AND TRANSFER TO A RACK IN A ROASTING PAN. ROAST FOR 30 MINUTES. BRUSH ROAST WITH 2 TBSP (30 ML) OF THE GLAZE, RESERVING THE REST. BAKE FOR 45 TO 55 MINUTES, BRUSHING AGAIN WITH GLAZE, UNTIL A MEAT THERMOMETER INSERTED IN THE THICKEST PART REGISTERS 155°F (68°C) AND JUST A HINT OF PINK REMAINS INSIDE. TRANSFER TO A CUTTING BOARD AND COVER LOOSELY WITH FOIL. (THE PORK WILL CONTINUE TO "COOK" IN ITS OWN HEAT, AND THE TEMPERATURE WILL

RISE BY ABOUT ANOTHER 5°F/3°C.) WHISK CHICKEN BROTH AND CORNSTARCH INTO THE RESERVED GLAZE. ADD TO ROASTING PAN, STIRRING TO SCRAPE UP BROWN BITS, AND SIMMER GENTLY ON THE STOVETOP, OVER LOW HEAT, FOR ABOUT 5 MINUTES OR UNTIL SLIGHTLY THICKENED. SEASON TO TASTE WITH SALT AND PEPPER. STRAIN INTO A SERVING BOWL. SLICE PORK AND ARRANGE ON A SERVING PLATTER. SERVE SAUCE SEPARATELY. MAKES 6 SERVINGS.

VARIATION: USE RED CURRANT JELLY (PAGE 118) IN PLACE OF THE BLACK CURRANT JELLY.

YOU KNOW YOU'RE OLD
IF THEY'VE DISCONTINUED YOUR
BLOOD TYPE. — PHYLLIS DILLER

RUM- AND LIME-GLAZED PORK RIBS

A TASTE OF THE CARIBBEAN!

SPICE RUB

1 TBSP	PAPRIKA	15 ML
1 TBSP	GROUND CORIANDER	15 ML
1 TBSP	GROUND CUMIN	15 ML
2 TSP	DRIED THYME	10 ML
2 TSP	SALT	10 ML
1 TSP	GROUND CINNAMON	5 ML
2 LBS	COUNTRY-STYLE PORK RIBS, CUT INTO INDIVIDUAL RIBS (SEE TIP, OPPOSITE)	1 KG
1/4 CUP	UNSWEETENED APPLE JUICE, CHICKEN BROTH OR WATER	60 ML

GLAZE

1 CUP	APRICOT JAM (PAGE 38) OR PINEAPPLE AND MANGO JAM (PAGE 88)	250 ML
1/4 CUP	DARK RUM	60 ML
1/4 CUP	FRESHLY SQUEEZED LIME JUICE	60 ML
2 TBSP	CIDER VINEGAR	30 ML

SPICE RUB: IN A BOWL, COMBINE PAPRIKA, CORIANDER, CUMIN, THYME, SALT AND CINNAMON.

PREHEAT OVEN TO 275°F (140°C). LINE A 13- BY 9-INCH (33 BY 23 CM) BAKING PAN OR A LARGE RIMMED BAKING SHEET WITH GREASED FOIL. RUB RIBS LIBERALLY WITH SPICE MIXTURE. PLACE IN A SINGLE LAYER IN PREPARED PAN. DRIZZLE APPLE JUICE OVER RIBS AND COVER TIGHTLY

WITH FOIL. BAKE FOR ABOUT 2 HOURS OR UNTIL RIBS ARE
FORK-TENDER AND THE MEAT IS STARTING TO FALL OFF
THE BONE.

GLAZE: IN A SMALL SAUCEPAN, COMBINE JAM, RUM, LIME
JUICE AND VINEGAR; BRING TO A BOIL OVER HIGH HEAT.
REDUCE HEAT AND SIMMER FOR 1 MINUTE. REMOVE FROM
HEAT AND KEEP WARM.

PREHEAT BARBECUE GRILL TO MEDIUM-HIGH AND
LIGHTLY GREASE THE RACK. TRANSFER RIBS TO A
LARGE PLATE AND BRUSH WITH GLAZE. GRILL FOR 5 TO
8 MINUTES, TURNING FREQUENTLY AND BRUSHING WITH
GLAZE, UNTIL CRISPY. MAKES 4 SERVINGS.

TIP: COUNTRY-STYLE RIBS ARE MEATIER THAN BABY BACK
OR SPARERIBS. YOU CAN USE THOSE CUTS WITH THIS
RECIPE, IF YOU PREFER. YOU'LL NEED 4 LBS (2 KG) FOR
4 SERVINGS.

MY WIFE AND I HAD WORDS,
BUT I DIDN'T GET TO USE MINE.

STICKY BAKED CHICKEN

IF YOU HAVE TO LOOK GOOD IN AN HOUR . . .

1 CUP	SPICED PEACH JAM (PAGE 53)	250 ML
1/2 CUP	CLASSIC BARBECUE SAUCE (PAGE 250)	125 ML
1/2 CUP	CHOPPED ONION	125 ML
2 TBSP	SOY SAUCE	30 ML
1	CHICKEN, CUT INTO 8 PIECES (OR 3 LBS/1.5 KG BONE-IN, SKIN-ON CHICKEN PIECES)	1

PREHEAT OVEN TO 325°F (160°C). IN A SAUCEPAN, COMBINE JAM, BARBECUE SAUCE, ONION AND SOY SAUCE. HEAT OVER MEDIUM HEAT, STIRRING OFTEN, UNTIL WELL BLENDED. PLACE CHICKEN PIECES IN A SHALLOW 13- BY 9-INCH (33 BY 23 CM) BAKING DISH AND POUR SAUCE OVER TOP. BAKE FOR 1 HOUR, BASTING DURING THE LAST 30 MINUTES OF COOKING. MAKES 6 SERVINGS.

WELL DONE IS BETTER THAN WELL SAID.

TURKEY, BRIE AND CRANBERRY PANINI

THE DAY AFTER THANKSGIVING OR CHRISTMAS, THESE SANDWICHES WILL BE A BIG HIT WITH THE WHOLE FAMILY. PANINI ARE ITALY'S VERSION OF GRILLED CHEESE SANDWICHES. COOK THESE DINNER-SIZED SANDWICHES IN AN ELECTRIC SANDWICH MAKER, IF YOU HAVE ONE; IF YOU DON'T, A SKILLET WILL WORK JUST FINE (SEE TIP, BELOW).

2 TBSP	BUTTER, AT ROOM TEMPERATURE	30 ML
4	THICK SLICES WHOLE-GRAIN BREAD	4
4	THIN SLICES LEFTOVER OR DELI TURKEY	4
4 to 6 OZ	BRIE CHEESE, THINLY SLICED	125 to 175 G
4 TBSP	CRANBERRY PORT JELLY (PAGE 124) OR CRANBERRY PEAR CHUTNEY (PAGE 168)	60 ML
	SALT AND BLACK PEPPER	

PREHEAT SANDWICH MAKER TO MEDIUM-HIGH. LIGHTLY SPREAD BUTTER ON ONE SIDE OF EACH BREAD SLICE. PLACE BREAD ON A WORK SURFACE, BUTTERED SIDE DOWN. ON BOTTOM HALVES, LAYER WITH 1 TURKEY SLICE, BRIE, CRANBERRY JELLY AND ANOTHER TURKEY SLICE. SEASON TO TASTE WITH SALT AND PEPPER. COVER WITH TOP HALVES. PLACE SANDWICHES IN GRILL AND COOK FOR 3 TO 4 MINUTES OR UNTIL BREAD IS BROWNED AND CHEESE IS MELTING. MAKES 2 SERVINGS.

TIP: IF YOU DON'T HAVE A PANINI GRILL OR OTHER ELECTRIC SANDWICH MAKER, COOK THE SANDWICHES IN A LARGE NONSTICK SKILLET, PRESSING DOWN GENTLY WITH A SPATULA AND TURNING ONCE.

CRISPY SOLE FINGERS WITH TARTAR SAUCE

FISH STICKS, BUT BETTER. THE TARTAR SAUCE
CAN BE WHISKED TOGETHER IN MINUTES.

TARTAR SAUCE

1/2 CUP	MAYONNAISE	125 ML
2 TBSP	WHIPPING (35%) CREAM OR MILK	30 ML
2 TBSP	FINELY CHOPPED DILL PICKLES (PAGE 220) OR DILL CUCUMBER RELISH (PAGE 192)	30 ML
2 TBSP	FINELY CHOPPED GREEN ONION	30 ML
1 TBSP	CAPERS	15 ML
2 TSP	JUICE FROM CAPER JAR	10 ML
1/4 TSP	SALT	1 ML
	BLACK PEPPER	

SOLE FINGERS

1 LB	FRESH OR THAWED FROZEN SKINLESS SOLE FILLETS (4 TO 8)	500 G
1 CUP	ALL-PURPOSE FLOUR	250 ML
1 TSP	PAPRIKA	5 ML
1 TSP	SALT	5 ML
2	EGGS	2
3 TBSP	MILK	45 ML
2 CUPS	PANKO OR DRY BREAD CRUMBS	500 ML
1/4 CUP	VEGETABLE OIL	60 ML

TARTAR SAUCE: IN A SMALL BOWL, WHISK TOGETHER
MAYONNAISE, CREAM, PICKLES, GREEN ONION, CAPERS,
CAPER JUICE, SALT AND PEPPER TO TASTE. COVER AND
REFRIGERATE FOR 2 HOURS TO LET FLAVORS DEVELOP.

SOLE FINGERS: RINSE SOLE AND PAT DRY WITH PAPER TOWELS. (IF THE FISH HAS BEEN FROZEN AND THAWED, IT WILL BE QUITE WET, SO BE SURE TO DRY IT WELL.) CUT EACH FILLET IN HALF LENGTHWISE, THEN CUT EACH HALF INTO 2 TO 3 STRIPS, DEPENDING ON THE SIZE OF THE FILLET. EACH STRIP SHOULD BE NO MORE THAN 1 INCH (2.5 CM) WIDE. IN A SHALLOW DISH, COMBINE FLOUR, PAPRIKA AND SALT. IN ANOTHER DISH, WHISK TOGETHER EGGS AND MILK. PLACE PANKO IN A THIRD DISH. WORKING WITH A FEW STRIPS AT A TIME, DIP FISH IN SEASONED FLOUR, SHAKING OFF EXCESS, THEN IN THE EGG MIXTURE AND FINALLY IN PANKO, COATING EVENLY. REPEAT UNTIL ALL FISH STRIPS ARE COATED. IN A LARGE SKILLET, HEAT OIL OVER MEDIUM-HIGH HEAT. WORKING IN BATCHES, FRY FISH STRIPS FOR ABOUT 1 MINUTE PER SIDE OR UNTIL BATTER IS GOLDEN AND FISH FLAKES EASILY WITH A FORK. TRANSFER TO A PLATE LINED WITH PAPER TOWELS AND KEEP HOT WHILE COOKING THE REMAINING FISH. SERVE WITH TARTAR SAUCE. MAKES 4 SERVINGS.

MAKE AHEAD: THE TARTAR SAUCE CAN BE STORED IN THE REFRIGERATOR FOR UP TO 3 DAYS.

ACTUALLY, I AM THE BOSS OF YOU.

CHEESY BEAN QUESADILLAS

*THESE FULL-FLAVORED QUESADILLAS ARE
SO TASTY YOU WON'T EVEN MISS THE MEAT.*

1 TBSP	OLIVE OR VEGETABLE OIL	15 ML
1	GREEN OR RED BELL PEPPER, CHOPPED	1
3/4 CUP	FINELY CHOPPED ONION	175 ML
2	CLOVES GARLIC, MINCED	2
1 TSP	GROUND CUMIN	5 ML
1	CAN (19 OZ/ 540 ML) RED KIDNEY BEANS, DRAINED AND RINSED	1
1/2 to 3/4 CUP	MILD TOMATO SALSA (PAGE 258) OR HOT, HOT, HOT TOMATO SALSA (PAGE 260)	125 to 175 ML
1/2 to 1 TSP	PURÉED CANNED CHIPOTLE PEPPERS (SEE TIP, OPPOSITE)	2 to 5 ML
	SALT	
2 TBSP	CHOPPED FRESH CILANTRO	30 ML
4	9-INCH (23 CM) WHOLE WHEAT FLOUR TORTILLAS	4
1 1/2 CUPS	SHREDDED TEX-MEX CHEESE BLEND, JALAPEÑO JACK CHEESE OR JALAPEÑO HAVARTI CHEESE	375 ML
	SOUR CREAM AND ADDITIONAL SALSA	

IN A LARGE NONSTICK SKILLET, HEAT OIL OVER MEDIUM HEAT. SAUTÉ GREEN PEPPER AND ONION FOR ABOUT 5 MINUTES OR UNTIL SOFTENED. ADD GARLIC AND CUMIN; SAUTÉ FOR 15 SECONDS OR UNTIL FRAGRANT. STIR IN BEANS AND LIGHTLY CRUSH THEM WITH A POTATO MASHER. ADD 1/2 CUP (125 ML) OF THE SALSA, CHIPOTLE PEPPERS TO TASTE AND 1/2 TSP (2 ML) SALT; COOK, STIRRING, UNTIL HEATED THROUGH. STIR IN CILANTRO.

ADJUST CONSISTENCY WITH MORE SALSA, IF DESIRED. TASTE AND ADJUST SEASONING WITH SALT, IF DESIRED. LAY 2 TORTILLAS ON A WORK SURFACE. SPREAD BEAN FILLING OVER BOTH TORTILLAS, THEN SPRINKLE WITH CHEESE. TOP WITH THE REMAINING TORTILLAS. HEAT A CLEAN NONSTICK SKILLET OVER MEDIUM-HIGH HEAT. COOK QUESADILLAS, ONE AT A TIME, PRESSING DOWN GENTLY WITH A SPATULA AND TURNING ONCE, FOR 3 TO 4 MINUTES PER SIDE OR UNTIL BROWNED ON BOTH SIDES AND CHEESE IS MELTED. TRANSFER TO A CUTTING BOARD AND CUT INTO LARGE WEDGES. SERVE WITH SOUR CREAM AND SALSA FOR DIPPING. MAKES 2 LARGE SERVINGS OR 4 SMALLER ONES.

TIP: CHIPOTLE PEPPERS ARE SMOKED JALAPEÑO PEPPERS, AND THEY'RE OFTEN SOLD PACKED IN MEXICAN ADOBO SAUCE. TYPICALLY, THE SMALL CANS CAN BE FOUND NEAR OTHER MEXICAN FOODS IN THE SUPERMARKET. LEFTOVER CHIPOTLES CAN BE PURÉED, TRANSFERRED TO AN AIRTIGHT CONTAINER AND REFRIGERATED FOR UP TO 4 WEEKS OR FROZEN FOR UP TO 6 MONTHS. YOU COULD USE AN EQUAL AMOUNT OF SMOKED OR SWEET PAPRIKA INSTEAD OF THE CHIPOTLES, BUT THE QUESADILLAS WILL TASTE DIFFERENT.

TIP: FEEL FREE TO SUBSTITUTE YOUR FAVORITE FLAVOR OF FLOUR TORTILLAS FOR THE WHOLE WHEAT.

MAKE AHEAD: THE BEAN FILLING CAN BE MADE AHEAD. LET COOL COMPLETELY AND REFRIGERATE IN AN AIRTIGHT CONTAINER FOR UP TO 2 DAYS OR FREEZE FOR UP TO 1 MONTH. THAW IN THE MICROWAVE OR OVERNIGHT IN THE REFRIGERATOR BEFORE ASSEMBLING QUESADILLAS.

FRESH RASPBERRY HAZELNUT TART

CRUST

1 CUP	ALL-PURPOSE FLOUR	250 ML
1/3 CUP	GROUND HAZELNUTS OR ALMONDS	75 ML
1/4 CUP	GRANULATED SUGAR	60 ML
1/4 TSP	SALT	1 ML
1/2 CUP	COLD UNSALTED BUTTER, CUT INTO CUBES	125 ML
1	EGG YOLK	1
1 to 2 TBSP	COLD WATER	15 to 30 ML

FILLING

1/2 CUP	RASPBERRY JELLY (PAGE 128) OR RED CURRANT JELLY (PAGE 118), DIVIDED	125 ML
1 CUP	MASCARPONE CHEESE, AT ROOM TEMPERATURE	250 ML
2 TBSP	CONFECTIONERS' (ICING) SUGAR	30 ML
2/3 CUP	HEAVY OR WHIPPING (35%) CREAM	150 ML
3 CUPS	RASPBERRIES	750 ML
1/3 CUP	CHOPPED TOASTED HAZELNUTS OR ALMONDS (OPTIONAL)	75 ML

CRUST: PLACE A 10-INCH (25 CM) TART PAN WITH A REMOVABLE BOTTOM ON A LARGE BAKING SHEET. IN A FOOD PROCESSOR, COMBINE FLOUR, HAZELNUTS, SUGAR, SALT AND BUTTER; PROCESS UNTIL MIXTURE RESEMBLES FINE BREAD CRUMBS. ADD EGG YOLK AND 1 TBSP (15 ML) COLD WATER; PULSE, ADDING MORE WATER 1 TSP (5 ML) AT A TIME IF NECESSARY, UNTIL IT JUST STARTS TO COME TOGETHER AS A BALL OF DOUGH. TURN OUT ONTO A LIGHTLY FLOURED WORK SURFACE AND KNEAD LIGHTLY

INTO A 6-INCH (15 CM) DISC. (AT THIS POINT THE DOUGH CAN BE WRAPPED IN PLASTIC WRAP AND REFRIGERATED FOR UP TO 3 DAYS. LET STAND AT ROOM TEMPERATURE FOR 15 MINUTES BEFORE ROLLING OUT.)

ROLL DOUGH OUT TO A CIRCLE ABOUT 12 INCHES (30 CM) IN DIAMETER. LIFT DOUGH INTO THE PAN (IT IS VERY PLIABLE) AND PRESS TO FIT THE BOTTOM AND SIDES. (IF THE PASTRY CRACKS, JUST PATCH IT IN THE PAN — NO ONE WILL EVER KNOW.) TRIM THE EDGES. REFRIGERATE FOR 15 MINUTES. MEANWHILE, PREHEAT OVEN TO 375°F (190°C). PRICK THE BOTTOM AND SIDES OF THE PASTRY WITH A FORK. BAKE FOR 20 TO 25 MINUTES OR UNTIL LIGHTLY BROWNED. CHECK AFTER 10 MINUTES; IF THE BOTTOM IS PUFFING UP, LIGHTLY PRICK A FEW MORE TIMES. LET COOL COMPLETELY IN PAN ON A WIRE RACK.

FILLING: PLACE JELLY IN A MICROWAVE-SAFE BOWL. MICROWAVE ON HIGH FOR ABOUT 30 SECONDS, UNTIL MELTED. LET COOL BUT DO NOT LET RESET. IN A LARGE BOWL, BEAT MASCARPONE WITH CONFECTIONERS' SUGAR TO LOOSEN IT SLIGHTLY. STIR IN 2 TBSP (30 ML) MELTED JELLY. IN ANOTHER LARGE BOWL, WHIP CREAM UNTIL SOFT PEAKS FORM. FOLD INTO MASCARPONE MIXTURE. SPOON INTO COOLED CRUST, LEVELING TOP WITH A SPATULA OR SPOON. IN ANOTHER BOWL, TOSS RASPBERRIES WITH THE REMAINING MELTED JELLY. TUMBLE OVER TOP OF MASCARPONE MIXTURE. SPRINKLE WITH HAZELNUTS, IF DESIRED. REFRIGERATE FOR AT LEAST 1 HOUR OR FOR UP TO 4 HOURS. MAKES 8 SERVINGS.

CHOCOLATE STRAWBERRY TORTE

*GOD MADE CHOCOLATE AND
THE DEVIL THREW THE CALORIES IN!
THIS TASTES AS GOOD AS IT LOOKS.*

CAKE

2 CUPS	ALL-PURPOSE FLOUR	500 ML
2 TSP	BAKING SODA	10 ML
1/2 TSP	SALT	2 ML
1/2 TSP	BAKING POWDER	2 ML
3 OZ	UNSWEETENED CHOCOLATE	90 G
1/2 CUP	BUTTER	125 ML
2 CUPS	PACKED BROWN SUGAR	500 ML
3	EGGS	3
1 1/2 TSP	VANILLA EXTRACT	7 ML
3/4 CUP	SOUR CREAM	175 ML
1/2 CUP	STRONG COFFEE	125 ML
1/2 CUP	COFFEE-FLAVORED LIQUEUR (KAHLÚA)	125 ML

FILLING

1 CUP	WHIPPING (35%) CREAM	250 ML
2 TBSP	CONFECTIONERS' (ICING) SUGAR	30 ML
1 1/2 CUPS	STRAWBERRY JAM (PAGE 66 OR 67) OR RASPBERRY JAM (PAGE 59 OR 60)	375 ML

FROSTING

1 1/2 CUPS	CHOCOLATE CHIPS	375 ML
3/4 CUP	SOUR CREAM	175 ML
PINCH	SALT	PINCH
	CHOCOLATE CURLS	
	STRAWBERRIES OR RASPBERRIES	

CAKE: PREHEAT OVEN TO 350°F (180°C). GREASE AND FLOUR TWO 9-INCH (23 CM) CAKE PANS. MIX FLOUR, BAKING SODA, SALT AND BAKING POWDER. MELT CHOCOLATE AND LET COOL. IN A LARGE BOWL, BEAT BUTTER, BROWN SUGAR AND EGGS AT HIGH SPEED UNTIL LIGHT AND FLUFFY, ABOUT 5 MINUTES. BEAT IN MELTED CHOCOLATE AND VANILLA. AT LOW SPEED, BEAT IN FLOUR MIXTURE (IN FOURTHS), ALTERNATING WITH SOUR CREAM (IN THIRDS). ADD COFFEE AND LIQUEUR, BLENDING UNTIL SMOOTH. POUR BATTER INTO PANS AND BAKE FOR 30 TO 35 MINUTES OR UNTIL SURFACE SPRINGS BACK. COOL IN PANS FOR 10 MINUTES, THEN REMOVE FROM PANS AND COOL ON WIRE RACKS.

FILLING: BEAT CREAM UNTIL IT BEGINS TO THICKEN. SPRINKLE IN CONFECTIONERS' SUGAR AND BEAT UNTIL STIFF. REFRIGERATE. SLICE CAKE LAYERS IN HALF HORIZONTALLY TO MAKE FOUR LAYERS (CAKE LAYERS CUT MORE EASILY IF FROZEN FIRST). PLACE ONE LAYER, CUT SIDE UP, ON CAKE PLATE. SPREAD WITH $1/2$ CUP (125 ML) STRAWBERRY JAM AND $1/2$ CUP (125 ML) WHIPPED CREAM. REPEAT WITH REMAINING LAYERS, ENDING WITH TOP LAYER CUT SIDE DOWN.

FROSTING: MELT CHOCOLATE CHIPS IN TOP OF DOUBLE BOILER. ADD SOUR CREAM AND SALT AND BEAT UNTIL FROSTING IS CREAMY AND SMOOTH. FROST TOP AND SIDES OF CAKE. GARNISH WITH CHOCOLATE CURLS AND FRESH BERRIES. MAKES 10 TO 12 SERVINGS.

TIP: TO MAKE CHOCOLATE CURLS, WARM A GOOD-QUALITY CHOCOLATE BAR TO ROOM TEMPERATURE, THEN USE A VEGETABLE PEELER TO SHAVE OFF CURLS.

BLACK CURRANT LINZER SLICES

A SPIN ON A CLASSIC LINZERTORTE. ALTHOUGH RASPBERRY JAM IS TRADITIONALLY USED WITH A LINZERTORTE, WE LOVE THIS COMBINATION OF SLIGHTLY TART BLACK CURRANT JAM WITH THE BUTTERY SHORTBREAD BASE.

BASE

1 CUP	ALL-PURPOSE FLOUR	250 ML
1/4 CUP	GRANULATED SUGAR	60 ML
1 TSP	GROUND CINNAMON	5 ML
1/2 CUP	COLD UNSALTED BUTTER, CUT INTO CUBES	125 ML

TOPPING

1 CUP	BLACK CURRANT JAM (PAGE 41)	250 ML
3 TBSP	TOASTED SLICED OR SLIVERED ALMONDS (SEE BOX, PAGE 145)	45 ML
2 TSP	GRANULATED SUGAR	10 ML

BASE: PREHEAT OVEN TO 350°F (180°C). GREASE AN 8-INCH (20 CM) SQUARE BAKING PAN AND LINE WITH PARCHMENT PAPER. IN A FOOD PROCESSOR, PULSE FLOUR, SUGAR, CINNAMON AND BUTTER TO FINE CRUMBS. (YOU CAN ALSO DO THIS IN A LARGE BOWL BY RUBBING THE MIXTURE THROUGH YOUR FINGERS OR CUTTING THE BUTTER IN WITH A PASTRY BLENDER.) REMOVE 1/4 CUP (60 ML) OF THE MIXTURE AND SET ASIDE. PAT THE REMAINING MIXTURE INTO BOTTOM OF PREPARED PAN. BAKE FOR ABOUT 15 MINUTES OR UNTIL BASE IS SET AND LIGHTLY BROWNED. REMOVE FROM OVEN, LEAVING OVEN ON.

TOPPING: PLACE JAM IN A SMALL MICROWAVE-SAFE BOWL. MICROWAVE ON HIGH FOR 20 SECONDS TO LOOSEN SLIGHTLY. SPREAD EVENLY OVER BAKED BASE. IN A SMALL BOWL, COMBINE RESERVED BASE MIXTURE AND ALMONDS. SPRINKLE OVER JAM. BAKE FOR 10 TO 15 MINUTES OR UNTIL JAM IS BUBBLING AND TOPPING IS GOLDEN. SPRINKLE WITH SUGAR. LET COOL COMPLETELY IN PAN ON A WIRE RACK. CUT INTO SQUARES. MAKES 16 SQUARES.

MAKE AHEAD: STORE IN AN AIRTIGHT CONTAINER AT ROOM TEMPERATURE FOR UP TO 2 DAYS, OR PLACE BETWEEN LAYERS OF WAXED PAPER IN AN AIRTIGHT CONTAINER AND FREEZE FOR UP TO 2 WEEKS.

VARIATION: IN PLACE OF THE BLACK CURRANT JAM, YOU CAN USE ANY OF THE JAMS IN THIS BOOK (PAGES 38-95).

THE ONLY FOOD THAT DOESN'T SPOIL: HONEY.

JOLLY GOOD BREAD AND BUTTER PUDDING

WHEN IT COMES TO BREAD PUDDING,
BRITS KNOW BEST!

1/4 CUP	UNSALTED BUTTER, SOFTENED	60 ML
8	THICK SLICES RAISIN BREAD	8
1/2 CUP	SEVILLE ORANGE MARMALADE (PAGE 96) OR BLOOD ORANGE MARMALADE (PAGE 98)	125 ML
1/2 CUP	RAISINS	125 ML
1/4 CUP	GRANULATED SUGAR, DIVIDED	60 ML
1/4 TSP	GROUND NUTMEG	1 ML
	FINELY GRATED ZEST OF 1 ORANGE	
3	EGGS	3
1 CUP	MILK	250 ML
1/3 CUP	HEAVY OR WHIPPING (35%) CREAM	75 ML

BUTTER AN 8-INCH (20 CM) SQUARE BAKING DISH. BUTTER ONE SIDE OF EACH BREAD SLICE, THEN SPREAD MARMALADE THICKLY OVER BUTTER. CUT EACH SLICE IN HALF DIAGONALLY TO GET 2 TRIANGLES. ARRANGE HALF THE BREAD, BUTTERED SIDE UP, IN PREPARED DISH, OVERLAPPING AS NECESSARY. SPRINKLE WITH RAISINS. ARRANGE THE REMAINING BREAD, BUTTERED SIDE DOWN, ON TOP. IN A BOWL, WHISK TOGETHER 2 TBSP (30 ML) OF THE SUGAR, NUTMEG, ORANGE ZEST, EGGS, MILK AND CREAM. POUR OVER BREAD, PUSHING DOWN GENTLY WITH A SPOON TO ENSURE ALL BREAD IS SUBMERGED. SPRINKLE WITH THE REMAINING SUGAR. COVER AND REFRIGERATE FOR AT LEAST 30 MINUTES OR FOR UP TO 12 HOURS TO ALLOW EGG MIXTURE TO SOAK INTO BREAD.

MEANWHILE, PREHEAT OVEN TO 350°F (180°C). BAKE, UNCOVERED, FOR 30 TO 40 MINUTES OR UNTIL GOLDEN BROWN AND PUFFY AND A TESTER INSERTED IN THE CENTER COMES OUT CLEAN. LET COOL IN DISH FOR 15 MINUTES BEFORE SLICING. MAKES 4 TO 6 SERVINGS.

LIFE IS SHORT. GET THE SHOES.

PRODUCE PURCHASE AND PREPARATION GUIDE

USE THE FOLLOWING TABLE TO FIGURE OUT HOW MUCH PRODUCE TO BUY FOR THE RECIPES IN THIS BOOK. IT'S ALWAYS BEST TO PURCHASE A LITTLE MORE THAN YOU THINK YOU NEED, JUST TO MAKE SURE YOU HAVE ENOUGH FOR YOUR RECIPE. YOU CAN ALWAYS EAT OR FREEZE THE EXTRA!

FRESH FRUITS	QUANTITY	WEIGHT	PREPARED VOLUME
Apples	1 large	8 oz (250 g)	1 cup (250 mL) chopped; $^2/_3$ cup (150 mL) grated
Apricots	3 medium		1 cup (250 mL) chopped
Berries			
Blackberries		4 oz (125 g)	1 cup (250 mL) whole
Blueberries		4 oz (125 g)	1 cup (250 mL) whole; $^1/_2$ cup (125 mL) crushed
Boysenberries		4 oz (125 g)	1 cup (250 mL) whole
Cranberries	1 bag	12 oz (340 g)	3 cups (750 mL) whole
Elderberries		4 oz (125 g)	1 cup (250 mL) whole
Gooseberries		5 oz (150 g)	1 cup (250 mL) whole
Raspberries		4 oz (125 g)	1 cup (250 mL) whole
Saskatoon berries		4 oz (125 g)	1 cup (250 mL) whole
Strawberries		8 oz (250 g)	1 cup (250 mL) sliced; $^1/_2$ cup (125 mL) crushed
Cherries		8 oz (250 g)	1 cup (250 mL) chopped
Crabapples		4 oz (125 g)	1 cup (250 mL) whole
Currants (black and red)		6 oz (175 g)	1 cup (250 mL) whole
Figs	12	1 lb (500 g)	$2^1/_2$ cups (625 mL) chopped
Grapefruit	1 medium		1 cup (250 mL) chopped, with juices
Grapes (all varieties)		6 oz (175 g)	1 cup (250 mL)
Kiwifruit	3 medium		1 cup (250 mL) chopped
Lemons	1 medium		$^1/_3$ cup (75 mL) juice; 1 tbsp (15 mL) grated peel

FRESH FRUITS	QUANTITY	WEIGHT	PREPARED VOLUME
Limes	1 medium		3 tbsp (45 mL) juice; 1 tsp (5 mL) grated peel
Mangos			
Regular	1 large		1 cup (250 mL) chopped
Ataulfo	1 medium		³/₄ cup (175 mL) chopped
Nectarines	2 medium	8 oz (250 g)	1 cup (250 mL) chopped
Oranges	1 medium		¹/₃ cup (75 mL) juice; 4 tsp (20 mL) grated peel; ¹/₂ cup (125 mL) chopped
Papaya	1 medium	2 lbs (1 kg)	2 cups (500 mL) chopped
Peaches	2 medium	8 oz (250 g)	1 cup (250 mL) chopped
Pears	2 large	1 lb (500 g)	1 cup (250 mL) chopped
Pineapple	1 medium	4 lbs (2 kg)	4 cups (1 L) chopped
Plumcots		8 oz (250 g)	1 cup (250 mL) chopped
Plums			
Black, red or yellow	3 or 4 large	8 oz (250 g)	1 cup (250 mL) chopped
Prune (blue)	4 medium	8 oz (250 g)	1 cup (250 mL) chopped
Shiro (small yellow, sugar plums)		12 oz (375 g)	1 cup (250 mL) chopped
DRIED FRUITS	**QUANTITY**	**WEIGHT**	**PREPARED VOLUME**
Apricots		7 oz (210 g)	1 cup (250 mL) chopped
Cranberries		2 oz (60 g)	¹/₂ cup (125 mL)
Currants		2.7 oz (80 g)	¹/₂ cup (125 mL)
Dates		8 oz (250 g)	1 cup (250 mL) chopped
Figs	40	1 lb (500 g)	3 cups (750 mL) chopped
Raisins		3 oz (90 g)	¹/₂ cup (125 mL)
VEGETABLES	**QUANTITY**	**WEIGHT**	**PREPARED VOLUME**
Beans, green or yellow (wax)	2 quarts (2 L)	1 lb (500 g)	
Beets	3 medium	1 lb (500 g)	1¹/₂ cups (375 mL) cooked, peeled and chopped or shredded
Carrots	5 to 6 medium	1 lb (500 g)	2¹/₂ cups (625 mL) shredded; 3¹/₃ cups (825 mL) chopped
Corn	1 medium cob		¹/₂ cup (125 mL) kernels

VEGETABLES	QUANTITY	WEIGHT	PREPARED VOLUME
Cucumbers, pickling	Eleven to fourteen 3- to 4-inch (7.5 to 10 cm) or twenty-two 2½- to 3-inch (6 to 7.5 cm)	1 lb (500 g)	3 cups (750 mL) ¼-inch (0.5 cm) crosswise slices or finely chopped
Garlic	3 large heads		¼ cup (60 mL) minced or roasted
Gingerroot	1-inch (2.5 cm) piece	1 oz (30 g)	1 tbsp (15 mL) finely chopped
Onions			
Yellow (cooking)	1 medium		1 cup (250 mL) chopped
Red or white sweet	1 large		2 cups (500 mL) thinly sliced; 1½ cups (375 mL) chopped
Peppers			
Bell (sweet)	1 large	6 to 8 oz (175 to 250 g)	1¼ cups (300 mL) chopped
Habanero	5 to 6 large		½ cup (125 mL) minced
Jalapeño	1 medium		2 tbsp (30 mL) minced
Rhubarb		6 oz (175 g)	1 cup (250 mL) chopped
Tomatoes			
Green	3 medium or 1 large	1 lb (500 g)	2½ cups (625 mL) chopped
Plum (Roma)	5 medium	1 lb (500 g)	2 cups (500 mL) peeled and chopped
Zucchini	one 6-inch (15 cm)	5 oz (150 g)	1 cup (250 mL) shredded; 1⅓ cups (325 mL) finely chopped or thinly sliced

The Best of Bridge Publishing Ltd.
The Rest of the Best and More
Recipes from this book can be found on pages 166–67 and 218–21.

Karen Brimacombe, Mary Halpen, Helen Miles, Valerie Robinson and Joan Wilson
The Complete Best of Bridge Cookbooks, Volume 1
Recipes from this book can be found on pages 114–15, 188–89, 202–3 and 214–15.

Karen Brimacombe, Mary Halpen, Helen Miles, Valerie Robinson and Joan Wilson
The Complete Best of Bridge Cookbooks, Volume 2
Recipes from this book can be found on pages 112–13, 132–33, 136–37, 194–95, 198–99, 204–7, 271 and 284–85.

Karen Brimacombe, Mary Halpen, Helen Miles, Valerie Robinson and Joan Wilson
The Complete Best of Bridge Cookbooks, Volume 3
Recipes from this book can be found on pages 110–11, 168–69, 224–25, 244–45, 266, 270 and 276.

Jennifer MacKenzie
The Complete Book of Pickling
Recipes from this book can be found on pages 170–75, 178–81, 184–85, 190–93, 196–97, 200–201, 222–23, 226–43 and 246–65.

Yvonne Tremblay
250 Home Preserving Favorites
Recipes from this book can be found on pages 38–52, 54–77, 79–109, 116–23, 126–31, 134–35, 140–65 and 186–87.

Sally Vaughan-Johnston and the Best of Bridge Publishing Ltd.
Bravo! Best of Bridge Cookbook
Recipes from this book can be found on pages 267–69, 272–73 and 277–79.

Sally Vaughan-Johnston and the Best of Bridge Publishing Ltd.
Fan Fare! Best of Bridge Cookbook
Recipes from this book can be found on pages 274–75, 280–83 and 286–89.

Sally Vaughan-Johnston and the Best of Bridge Publishing Ltd.
[unpublished]
Recipes under this copyright can be found on pages 53, 78, 124–25, 138–39, 176–77, 182–83, 208–13 and 216–17.

Library and Archives Canada Cataloguing in Publication

Best of Bridge home preserving : 120 recipes for jams, jellies, marmalades, pickles & more / Best of Bridge.

Includes index.
ISBN 978-0-7788-0482-6 (bound)

1. Jam. 2. Jelly. 3. Marmalade. 4. Pickles. I. Best of Bridge Publishing Ltd., author

TX612.J3B48 2014   641.85'2   C2013-908153-4

INDEX

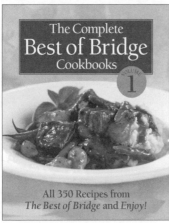

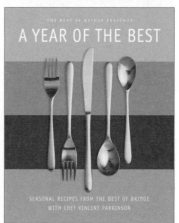

More Great Books
from Robert Rose

Bestsellers

- The Juicing Bible, Second Edition
  by Pat Crocker
- 175 Best Babycakes™ Cupcake Maker Recipes
  by Kathy Moore and Roxanne Wyss
- 175 Best Babycakes™ Cake Pop Maker Recipes
  by Kathy Moore and Roxanne Wyss
- Eat Raw, Eat Well
  by Douglas McNish
- The Smoothies Bible, Second Edition
  by Pat Crocker
- The Food Substitutions Bible, Second Edition
  by David Joachim
- Zwilling J.A. Henckels Complete Book of Knife Skills
  by Jeffrey Elliot and James P. DeWan

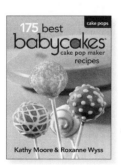

Appliance Bestsellers

- 225 Best Pressure Cooker Recipes
  by Cinda Chavich
- 200 Best Panini Recipes
  by Tiffany Collins
- 125 Best Indoor Grill Recipes
  by Ilana Simon
- The Convection Oven Bible
  by Linda Stephen
- The Fondue Bible
  by Ilana Simon

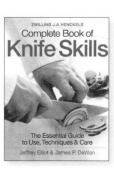

- 150 Best Indian, Thai, Vietnamese & More Slow Cooker Recipes
  by Sunil Vijayakar
- The 150 Best Slow Cooker Recipes, Second Edition
  by Judith Finlayson
- The Vegetarian Slow Cooker
  by Judith Finlayson
- 175 Essential Slow Cooker Classics
  by Judith Finlayson
- The Healthy Slow Cooker
  by Judith Finlayson
- Slow Cooker Winners
  by Donna-Marie Pye
- Canada's Slow Cooker Winners
  by Donna-Marie Pye
- 300 Best Rice Cooker Recipes
  by Katie Chin
- 650 Best Food Processor Recipes
  by George Geary and Judith Finlayson
- The Mixer Bible, Third Edition
  by Meredith Deeds and Carla Snyder
- 300 Best Bread Machine Recipes
  by Donna Washburn and Heather Butt
- 300 Best Canadian Bread Machine Recipes
  by Donna Washburn and Heather Butt

Baking Bestsellers

- 150 Best Gluten-Free Muffin Recipes
  by Camilla V. Saulsbury
- 150 Best Vegan Muffin Recipes
  by Camilla V. Saulsbury
- Piece of Cake!
  by Camilla V. Saulsbury
- 400 Sensational Cookies
  by Linda J. Amendt
- Complete Cake Mix Magic
  by Jill Snider
- 750 Best Muffin Recipes
  by Camilla V. Saulsbury
- 200 Fast & Easy Artisan Breads
  by Judith Fertig

Healthy Cooking Bestsellers

- Canada's Diabetes Meals for Good Health, Second Edition
  by Karen Graham
- Diabetes Meals for Good Health, Second Edition
  by Karen Graham
- 5 Easy Steps to Healthy Cooking
  by Camilla V. Saulsbury
- 350 Best Vegan Recipes
  by Deb Roussou
- The Vegan Cook's Bible
  by Pat Crocker
- The Gluten-Free Baking Book
  by Donna Washburn and Heather Butt

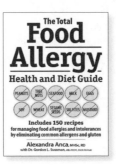

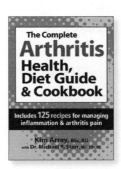

- Complete Gluten-Free Cookbook
  by Donna Washburn and Heather Butt
- 250 Gluten-Free Favorites
  by Donna Washburn and Heather Butt
- Complete Gluten-Free Diet & Nutrition Guide
  by Alexandra Anca and Theresa Santandrea-Cull
- The Complete Gluten-Free Whole Grains Cookbook
  by Judith Finlayson
- The Vegetarian Kitchen Table Cookbook
  by Igor Brotto and Olivier Guiriec

Health Bestsellers

- The Total Food Allergy Health and Diet Guide
  by Alexandra Anca with Dr. Gordon L. Sussman
- The Complete Arthritis Health, Diet Guide & Cookbook
  by Kim Arrey with Dr. Michael R. Starr
- The Essential Cancer Treatment Nutrition Guide & Cookbook
  by Jean LaMantia with Dr. Neil Berinstein
- The Complete Weight-Loss Surgery Guide & Diet Program
  by Sue Ekserci with Dr. Laz Klein
- The PCOS Health & Nutrition Guide
  by Dr. Jillian Stansbury with Dr. Sheila Mitchell

For more great books, see previous pages

Visit us at www.robertrose.ca